SOCIAL INSURANCE IN GERMANY, 1883-1911

ITS HISTORY, OPERATION, RESULTS

AND A COMPARISON WITH
THE NATIONAL INSURANCE ACT, 1911

BY
WILLIAM HARBUTT DAWSON
AUTHOR OF "THE EVOLUTION OF MODERN GERMANY,"
"GERMAN SOCIALISM AND FERDINAND LASSALLE,"
"PRINCE BISMARCK AND STATE SOCIALISM," "THE
GERMAN WORKMAN," ETC., ETC.

WITH TEN ILLUSTRATIONS

GREENWOOD PRESS, PUBLISHERS
WESTPORT, CONNECTICUT

Library of Congress Cataloging in Publication Data

Dawson, William Harbutt, 1860-1948.
  Social insurance in Germany, 1883-1911.

  Reprint of the 1912 ed. published by Scribner,
New York.
  Includes index.
  1. Social security--Germany--History. I. Title.
HD7179.D3 1979   368.4'0943   78-32002
ISBN 0-8371-5446-4

PUBLISHER'S NOTE

Because of the scholarly importance of this work and its un-
availability through antiquarian and other book sources, we
have reprinted this volume from a microfilm copy of the
original edition housed at the Library of Congress.

First published in 1912 by Charles Scribner's Sons,
New York, and T. Fisher Unwin, London

Reprinted in 1979 by Greenwood Press, Inc.
51 Riverside Avenue, Westport, CT 06880

Printed in the United States of America

10 9 8 7 6 5 4 3 2 1

PREFACE

It is the purpose of this book to state, in language as summary and as little technical as possible, the principal provisions of the German Social Insurance Legislation in its present form—that is, as amended by the Insurance Consolidation Act (literally, "Imperial Insurance Ordinance") of July 19, 1911.

The book has been written less for insurance experts than for the large and growing class of publicists and students who are seriously interested in social reform movements abroad, and who, in view of recent insurance legislation in this country, will be likely to welcome the opportunity of comparing the principles and methods embodied in that legislation with those which Germany adopted when it approached the same problem nearly thirty years ago and has continued, with slight modifications, until the present time. In order to facilitate such comparison the provisions of the German laws on sickness, accident, and invalidity and old age insurance, as explained in Chapters II. to VI., are supplemented in footnotes by the corresponding provisions, where such exist, contained in the National Insurance Act (Part I.) of 1911, the Old Age Pensions Act of 1908, and the Workmen's Compensation Act of 1906.

It did not seem expedient to institute comparisons

v

Preface

between the provisions of the National Insurance Act (Part II.) relating to unemployment and the German methods of dealing with this question. Such comparisons would have had little interest and no practical value, inasmuch as the few local experiments in unemployment insurance so far attempted in Germany have been made solely by municipal authorities or philanthropic associations; for no legislation, either Imperial or State, has yet been passed on the subject, and at present none appears to be contemplated.

Chapters are added in which such questions as the aggregate cost of German social insurance, its incidence as between employers, workpeople, and the State, the attitude of employers and workpeople towards the insurance legislation and their willingness to bear the necessary burdens, and the influence of insurance upon national health and thrift are considered in the light of the most reliable evidence procurable.

The writer's high opinion of the benefits of obligatory insurance, as practised in Germany now for nearly a generation, is candidly avowed in the following pages; yet while no formal attempt is made to estimate the relative advantages conferred upon the working classes by the three independent systems of insurance—against sickness, accident, and invalidity and old age respectively—special emphasis has been laid, and laid with right, upon the measures which are adopted, with yearly increasing persistence, method, and success, to prevent and eradicate the evils which monetary benefits at best can only minimise and palliate. No one who has followed the development of the German social insurance systems and who knows the immense educative influence

Preface

which they have exerted upon the working classes can doubt or wonder that it is the preventive work of the insurance organisations—as applied alike to disease and accident—which most appeals to the imagination, sympathy, and confidence of those in whose interest these laws have been passed. For, after all, in Germany, as here and everywhere, what the self-reliant workman values more highly than distress benefits is a fair and full use of his faculties. What he wants is not sickness pay, but a healthy life; not accident compensation, but sound limbs and unimpaired energies; not infirmity pensions, but the opportunity and the power to follow as long as possible the employment of his choice. Hence in their aggressive campaign against disease and their constant endeavour to lessen the risks to limb and life in industrial occupations the insurance authorities have from the first been conscious of the goodwill of the working classes, and have from no quarter received greater encouragement and praise than from the recognised leaders of organised labour. It is not too much to say that the many-sided preventive work which is being done by these authorities constitutes so far the peculiar distinction of the German system of social insurance.

The wider effects and influences of social insurance have never, perhaps, been stated with greater clearness and force than in the following words of that keen economic thinker and philosopher, the late Dr. Albert von Schäffle:—

"The supreme aim of statesmanship is not the wealth and efficiency of the few, but the greatest physical, material, and moral force of the entire community, by which a nation main-

Preface

tains its position in the struggle for existence. From this standpoint everything that makes the masses of the population secure against need, and therefore on the lowest plane contented, that strengthens a people by its own co-operative effort, that creates social peace and prevents violent agitation, that transforms the spirit of mendicancy into a consciousness of State-directed, collective self-help, and that raises the entire moral and political level of the lower classes, is of incalculable worth. And all this is done by the system of obligatory self-insurance against want and distress." *

For the illustrations which accompany the text reader and writer are indebted to the courtesy of Dr. R. Freund, President of the Berlin Pension Board (the four illustrations of the Beelitz Sanatorium belonging to that Board); Dr. von Hilbert, President of the Würtemberg Pension Board (the two illustrations of the Überruh Sanatorium belonging to that Board); Dr. Stoecker, President of the Mutual Association established under the Accident Insurance Law for the mining industry in Westphalia (the illustration of the Bergmannsheil Hospital belonging to that Association); and Dr. Hoeftman, of Königsberg (the four illustrations—chosen from a large collection kindly placed by him at my disposal—of labour appliances supplied to maimed workpeople). Some of the photographs from which illustrations have been produced were made specially for this book.

It has been thought advisable to state money values in German currency; in the few cases in which an exception has been made the German mark has for convenience been taken as the equivalent of the English shilling.

* "Aus meinen Leben," 1905.

viii

CONTENTS

ix

LIST OF ILLUSTRATIONS

Social Insurance in Germany

CHAPTER I

EARLY EXPERIMENTS IN INSURANCE

IT is impossible to assign the origin of the German
Insurance Legislation definitely to any one set of conditions or even to a precise period. In its entire spirit this
legislation clearly carried forward ideas and tendencies
which had been peculiar to German State policy for
many generations. A policy of social reform on a broad
national scale was only possible, indeed, after the establishment of the Empire in 1871, and the concurrent institution of an Imperial Legislature. All the statutory
measures hitherto adopted for the welfare of the working
classes had been of necessity of a partial character, owing
their existence to the enlightenment and good will of the
rulers and Governments of the independent States.

In Prussia, in particular, the domestic policy of the
dynasty had for centuries been that of a benevolent
patriarchalism conjoined with a very decided assertion of
the Sovereign's right to give or withhold social benefits
at will. Prince Bismarck used no hollow boast when he
said in 1882: "It is the tradition of the dynasty which

B

Social Insurance in Germany

I serve that it takes the part of the weaker ones in the
economic struggle." Long before the era of constitu-
tional government and Parliamentary systems, wise
rulers and far-seeing Ministers were always ready, when
social evils became acute and new conditions and needs
arose, to take occasion by the hand and readjust dis-
cordant relationships even in the absence of the active
pressure of popular demand. It was one of the apothegms
of Frederick the Great that " It is the business of a Sovereign, great or small, to alleviate human misery," and the
story of his own manifold social activities, as brought to
light by the investigations of the Prussian historiographers,
bears striking testimony to the sincere concern of a well-
nigh absolute ruler for the welfare of his subjects, and of
his genuine desire to hold the balance fairly between
conflicting classes and interests.

Later Prussian Sovereigns maintained the healthy
tradition that the State's first citizen should lead the
way in public spirit and the willing recognition of social
obligations. The entire system of serfage, which had
so long oppressed the peasants of North Germany, was
swept away at the beginning of the 19th century at the
word of an autocratic prince who, though gifted with
neither a strong nor even a discerning mind, had the
good sense to follow, at least for a time, the advice of
sagacious statesmen like Stein and Hardenberg. It is note-
worthy, too, that the Prussian Common Law, as promulgated in 1794, embodied all the principles of our early
English Poor Law regarding the relief of destitution, the
provision of employment for the workless, and the detention at forced labour of the idle and vicious. Hence
when Prince Bismarck on one occasion was reproached

2

Early Experiments in Insurance

with preaching the insidious doctrine of a "right to work," he promptly replied that the doctrine was not his at all, for it was part of the immemorial law of the land.

So, too, the regulation of factory labour began before there were Parliaments to pass factory laws. As early as 1839 a Prussian Royal decree restricted the employment of children in the factories and mines which were fast springing up in the industrial districts on the Rhine ;[1] and similar regulations were issued in Bavaria and Baden in 1840. In 1845, still before the creation of a national Legislature, a formal Industrial Code, containing many regulations for the welfare of the wage-earning classes, was promulgated for Prussia.

One of the first acts of the Diet of the North German Confederation, constituted in 1869, was the application of this Prussian Code to all the federated States. When the Empire was established two years later the Code became an Imperial law, and during the next few years it was repeatedly amended. Most of the important legal provisions of later date regulating the hours and conditions of labour have taken the form of alterations of or additions to this compendious statute.

The early years of the new Empire, however, were not favourable to the inauguration of any energetic policy of social reform, even had the need for such a policy been strongly felt. At that time political questions were uppermost, and their urgency indisposed or incapacitated the Central Government—dominated as it was by one

[1] Children under 9 years were not to be employed at all; those between 9 and 16 years might not be employed during the night; and the maximum day's work for children was fixed at 10 hours.

Social Insurance in Germany

masterful personality, whose genius found its natural outlet in foreign affairs—from recognising the existence of a social problem.

Recalling the continuity in Prussian social policy to which reference has been made, it is interesting to know that the Insurance Legislation itself is only a development of old-established usage. The germ of the three later systems of industrial insurance was contained in the ancient institution of the *Knappschaftskasse* (corresponding to the *Brüderladen* of Austria), an organisation of miners for mutual aid. The age of this institution is uncertain. Originally the *Knappschaft* was the gang of *Knappen*,[2] or associates, who worked a mine on the partnership principle. They formed funds or *Kassen*, from which grants were made to needy members in time of sickness, accident, and infirmity, as well as to their widows and orphans. These fraternities were greatly encouraged by Frederick the Great in Prussia, but they also existed in other German States. The principal modern development of the Prussian miners' societies, prior to the introduction of general compulsory insurance for the working classes, took place after the passing of a law of April 10, 1854 (embodied in the General Mining Law of June 24, 1865), the object of which was to strengthen the societies and to increase their efficiency and utility.

The main feature of this law was that it made compulsory the formation of provident funds for all work-

[2] The word *Knappe* itself had originally a broader and more distinguished signification. In mediæval times the *Knappe* was the attendant of a German *Ritter*, or Knight, and answered to the English squire.

4

Early Experiments in Insurance

people employed in the mines, smelting works, and salt works of the kingdom. The cost of insurance was to be defrayed out of contributions by the miners and the mine-owners, forming either a fixed or a variable percentage of the wages, and the mine-owners were required to pay at least half as much as the men ; while the executive bodies were to be chosen by the two parties in equal numbers. At that time 53 miners' funds existed in Prussia, and it was estimated that they had 56,500 members, or over 80 per cent. of the 68,300 workpeople employed in the mines and salt works of the kingdom.

Inasmuch as these miners' funds fulfilled already, in a more or less effective manner, the objects of the general sickness and infirmity insurance legislation enacted during the 'eighties of last century, they were accepted as the proper organisations through which to work this legislation for the benefit of miners, smelters, and salt workers. As to sickness insurance in particular, in view of their wide basis and the liberal benefits which they had been in the habit of offering to their members, their operations were interfered with as little as possible.

But the miners' mutual aid societies were not the only provident agencies already serving the special interests of the working classes. A system of benefit funds providing against sickness, need, and death had been created by the Prussian Industrial Code of 1845, which empowered local authorities to require journeymen in the handicrafts and other workmen to join funds of this kind at their own expense. In 1849 these authorities were empowered to require factory owners and master craftsmen to insure their workmen against sickness ; they were to contribute towards the cost half as much as their men, and were to

Social Insurance in Germany

deduct the latter's contributions from their wages—two provisions which provided useful precedents when the time had ripened for general sickness insurance legislation.

Under the influence of the English Friendly Society movement an important law was passed in Prussia in 1854 (April 3rd) empowering local authorities by by-laws to require dependent workpeople to join benefit societies. Under this law a great increase in the provision for sickness took place. In 1874 it was estimated that some 5,000 societies, with a membership of 800,000, a revenue of £150,000, and accumulated funds of £650,000, existed in Prussia. Sickness funds existed in large numbers also in connexion with the Trade Guilds, being supported and managed by masters and men on equal terms.

Similarly in the South German States—Bavaria, Wurtemberg, and Baden—a form of parochial sickness insurance existed more than half a century ago in virtue of laws enabling local authorities to levy a small weekly charge on unmarried workpeople and domestic servants, in return for which they were cared for when ill and disabled. Legislation on somewhat similar lines was passed in Saxony, Brunswick, and Hanover.

Special statutory provision was made for particular sections of wage-earners. Thus the German Commercial Code of May 31, 1861, gave shop assistants a right to the continuance of their wages during six weeks of sickness in a year, and this provision was continued in the revised law of May 10, 1897.[3] Seamen were protected by laws

[3] The Sickness Insurance Amendment Act of 1903 brought this class of workers, and also apprentices, within the scope of obligatory insurance.

6

Early Experiments in Insurance

which made the shipowners responsible for their maintenance in the event of sickness or accident during a voyage and for a certain provision for their relatives in the event of their death.

Finally, there had come into existence a large class of voluntary aid or benefit societies (*Hilfskassen*), formed more or less on the model of the English Friendly Societies, and for the development of which the Imperial law of April 7, 1876, was passed, providing for registration, restricting the functions of such societies to the granting of sickness and funeral benefits, fixing the rates of contributions and benefits, and providing for the security of funds.

About this time it was estimated that the benefit societies of all kinds in operation in Germany numbered 12,000 and their membership over 2,000,000. In Prussia alone the members of the registered benefit societies numbered 840,000, those of the unregistered societies and clubs 200,000, and those of the miners' societies 220,000.

An investigation into the influence of the compulsory insurance laws upon the Poor Law made by the German Poor Law Association in 1893-4 brought to light the extent to which the working classes of industrial towns were insured against sickness prior to the passing of these laws. Some of the replies then received are quoted:—

BIELEFELD.—"The major part of the factory operatives were insured against sickness and a large part of them against accident before the passing of the obligatory system of insurance."

COLMAR (Alsace).—"Before the laws were passed a

large part of the workers were already insured against sickness."

ERFURT.—"A large part of the industrial population was insured against sickness and a part against accident before the laws were passed."

HALLE.—"The larger part of the workers were already insured against sickness."

KAISERSLAUTERN.—"A large part of the workers were already insured against sickness."

PLAUEN.—"About one quarter of the workers were already insured against sickness."

ZITTAU.—"A large part of the workers (2,800 out of 7,500) were already insured against sickness, accident, and infirmity and old age."

ESSEN.—"Before the issue of the obligatory laws voluntary funds afforded the workers about the same benefits to which they have now a legal claim, except in the case of old age pensions."

Nevertheless, on the whole, the existing provident agencies had for various reasons failed to keep pace with the altered needs of the times, and when in 1882 a general obligatory scheme of sickness insurance was proposed the Government pleaded in its support that "Experience has abundantly shown that the universal adoption of sickness insurance, which must be characterised as one of the most important measures for the improvement of the condition of the working classes, cannot be effected on the lines of the [voluntary] legislation of 1876."

The way had been prepared likewise for a general measure of accident insurance. As early as 1838 Prussia replaced the common law on the subject of liability for injuries by a formal Employers' Liability Act (*Haft-*

Early Experiments in Insurance

pflichtgesetz) (November 3rd), applicable to the railway service, and several of the minor States followed Prussia's example. It was not until 1871 that a law was passed (June 7th) for the whole Empire, applying the same principle to new classes of workpeople—those employed in factories, mines, and quarries. Even this law was limited in scope, however, and it worked cumbrously, uncertainly, and unequally. Liability could only be established where negligence was proved, and often a workman obtained compensation only after long, wearisome, and costly litigation. On the other hand, in the absence of mutual liability the compensation awarded proved at times an intolerable burden to small employers, many of whom were ruined in consequence. The law, in fact, pleased neither workpeople nor employers, and no one grumbled when it was proposed to replace it by a comprehensive and more business-like measure. When relating to me on one occasion the origin of the insurance legislation, Prince Bismarck said of this law :—

"Something had been done in regard to compensation for injuries before I introduced the Accident Insurance Law. There was the old Employers' Liability Act, but it was unjust and inadequate. I could see myself, in my private capacity, how unfairly this law worked. It did, indeed, award workpeople of certain classes compensation for injuries sustained under fixed circumstances, but their claims entailed endless litigation of a costly kind, with the result that the claimants seldom got their due."

A little later compensation for accidents was secured to seamen by a special law (of 1877), which established Marine Boards for the purpose of investigating liability in every individual case.

9

Social Insurance in Germany

On the whole, the existing provision against infirmity and old age was more inadequate than that against sickness and accidents. The miners of Prussia were protected to some extent by their " Knappschaft " funds, but the corresponding organisations in the other States did not go beyond sickness. Many factory pension funds existed also, particularly in the large industrial towns, but the help which they were able to afford was often uncertain and generally insufficient. For the rest, the horizon of the working man whose earnings did not allow of substantial saving was bounded by the Poor Law.

But, further, the existing insurance agencies failed to take account of the changed conditions of industrial life, which exposed the working classes to risks and vicissitudes of a kind not experienced before. The old home industries were fast giving way to the factory system, and the leisurely methods of hand production had largely been supplanted by machinery and steam power. It may be true that the German factory worker never trod the dark paths which led the Lancashire and Yorkshire factory operative tardily to the statute of 1833 and its followers, regulating the hours of labour; yet even in Germany the coming of the factory system crowded the battle-field of industry with victims. The special hazards to the worker's life and health were on the one hand accidents, and on the other hand sickness and infirmity arising out of exhausting and unhealthy occupations and the general pressure of industrial life. A genuine desire to ameliorate the effects of these hazards, and to lessen the risks themselves, by preventive measures, explains much of the enthusiasm which carried the insurance legislation so speedily and triumphantly on its way. It was

Early Experiments in Insurance

not enough, as Prince Bismarck said at that time, to think of the workman's need for protection when recruits were wanted for the army and taxpayers for the national treasury; the statesman and the legislator must accustom themselves to think of the workman all the time, and to make his welfare a direct object of national policy.

There is no need to disguise the fact—for Prince Bismarck himself avowed it—that a strong motive of expediency also played a part in determining the legislation of that era of large social ideas. Bismarck's idea was, in fact, " to bribe the working classes, or, if you like, to win them over "—I recall words which he spoke to myself—" to regard the State as a social institution existing for their sake and interested in their welfare."

For Socialism had already made an ominous entrance not only into Germany, but into its Imperial Parliament. In the first Diet of the new Empire, elected in 1871, the Socialists were represented by only two members; but in 1874 there were seven and in 1877 twelve, while the votes recorded for these members in the elections increased in six years from 124,700, or 3 per cent. of the aggregate poll, to 493,300, or 9 per cent.

With his characteristic faith in measures of force, Bismarck did not hesitate, even at this early stage in the growth of Socialism, to propose repressive legislation. Most parties in the Diet, however, looked askance at any experiment of the kind until the attempted assassination of the aged Emperor William I. on May 11, 1878. Two days after that occurrence a Bill for the " checking of Social Democratic excesses " was introduced in the Reichstag. The measure was urged on the assembly by the full force of Bismarck's eloquence and conviction; yet

Social Insurance in Germany

it was not popular, and it was thrown out by an over-whelming majority. A few days later, on June 2nd, followed the second attempt on the Emperor's life. Without asking the Reichstag to reconsider its attitude towards Socialist agitation, Bismarck appealed to the nation for a more tractable House. The new Diet accepted an amended measure of repression, which became law in October of the same year, and continued in force for twelve years.

No sooner was the Socialist Law passed than the promise of social reform legislation was made. At the opening of the Reichstag in February, 1879, the Emperor in his speech from the throne expressed the hope that the Legislature would co-operate with the Government in remedying social ills by legislation, for " a remedy cannot be sought merely in the repression of Socialistic excesses—there must be simultaneously a positive advancement of the welfare of the working classes."

The Insurance Laws were the immediate outcome of the new social policy foreshadowed in these words. They were not meant to mollify the effects of the Anti-Socialist Law, but rather to establish in the old monarchical faith and in attachment to the existing social order that part of the proletariate—still by far the greater part—which had not been won over to the party of subversion.

Already a small and influential social reform group, imbued with a sincere solicitude for the welfare of the working classes, yet also with a strong patriarchal spirit, had been formed in the Reichstag, and in 1878 this group petitioned the Government to enact an obligatory measure of insurance against old age and infirmity, taking the constitution and provisions of the miners' aid societies

12

Early Experiments in Insurance

as their model. The reply was sympathetic yet reserved. "The Government," it was said, "accepts the theory that the working man who has become incapacitated through age or in consequence of his work should not fall upon the Poor Law, but should be provided for by other institutions. It is, however, difficult to say how."

Soon after the Government were working on sickness and accident insurance schemes on their own account, and the first of these was laid before the Reichstag in 1881. The speech from the throne on February 15th again recalled the insufficiency of the Socialist Law as a remedy for social discontent, and added:—

"The care of those workpeople who are incapable of earning their livelihood is of the first importance. In their interest the Emperor has caused a Bill for the insurance of workpeople against the consequences of accident to be sent to the Federal Council—a Bill which, it is hoped, will meet a need felt both by workpeople and employers. His Majesty hopes that the measure will in principle receive the assent of the Federal Governments, and that it will be welcomed by the Reichstag as a complement of the legislation affording protection against Social Democratic movements."

The Bill as introduced bore date March 8, 1881, and the *exposé des motifs* which accompanied it avowed that it had been conceived in the spirit of State Socialism, yet defended that form of Socialism as inherent in the Christian theory of society and the State. It was declared to be expedient, as well as right, that the State should justify itself to the working classes as "not merely a necessary, but a beneficent institution."

"These classes must be led, by the evident and direct

13

advantages which are secured to them by legislative measures,' to regard the State not as an institution contrived for the protection of the better classes of society, but as one serving their own needs and interests. The apprehension that a Socialistic element might be introduced into legislation if this end were followed should not deter us. So far as that may be the case, it will not be an innovation, but the further development of the modern idea of the State, the result of Christian ethics, according to which the State should discharge, besides the defensive duty of protecting existing rights, the positive duty of promoting the welfare of all its members, and especially those who are weak and in need of help, by means of judicious institutions and the employment of those resources of the community which are at its disposal."

In the course of the debate on the first reading (April 1st), Prince Bismarck foreshadowed a still larger measure. "The end I have in view," he said, "is to relieve the parishes of a large part of their Poor Law charges by the establishment of an institution, having State support and extending to the whole Empire, for the maintenance of old and infirm persons." In a further speech (April 2nd) he said :—

" The domain of legislation which we enter with this law . . . deals with a question which will not soon disappear from the order of the day. For fifty years we have been speaking of a social question. Since the passing of the Socialist Law I have continually been reminded that a promise was then given that something positive should also be done to remove the legitimate causes of Socialism. I have had the reminder in mind

Early Experiments in Insurance

tota die up to this very moment, and I do not believe that either our sons or grandsons will quite dispose of the social question which has been hovering before us for fifty years. No political question can be. brought to a perfect mathematical conclusion, so that book balances can be drawn up ; these questions rise up, have their day, and then disappear among other questions of history ; that is the way of organic development."

Bismarck now for the first time appealed to the Reichstag to help him to elaborate and enact a triple system of compulsory insurance—against accident, sickness, and old age.

The first Accident Insurance Bill—for three several schemes were prepared before the Reichstag was satisfied—proposed a system of insurance through the Empire and the federal States, assisted by the higher administrative authorities. The entire organisation was to be bureaucratic ; neither employers nor workpeople were to share in administration. The workpeople were to be divided into three wages classes ; in the case of those with wages not exceeding 750 marks (£37 10s.) annually the employer was to pay two-thirds of the contributions and the provincial Poor Law authority the remainder ; in the case of those with incomes between 750 and 1,200 marks (£37 10s. and £60) the employers were to pay two-thirds and the workpeople one-third ; and where the income was between 1,200 and 2,000 marks (£60 and £100), each party was to pay one-half. Undertakings were to be grouped in "danger classes," employers subject to the same risk were to be allowed to insure on the mutual prin-

15

ciple, and the capital value of the liabilities incurred each year was to be raised in that year (the so-called *Kapitaldeckungsverfahren*, introduced in the later Austrian legislation). The pensions for accident were to range from a quarter to two-thirds of the usual wages of the injured person. In the course of discussion in Committee the Bill was modified greatly, particularly by an amendment placing the entire cost of insurance upon the employers, a proposal to which Bismarck was then strongly opposed, and the measure was withdrawn.

Soon afterwards followed the promulgation of the historical Imperial Message of November 17, 1881, laying down the principles of future German social policy. It stated :—

"The cure of social ills must be sought not exclusively in the repression of Social Democratic excesses, but simultaneously in the positive advancement of the welfare of the working classes. We regard it as our imperial duty to urge this task again upon the Reichstag, and we should look back with the greater satisfaction upon all the successes with which God has visibly blessed our government if we were able one day to take with us the consciousness that we left to the Fatherland new and lasting sureties for its internal peace, and to those needing help greater security and liberality in the assistance to which they can lay claim. Our efforts in this direction are certain of the approval of all the federal Governments, and we confidently rely on the support of the Reichstag, without distinction of parties. In order to realise these views a Bill for the insurance of workmen against industrial accidents will first be laid

Early Experiments in Insurance

before you, after which a supplementary measure will be submitted providing for a general organisation of industrial sickness insurance. But likewise those who are disabled in consequence of old age or invalidity possess a well-founded claim to a more ample relief on the part of the State than they have hitherto enjoyed. To find the proper ways and means for making such provision is a difficult task, yet is one of the highest obligations of every community based on the ethical foundations of a Christian national life. The closer union of the practical forces of this national life and their combination in the form of corporate associations, with State patronage and help, will, we hope, render possible the discharge of tasks to which the Executive alone might prove unequal."

The second Accident Insurance Bill, of 1882, fared no better than the first, for Bismarck would not abandon the idea of a bureaucratic institution, subsidised by the State. The Bill was an improvement upon its predecessor in that it fully accepted the mutual principle and adopted the principle of yearly levies according to the actual expenditure of the year (*Umlagererfahren*) in place of the method of capitalising all liabilities incurred during the year (*Kapitaldeckungsverfahren*).

The Bill was introduced almost simultaneously with a Sickness Insurance Bill (April 29th), inasmuch as it was now proposed that the care of persons injured should fall during the first 13 weeks on the sickness funds to be established, and to the cost of which the employers were to contribute one-third. Of the two Bills only that dealing with sickness was dealt with during that session. It passed the Reichstag on May 31, and was pro-

Social Insurance in Germany

mulgated June 15, 1883, but the date of its coming into operation was deferred until December 1, 1884, so as to give time for the passing of the complementary Accident Insurance Law. The Sickness Insurance Law applied to industrial workers generally, and provided benefits of 13 weeks' duration ; the extension to 26 weeks came only 20 years later.

In the session of 1884 the Accident Insurance Bill was reintroduced with amendments, the principal of which gave to the Mutual Associations complete autonomy, while subjecting them to the supervision of an Imperial Insurance Office, established by the Bill, and the measure became law on July 6, 1884, coming into force on October 1, 1885.

A law of May 28, 1885 (in force from October 1st of the same year) extended both the Sickness and Accident Insurance Laws to inland transport undertakings, and made special provision for the insurance of employees engaged in State undertakings (*i.e.* railway, post, and telegraph services), and to those engaged on canals and rivers ; while the Sickness Insurance Law was amended by supplementary laws of April 10, 1892, June 30, 1900, and May 25, 1903.

Further amendments of the Accident Insurance Law extended obligatory insurance to civil servants employed in naval and military establishments (March 15, 1886) ; to agriculture and forestry (May 5, 1886, in force from April 1, 1888) ; to civil engineering works (July 11, 1887, in force from January 1, 1888) ; to seamen (July 13, 1887, in force from January 1, 1888); and to prisoners (June 30, 1900). A law of June 30 (operative from October 1st), 1900, amended the parent statute.

Early Experiments in Insurance

A measure for providing pensions in time of infirmity and old age was promised in an Imperial Message of April 14, 1883, but the promise only took practical shape in 1888. Of the trio of insurance schemes this was undoubtedly nearest to Prince Bismarck's sympathies, yet by the irony of fate it fell to another Chancellor to enact it, and to do so in a form different from that originally designed. The measure as passed divided the actual cost of insurance between employers and workpeople, the Imperial Treasury making an addition of a fixed amount, whereas it was Bismarck's intention to relieve the workpeople altogether from liability. The Government also intended to work this system of insurance through the Mutual Associations created by the Accident Insurance Law, but in face of the opposition of the employers this proposal did not appear in the draft laid before the Reichstag on November 22, 1888; and territorial Insurance or Pension Boards (*Versicherungsanstalten*), organised on a bureaucratic basis, were introduced instead, representation being given to employers and workpeople in the form of committees. In view of the later strengthening of the official element in the administration of the insurance systems, it is of special interest to know that government from the outside was not Bismarck's intention. Speaking of the Insurance Laws as a whole, he said to me, "We have too much bureaucracy (*Beamtentum*) in them."

The Bill became law as the Old Age and Invalidity Insurance Act on June 22, 1889, and entered into force on January 1, 1891. The only later amendment of importance until 1911 was that of July 13, 1899, in

Social Insurance in Germany

force as from January 1, 1900. This law was called the "Invalidity Insurance Act," a change which was deemed prudent owing to the fact that the number of pensions granted simply on account of old age had become quite insignificant when compared with the number granted by reason of invalidity. In 1899 only one pension in every seven was granted on account of old age, and of the new pensions granted in 1910 only one in twelve was an old age pension.

It is significant of the progress in public favour made in the meantime by the insurance principle that whereas the earlier law was only adopted with a majority of twenty votes, the amending law was passed with the approval of an almost unanimous House, only five votes being recorded against the third reading. Further, the Social Democrats now for the first time voted as a party for an insurance law, instead of maintaining its old attitude of grudging tolerance, as evidenced by endless criticism of a captious kind, followed by abstention from the division lobby.

Two other measures, passed in 1911, must be named, in order to complete this brief historical review of German social insurance legislation. One is the Insurance Consolidation Act (*Reichsversicherungsordnung*), which brings all the insurance systems into one statute, and besides extending the scope of sickness insurance grafts upon the invalidity insurance scheme a small provision for the widows (or widowers respectively) and orphans of persons insured under that scheme. This supplementary measure of insurance was promised by the Government during the passage of the Customs Tariff Law of 1902. Section 15 of that Act stipulated that

BERGMANNSHEIL. HOSPITAL OF THE ACCIDENT INSURANCE ASSOCIATION FOR THE WESTPHALIAN MINING INDUSTRY.

Early Experiments in Insurance

in so far as the net yield per head of the population of the higher duties on rye, wheat, spelt, cattle, sheep, &c. exceeded the average of the years 1898 to 1903, the excess should be applied towards facilitating such a scheme of insurance, and the fund so ear-marked was to accumulate until a law on the subject could be prepared. Had expectations been realised, a sum of some twenty-five million pounds would have accrued up to the present time, but in fact barely one-tenth of this amount has been realised, and it has been found necessary to work out a scheme on business principles, and to throw the cost upon workpeople, employers, and the Imperial Treasury jointly. The other measure of insurance is one providing retirement allowances to salaried *employés* (in the French sense of the word) and pensions to their survivors.

The main provisions of the first of these extensions of the insurance principle are explained in the chapter dealing with Invalidity Insurance, and those of the second form the subject of a separate chapter.

CHAPTER II

SICKNESS INSURANCE—I. ORGÁNISATION, CONTRI-BUTIONS, AND BENEFITS

PROVISION against sickness is the oldest part of the threefold system of insurance, and it may also be regarded as the practical basis of that system. For not only does this provision meet the most pressing needs of the working classes, and meet them most expeditiously, but the extent of the demands made upon the two other branches of insurance is largely determined by the efficiency and success with which the sickness insurance funds protect the health and strength of their members during the period of their highest earning capacity.

I. SCOPE OF INSURANCE.

Prior to the law of 1911 insurance against sickness was already obligatory upon the great majority of wage-earners regularly engaged in industrial and commercial undertakings, in so far as their employment was "not limited by the nature of its object, or otherwise by the contract of service in advance, to a period of less than a week." This limitation was imposed owing to the assumption that to extend liability to insurance to every temporary employment would make difficult or impos-

Sickness Insurance

sible of enforcement the employer's obligation to notify such employment. Subject to this condition the liability to insure was extended to persons of both sexes employed for remuneration (this including all money considerations and payments in kind) in factories and workshops, iron-works, mines and quarries, shipbuilding yards, the building trades, the inland transportation services (railways, navigation, &c.), undertakings connected with the postal and telegraph services and military and naval establishments, trade and commerce, the handicrafts, and all undertakings employing mechanical motive power. Works officials, foremen, and shop assistants were only liable to insurance if their remuneration did not exceed 6s. 8d. a day, or, if they were paid by periods, 2,000 marks or £100 a year.

The pre-supposition of liability to insure being a direct wages relationship, persons in an independent position were exempted. Other classes excluded were military persons and State and communal employees who had a claim against the State or communes respectively in the event of sickness, also agricultural and forest labourers and domestic servants.

Provision was made, however, both for the extension of obligatory insurance to certain classes of persons and for the exemption of others ordinarily liable, also for voluntary insurance.

The exclusion from the earlier law of domestic servants was justified at the time by the fact that many of the States had partial laws making provision for them during sickness, while the Civil Code makes employers responsible for the care of their servants during six weeks of illness or until the expiration of the term of service,

23

Social Insurance in Germany

should this period be shorter, though it does not allow a master to evade liability by discharging a servant during illness. It was not pretended, however, that this provision was adequate. Sick servants often found themselves without legal claim upon their employers for care and maintenance—for example, if sickness had begun the day before they received notice, or in the case of sickness due to intent or to gross negligence. Furthermore, an employer was empowered to deduct the cost of curative treatment from a servant's wages for the time of sickness unless (as in Prussia) the sickness had been actually caused by employment. The possible hardships to which servants were exposed led the legislature, while deferring their admission to the national system of insurance, to give them the option of becoming insured with the parochial authorities, and even empowered these authorities to require their insurance in this way.

The omission of agricultural labourers from the compulsory provisions of the law was similarly justified by the obligation resting upon employers under the ancient Rural Servants' Ordinances (*Gesindeordnungen*) of the various States to provide for their dependants in time of sickness and by the provisions of the Civil Code already noted.

The Insurance Consolidation Act of 1911 has both extended and amended the Sickness Insurance legislation more than that relating either to accident or invalidity. The old catalogue of trades and occupations liable to insurance has given place to the following more comprehensive list :—

1. Workpeople, assistants, journeymen, apprentices, servants;

Sickness Insurance

2. Works officials, foremen, and other employees in a similar leading position, all in so far as this employment forms their principal occupation;

3. Assistants and apprentices in shops and pharmacies;

4. Members of theatrical and orchestral companies, regardless of the artistic value of their performances;

5. Teachers and tutors;

6. Out-workers;

7. Crews of German sea-going vessels in so far as they are not protected by the Merchant Shipping Act and the Commercial Code, and those engaged in inland navigation.[1]

Insurance is compulsory, irrespective of age, and there is no wages limit in the case of workpeople; but classes 2 and 5 in the foregoing list, as well as ships' captains, are only liable to insurance if their ordinary yearly earnings do not exceed 2,500 marks, or £125.[2]

[1] *National Insurance Act.*—Special provisions apply to the insurance of persons in the naval and military services of the Crown and to seamen, the contributions and benefits in both cases being adjusted to the peculiar conditions of their employment (Sections 46 and 48). As to seamen, see p. 70, note.

[2] *National Insurance Act.*—The Act recognises two classes of insurers, employed and voluntary insurers. Subject to certain exemptions, the compulsory provisions apply to all persons within the ages of 16 and 70 employed within the meaning of the Act whose income (except from manual labour, in which case the condition does not apply) does not exceed £160 a year. At age 70 both contributions and benefits (except medical benefit) cease, since old age pensions are then claimable under the Act of 1908. Persons aged 65 or

Social Insurance in Germany

The classes of employed persons added and their estimated numbers are as follows: Labourers engaged in agriculture and forestry, 2,986,000; domestic servants, 1,105,000; casual labourers, 356,000; itinerant workers,

upwards at the time of the coming into operation of the Act will not have the benefit of full insurance, but employers will pay contributions in respect of them and they will receive such benefits as these contributions and the subsidy to be paid by the State will provide. (Sections 1 (4) and 49, and Part I. of 1st Schedule.)

The employments specified for inclusion in Part I. of the first Schedule are:—(a) Employment in the United Kingdom under any contract of service or apprenticeship, written or oral, whether expressed or implied, and whether the employed person is paid by the employer or some other person, and whether under one or more employers, and whether paid by time or by the piece or partly by time and partly by the piece or otherwise, or, except in the case of a contract of apprenticeship, without any money payment; (b) employment under such a contract as aforesaid as master or a member of the crew of any ship registered in the United Kingdom or of any other British ship or vessel of which the owner, or, if there is more than one owner, the managing owner or manager, resides or has his principal place of business in the United Kingdom; (c) employment as an outworker unless excluded by a special order made by the Insurance Commissioners; and (d) employment in the United Kingdom in plying for hire with any vehicle or vessel the use of which is obtained from the owner thereof under contract in consideration of the payment of a fixed sum or a share in the earnings or otherwise.

In addition to the income limit of exemption (over £160 a year) applying to employed persons other than those engaged in manual labour (Section 1 (3)), the Insurance Committees may in all cases fix a limit of income beyond which medical benefit may not be given to insured persons on the terms and

26

Sickness Insurance

40,000; out-workers, 295,000; also chemists' assistants and apprentices, teachers and tutors, members of theatrical companies and orchestras, apprentices employed without payment, and others, to the estimated number of 250,000; giving a total of 5,041,000.

Special provisions apply to the insurance of persons employed in agriculture, domestic servants, casual labourers, those employed in itinerant trades, out-workers, and apprentices of all kinds employed without payment, and it is left to the Federal Council to decide how far casual employment shall be exempted from insurance

The law formally exempts certain classes of employees from liability to insurance, viz. :—[3]

conditions arranged with the doctors for others, in which case the Committees will pay to such excluded persons sums not exceeding in the aggregate the amounts which the Committees would otherwise have expended in providing medical benefit for them, leaving them to make their own arrangements with the doctors of their choice. (Section 15 (3).)

[3] *National Insurance Act.*—The exemptions specified in Part II. of the first Schedule are :—

(a) Sailors and soldiers (who are dealt with under a special scheme, forming part of the Act) ; (b) employees of the Crown, and of local or other public authorities where, by the terms of their employment, they secure a provision not less favourable than that made by the Act; (c) clerks and other salaried officials in the service of railway and other statutory companies subject to the same condition as in (b); (d) teachers with claim to pension ; (e) agents employed by commission, or fees, or share in profits, where mainly dependent for a livelihood on their earnings from some other occupation, or ordinarily employed as agents by more than one employer, and not mainly dependent for a livelihood on such employment;

Social Insurance in Germany

1. Officials of the State, communal bodies, and insurance authorities acting under the Insurance Laws, and teachers and tutors in public schools so long as they are being trained for their profession.

(*f*) employment in respect of which no wages or other money payment is made where the employer is the occupier of an agricultural holding and the employed person is employed thereon, or where the person employed is the child of, or is maintained by, the employer ; (*g*) employment otherwise than by way of manual labour and at a rate of remuneration exceeding in value £160 a year ; (*h*) casual employment otherwise than for the purposes of the employer's trade or business or of any game or recreation where the persons employed are engaged or paid through a club ; (*i*) employment subsidiary in character and not adopted as the principal means of livelihood ; (*j*) employment as an out-worker where the person so employed is the wife of an insured person and is not wholly or mainly dependent for her livelihood on her earnings in such employment ; (*k*) employment as a member of the crew of a fishing vessel remunerated by shares in the profits or the gross earnings ; and (*l*) employment in the service of the husband or wife of the employed person.

Exemption from liability to insurance may be claimed by persons employed within the meaning of the Act if they are in receipt of any pension or income of the annual value of £26 or upwards not dependent upon their personal exertions, or are ordinarily and mainly dependent for a livelihood upon other persons. Nevertheless, the employers of such exempted persons will pay the usual employers' contributions. (Section 2.)

Inmates of charitable or reformatory homes and there employed may be exempted from compulsory insurance, if they receive maintenance and medical attendance when sick. Where such inmates leave after staying in the home longer than six months, the managers must pay the sums necessary to allow of their entering or re-entering into insurance. (Section 51.)

28

Sickness Insurance

2. Military persons engaged in civil employments for the Crown.

3. Persons who during their scientific training for a future calling teach without remuneration.

4. Members of ecclesiastical societies, deaconesses, sisters, and similar persons who devote themselves to nursing, teaching, or other works of public welfare from religious or moral motives, and only receive free board and lodging by way of remuneration.

5. Persons employed in undertakings belonging to the State, communal bodies, and insurance authorities acting under the law, also teachers and tutors in public schools, provided they have a claim against their employers equivalent to the sickness benefits provided by the law or alternatively salary, retirement allowance, or other moneys equal to one and a half times the statutory sick-pay.

Persons employed by other public bodies or corporations may be exempted on the employer's application, on the condition just stated, and also if they are being trained for a calling. Other persons who may be exempted on the employer's application are apprentices in the service of their parents and persons employed in voluntary labour colonies and similar institutions.

Voluntary insurance is open to several classes of persons, so long as their total yearly income does not exceed £125, viz. :—⁴

1. Employees of the scheduled classes (Nos. 1 to 7, pp. 24, 25) who are not liable to compulsory insurance.

⁴ *National Insurance Act.*—Subject to an income limit of £160, voluntary insurance is open to persons not employed

29

Social Insurance in Germany

2. Members of an employer's family working in his business without a formal contract of service and without remuneration.

3. Tradesmen who do not regularly employ workpeople, or employ at the most two.

In these cases it is competent for a sickness fund to impose an age limit, and to require applicants to undergo medical examination.

Voluntary insurance lapses in all cases, however, when the "regular total yearly income" exceeds 4,000 marks, or £200.

It is estimated that 13,954,973 persons (10,291,532 males and 3,663,441 females) were insured under the old law in 1910; this represented about 21·5 per cent. of the total population, and 49·7 per cent. of the occupied population. It is impossible to estimate how large a proportion of the five million persons brought under liability to insure will in fact become members of sickness funds. If the whole came in, the proportion of the occupied population insured would be 67·6 per cent.[5]

The proportion which the voluntary members form of the whole is not known, but figures relating to funds containing nearly half a million members show the small

within the meaning of the Act, provided they are engaged in some regular occupation, and are wholly or mainly dependent for their livelihood upon the earnings derived by them from that occupation. But the income limit does not apply to persons who have been insured for five years. (Section 1 (3).)

[5] *National Insurance Act.*—It is estimated that the total number of persons who will be insured under the law from July, 1912, will be 13,918,000, made up as follows: Compulsory contributors 13,089,000, or 94 per cent.; voluntary con-

Sickness Insurance

percentage of 8. . The ratio does not vary greatly in these.
funds :—

	Compul-sory.	Per Cent.	Volun-tary.	Per Cent.	Total.
Berlin Sickness Funds (1911)	927,451	92·5	75,563	7·5	1,003,014
Leipzig Local Fund (1910)	168,948	92·4	13,950	7·6	182,898
Dresden Local Fund (1910)	104,310	87·4	15,109	12·6	119,419
Munich Local Fund (1910)	119,175	92·7	9,368	7·3	128,543
	1,319,884	92·0	113,990	8·0	1,433,874

tributors 829,000, or 6 per cent. The insurers may be classified
further as follows :—

	COMPULSORY.		VOLUNTARY.		TOGETHER.	
	Males.	Females.	Males.	Females.	Males.	Females.
Members of Approved Societies ...	8,579,000	3,628,000	625,000	204,000	9,204,000	3,832,000
Deposit Con-tributors ...	638,000	244,000	—	—	638,000	244,000
	9,217,000	3,872,000	625,000	204,000	9,842,000	4,076,000
	13,089,000	+	829,000	=	13,918,000	

No allowance is made here for possible voluntary deposit
contributors. The grand total may be placed roundly at
fourteen millions. This number would be equal to about 31
per cent. of the total population, and 77 per cent. of the
occupied population, of the United Kingdom.

Social Insurance in Germany

Insurance entails no formality whatever upon the workman. His membership of a sickness fund begins with the day of entrance into insurable employment, and a contingent claim to benefits begins at once, subject to the provision that no benefits can be claimed in respect of an illness which existed at the time of becoming a member, and that a waiting time may be imposed by rule in the case of voluntary insurers and casual labourers (six weeks) and members of miners' funds.[6] A fund is protected against "bad lives" by the unwillingness of employers to engage them, but in the case of voluntary insurers a fund may by rule apply a medical test and also impose an age limit.[7] An employer is required to notify all persons in his employment to the proper sickness fund within three days of the beginning and end of their employment, and an Insurance Office may establish offices for this purpose.

[6] *National Insurance Act.*—Medical benefit (medical attendance and medicine) cannot be claimed for six months after the coming into force of the Act, but beyond that no waiting time will be necessary. . For other benefits waiting times must be observed as follows: Sickness benefit (sick pay) 26 weeks, with 26 weekly contributions; disablement benefit, 104 weeks, with 104 weekly contributions; and maternity benefit, 26 (with voluntary insurance 52) weeks, with 26 (52) weekly contributions. (Section 8 (8).)

[7] *National Insurance Act.*—Medical examination is permitted, in consonance with the past usage of Friendly Societies, by the provision that "an approved society shall be entitled in accordance with its rules to admit or reject" any applicant for membership, provided that no application may be refused solely on the ground of age. (Section 30 (2).)

Sickness Insurance

II. The Insurance Funds.

When the first law was passed the Government endeavoured to use existing provident organisations as far as possible, only requiring that they should offer to their members a minimum scale of benefits. Thus although the execution of the law was entrusted to eight different types of sickness funds or institutions, only two of these were altogether new. The existing organisations which were recognised by the law were the old-established miners' brotherhood funds, or *Knappschaftskassen;* the factory and works funds, formed for individual undertakings, and henceforth sanctioned wherever more than fifty workpeople were employed ; the Guild funds established for the organised handicrafts under the Industrial Code of the Empire ; and two classes of free Mutual Aid or Friendly Societies, viz., those registered under the Imperial law of 1876, already referred to, and those established under the laws of the various States.

The new organisations were the " local " funds (*Ortskrankenkassen*) formed by the communes for special trades or for various trades carried on in the same locality, and building works funds formed *ad hoc* for special works of construction owing to the exceptional risks incurred, and in their nature of a temporary character. Finally, there was developed the South German system of parochial insurance, the local authorities being required to insure such persons coming under the law as were unable to join any of the statutory funds already enumerated.[8]

[8] *National Insurance Act.*—The now superseded communal system of insurance, into which persons not entitled or not

33   D

Social Insurance in Germany

In 1910 the numbers of funds in existence and their average membership were as follows :—

	Number of Funds.	Percentage of Total.	Average Membership.	Percentage of Total.
Parochial..	8,217	35·1	1,671,827	12·0
Local	4,752	20·4	6,845,940	49·1
Factory	7,957	34·0	3,273,710	23·5
Building	46	0·2	16,665	0·1
Guild	818	3·5	296,521	2·1
Registered Mutual Aid ..	1,262	5·4	928,606	6·7
State Aid	136	0·6	36,106	0·3
Mining	166	0·8	885,598	6·3
Total	23,354	—	13,954,973	—

The average membership of the various classes of funds in 1910 was as follows :—

Parochial 210, "local" 1,442, factory 415, building 417, Guild 370, registered Mutual Aid 739, State regulated Mutual Aid 265, mining 5,335; all funds together 597.

The new law aims at greater centralisation, with a view to superseding small and inefficient funds. Two able to obtain insurance elsewhere fell, have a distinct counterpart under this Act in the system of deposit insurance. In the interest of persons liable to insurance who fail, owing to bad health, irregularity of employment, or other reasons, to become members of approved societies, a system of Post Office deposit has been introduced; the contributions of such persons, their employers, and the State will go to individual accounts, and the amount thus accumulated, less deduction for medical and sanatorium benefit and cost of administration, may be drawn on in time of sickness until it is exhausted. This arrangement is temporary only and will expire on January 1, 1915. (Sections 42 and 43.)

Sickness Insurance

groups disappear entirely, viz., the parochial and building trade funds, which accounted for more than one-third
of all funds in existence in 1910, and two new types are
created. The funds now recognised by the law are the
following :—9

1. *General Local Funds.*—This new group of funds is
made the basis of the system of insurance. The existing
" local " funds for one or more trades or occupations will
be retained, but as " special local " funds, provided they
contain at least 250 members, do not threaten the
existence and efficiency of the "general local" and " rural "
funds of the district, offer benefits now or within six
months equivalent to those of the " general local " funds,
give proof of permanent efficiency, and do not carry
on operations beyond the district of the Insurance Office
affected. A " general local " or a " rural " fund is held to
be menaced if its membership would fall below 250 in
the event of " special local " funds being permitted.10

9 *National Insurance Act.*—The actual working of the insurance system is entrusted to " approved societies," consisting
exclusively of insured persons and in the fullest degree
autonomous. The existing friendly societies and trade unions,
together with societies or branches formed by the industrial
assurance societies and companies, will in the main provide
the machinery by which the Act will be worked. (Sections 14
and 23.) Medical and sanatorium benefits, however, will be
administered by Insurance Committees formed for the counties
and county boroughs, upon which the insured person through
their societies will have a majority of members. (Sections 14,
15, and 59.) The general administration of the Act will be
supervised by bodies of Insurance Commissioners for the
three Kingdoms and for Wales. (Sections 57 and 80-83.)

10 *National Insurance Act.*—The only provision as to a

35

Social Insurance in Germany

2. *Factory and Works, and* (3) *Guild Funds.*—The existing Factory or Works and Guild funds are also recognised, subject to a minimum membership of 100, except in the case of funds for undertakings connected with agriculture and inland navigation, which need only have 50 members ; new Works and Guild funds may also be formed, subject to a minimum membership of 150, unless they would endanger the existence and efficiency of existing "general local" funds, the test being the maintenance of the latter at a membership of over 1,000.

4. *Miners' Funds.*—As with all previous legislation on this subject, miners' funds are but little affected. Formed for a special class of workpeople, subject to exceptional conditions and needs, and having behind them a long and unbroken record of invaluable service in the interest of thrift, they are left to do their own work in their own way.

5. *Rural Funds.*—The parochial funds are replaced by rural (*Land*) funds, which will insure domestic servants, agricultural labourers, out-workers, and such other classes of persons as the Federal Council may decide. Both the "General local" funds and the "Rural" funds are intended as a rule to serve for definite areas—as a rule the district of an Insurance Office—though the State Governments have certain discretionary powers, as explained below.

6. *Mutual Aid Funds.*—Voluntary provident or mutual aid funds certified before April, 1909, may continue with

minimum membership of approved societies is that requiring societies which at the date of any valuation have less than 5,000 members to be associated with other societies for the purpose of such valuation. (Section 39.) In all other matters even the smallest societies will be independent.

Sickness Insurance

the name " substitutionary (*Ersatz*) funds." They must have a membership of over 1,000. No new funds of this kind may be formed.

The idea underlying the new organisation of sickness insurance is to pave the way for the eventual supremacy of two types of funds—the " general local " and " rural " funds, each unassailable within its own sphere of operations. These funds are to be formed for specified districts by resolution of the local government authorities. The State Legislatures are empowered to prohibit the formation of " rural " funds alongside of the " general local " funds, either within an entire State or certain areas of such State. In any case no " rural " fund may be formed alongside of a " general local " fund when such rural fund would not have at least 250 obligatory members, and in addition the Higher Insurance Office can prohibit the formation of a rural fund where it can be shown that no need exists. On the other hand, the formation of a " general local " fund alongside of a " rural " fund may be prohibited where the former would not have at least 250 obligatory members.

Persons liable to be insured who are not members of a mining fund, a " special local " fund, a works or factory fund, or a Guild fund, have to join the " general local " fund or the " rural " fund for their trade or place of employment respectively. Provision is made for amalgamating local and rural funds when the membership of either of them falls below 250, and for the dissolution of funds of all kinds under given circumstances.

Double insurance in " statutory funds " is not allowed ; but a workman may insure himself both in a statutory fund and a " substitutionary " fund, *i.e.*, a voluntary provident

37

Social Insurance in Germany

or mutual aid fund carried on at the sole cost of its members; and he may also insure himself outside the law at will.[11]

Certain general provisions common to all the funds, except those of the miners, which are governed by a special law, may now be summarised.

III. The Contributions.

(i) *Method of Payment.*—Now as before the contributions are in general borne to the extent of two-thirds by the workpeople and one-third by the employers.[12] The draft of the Insurance Consolidation Law proposed to

[11] *National Insurance Act.*—No person may be insured under the Act in two approved societies or be at once a member of such society and a deposit contributor. The benefits offered by the Act can only be claimed through one society, though it is open to any one to contribute to that or other societies for additional benefits outside the Act. (Section 34.)

[12] *National Insurance Act.*—The general basis of contribution is a uniform rate for males and females respectively. There are, however, important deviations from this rule. In general, the funds for providing the benefits conferred by the Act and for defraying the expenses of the administration of those benefits are derived as to seven-ninths (or, in the case of women, three-fourths) thereof from contributions made by or in respect of the contributors by themselves or their employers, and as to the remaining two-ninths (or, in the case of women, one quarter) thereof from moneys provided by Parliament.

For the actual rates of contribution see pp. 44, 45, note. (Section 3 and Second Schedule.)

Voluntary contributors who insure under the State scheme within six months after the commencement of the Act (July 15, 1912), and are then under 45 years of age, will pay the ordinary employed rates (both the employer's and their

38

Sickness Insurance

charge employers with one-half of the contribution, with
a view to giving them an equal voice in administration.
This proposal was strongly opposed by the Labour party,
and the smaller employers were also against it; hence
it was dropped, and the object aimed at was achieved
in another way. There are, however, certain variations
from the general rule of apportionment. In the case of
the miners' funds the matter is left to agreement, and
in practice the employers pay nearly as much as the
men; the rules of a Guild fund may provide for equal
payments; in the case of the mutual aid or "substitutionary" funds the workpeople bear the entire cost, but
their employers make contributions in respect of them to
the compulsory funds in which they would otherwise be
insured. Voluntary insurers pay the whole contribution
themselves. The contributions are paid in the first
instance by the employers, who deduct the workers' share
at the following pay-day, but arrears can only be deducted
in respect of one payment period, unless not caused by
the employer's fault.[13] The rules of a fund prescribe

own); those joining later and over 45 will pay rates proportionate to their age. But any one who has been an
employed contributor for five years and then becomes a
voluntary contributor will continue to pay the employed rate.
(Section 5.) Payment is by stamps, as in the case of German
invalidity insurance.

[13] *National Insurance Act.*—Contributions are payable at
weekly or other prescribed intervals. The employer, in the
first instance, pays both the contribution payable by himself
and that of the employed contributor, and is entitled to recover from the contributor by deduction from his wages or
otherwise the amount of the contribution so paid on his
behalf. (Section 4 and 3rd Schedule.)

Social Insurance in Germany

when an employer himself must pay over the contributions, but the intervals must not be longer than a month. No contributions are payable during sickness.[14]

A workman does not forfeit claim to any benefits under the the Sickness Insurance Law in the event of his employer having failed to pay contributions in respect of him, nor in such a case can arrears be claimed from him. Under the old law the defaulting employer might be required to make good all expenditure incurred by the fund and be fined up to 20 marks (£1). Under the new law omission to notify insurable persons is punishable with the same fine, and in addition the fund concerned claims from the employer all arrears of contributions and is empowered to levy upon him additional contributions to the amount of from 100 to 500 per cent. of the arrears.[15]

[14] *National Insurance Act.*—" In calculating arrears of contributions no account shall be taken of any arrears accruing (*a*) during any period when the person in question has been, or but for this section or any other provision of this Act disentitling a person to such benefit, would have been, in receipt of sickness benefit or disablement benefit; or (*b*) in the case of a woman who, being an insured person, is herself entitled to maternity benefit, during two weeks before and four weeks after her delivery, or in the case of maternity benefit payable in respect of the posthumous child of an insured person, during the period subsequent to the father's death." (Section 10 (4).)

[15] *National Insurance Act.*—It is provided that where an employer has failed or neglected to pay any contributions for which he is liable in respect of a person in his employment, so that such person has been deprived of benefits which would otherwise have been payable to him, the person so aggrieved

40

Sickness Insurance

(ii) *Lapse of Membership.*—Membership of a sickness fund may lapse, and claim to benefit be forfeited owing to several reasons. (*a*) Membership ceases automatically with cessation of employment unless the insured person continues as a voluntary contributor at his own expense.[16] (*b*) Membership of any particular fund lapses

shall be "entitled to take proceedings against the employer for the value of the right of which he has been so deprived, and in any such proceedings the employer may be ordered to pay to the Insurance Commissioners a sum equal to the value so ascertained, which sum when paid shall be carried to the credit of the society of which such person is a member, and thereupon such person shall thenceforth be entitled to receive from the society benefits at the same rate as he would have been entitled to had the contributions been properly paid, together with the difference between the amount of the benefits (if any) he has actually received and the benefits he would have received had the contributions been properly paid." (Section 70.)

In addition, the defaulting employer is liable on summary conviction to a fine not exceeding £10, as well as to pay to the Insurance Commissioners all arrears of contributions. (Section 69.)

[16] *National Insurance Act.*—Contributions are not payable during sickness or disablement or during unemployment not exceeding an average of 3 weeks a year reckoned upon the whole period of insurance; where the arrears do not exceed 13 weekly contributions a year on average there is a reduction of sickness benefit from the fourth week; where the arrears exceed 13 weekly contributions a year on average, sickness and disablement benefits are suspended; and where the arrears exceed 26 weekly contributions a year on average all benefits are suspended. Arrears may be paid up at will, so as to preserve claim to benefits. In the case of an insured woman who is entitled to maternity benefit arrears are not

41

when the insurer joins another fund recognised by the law, not being a "mutual aid" or provident society, since with this exception double insurance is not permissible. (c) Voluntary membership lapses if the contributions are not paid on two successive pay days, but four weeks must have expired since the first of these days.[17]

· Membership is not broken by sickness, however, and no contributions are levied during the receipt of sickness benefit owing to disablement. Further, a person ceasing to be a member of a fund owing to loss of employment retains a claim to the ordinary benefits provided by his fund in respect of sickness occurring during unemployment within three weeks of such lapse of membership, provided the person was insured for at least 26 weeks in the preceding twelve months or during at least 6 weeks immediately preceding. The claim is made contingent upon residence in Germany unless the rules of the fund provide to the contrary. Short intervals of unemployment occurring owing to change of employer do not count as breaking membership. Should a person

counted during two weeks before and four weeks after confinement, or in the case of maternity benefit payable in respect of the posthumous child of an insured person during the period subsequent to the father's death. (Section 10 (4) and Fifth Schedule.)

Reinsurance presumes the observance of the specified waiting times. (Section 8 (8).)

[17] *National Insurance Act.*—Where a voluntary contributor is in arrears he is liable to such proportionate reduction of benefits as may be prescribed; but the same allowances are made for arrears due to sickness and unemployment as in the case of compulsory contributors. (Section 10 (3).)

Sickness Insurance

cease to follow an employment in virtue of, which he is liable to insurance, he is allowed to continue his insurance by the payment of the full contributions (including the share which the employer would have borne had the insurer been employed) so long as he remains in the country, provided he notify his intention to that effect to the executive of the fund within a week of ceasing employment.[18] This right to continue insurance may be exercised even though the person concerned be unemployed or even disabled. It has been decided that the receipt of an invalidity pension does not invalidate the right. In order that membership under such circumstances may not lapse owing to inadvertence, the payment on the proper date of the full contributions is regarded as equivalent to formal notification so long as the date falls within the week's grace allowed for such notification. Membership lapses absolutely, however, if the contributions are not paid on two successive pay days.

(iii) *Scale of Contributions.*—The contributions are levied in the form of a percentage of wages.

Under the old law the combined contributions of workman and employer might not exceed 3 per cent. in the case of parochial insurance, and 6 per cent. in the case of the other funds. The wages adopted as the basis of calculation were computed in different ways. As a rule the basis was the average daily wage of the class of insurer

---

[18] *National Insurance Act.*—An employed contributor ceasing to be employed within the meaning of the Act may become a voluntary contributor, and if he has been an employed contributor for five years he will then continue to pay contributions at the employed rate. (Section 5 (1) (*b*).)

43

Social Insurance in Germany

for which the fund was established, to a maximum of 4s., or if the insurers were graded in income classes to a maximum of 5s., or it might be the actual daily earnings of the individual insurers to a maximum of 5s., all earnings above 5s. a day not being assessed. In the case of persons insured with the parochial authorities the basis accepted was the recognised local rate of wages for common day labour. This rate was periodically ascertained for every locality, for men, women, boys, and girls separately, by a State authority acting on the advice of experts. Whatever the income basis adopted for computing contributions, sickness benefit was paid on the same basis.

The new law requires both contributions and money benefits to be calculated according to a basal rate of wages (*Grundlohn*). This rate is intended to represent the average daily remuneration of the class of insured persons for which the fund is established to a maximum of 5s. for the working day; but a fund is empowered to adopt a graduated scale and go to a maximum of 6s., or to adopt the actual earnings of the individual insurer to the same maximum as the basal wages rate.[19]

[19] *National Insurance Act.*—The Act makes provision against sickness and permanent disablement as part of one system of mutual insurance, and accordingly one contribution covers both contingencies. The principle of contribution adopted by the Act is a flat rate of 4d. a week for male employed contributors, and 3d. a week for female employed contributors, with 3d. a week in each case from the employer; except that a differential scale applies to insured persons of the age of 21 years and upwards whose remuneration does not include board and lodging and does not exceed 2s. 6d. a working day, the contributions in such cases being as follows:—

Sickness Insurance

In the case of voluntary insurers for whom a basal wages rate cannot be determined on the foregoing plan, the rate is decided by the rules of the fund. In the case of "rural" funds the normal local rate of common day labour may be adopted as the basal wages rate.[20]

The contributions must in every case be so fixed as to cover, together with other receipts, the statutory expenditure of the fund. These extra receipts no longer include entrance fees.[21] On the establishment of a fund the

(a) Where the remuneration does not exceed 1s. 6d. a day —by employer 6d. for men and 5d. for women, by the State 1d. ;

(b) Where the remuneration exceeds 1s. 6d. but does not exceed 2s. a day—by the employer 5d. for men and 4d. for women, by the contributor 1d., and by the State 1d.

(c) Where the remuneration exceeds 2s. but does not exceed 2s. 6d. a day—by the employer 4d. for men and 3d. for women, by the contributor 3d.

Special rates apply to Ireland (where medical benefit is omitted from the scheduled benefits), to married women, persons in the naval and military services of the Crown, the mercantile marine, and in other cases where the benefits are modified owing to the special conditions of employment. (Sections 3, 4, 44, 46, 47, 48, 51, and 2nd Schedule.)

[20] For the method of calculation see Chapter VI., p. 166.

[21] *National Insurance Act.*—In addition to providing for a State contribution equal to the value of two-ninths of the benefits in the case of men and one-quarter in the case of women, the Act provides that if in any year the amount paid to an Insurance Committee from contributions in respect of all persons for the administration of whose medical benefit it is responsible is insufficient to meet the estimated expenditure thereon, the Treasury and the county council or the council of the county borough concerned may charge themselves with

joint contributions may only exceed 4½ per cent. of the wages when an increase is necessary in order to cover the normal benefits. Should the contributions be insufficient to meet the expenditure they must be increased or the benefits must be restricted to the normal benefits: If a levy of 6 per cent. is insufficient to meet the normal benefits in the case of a "local" fund the contributions can be further increased if both workpeople and employers agree; should this levy be similarly insufficient in the case of a "rural," a factory, or a Guild fund the excess must be borne by the local authority, the employer, or the Guild respectively.

(iv). *Special Assessment in Unhealthy Trades.*—The new law makes a serious attempt to adjust the liability of employers for the cost of sickness to the special risks of their trades or undertakings.[22] The old law empowered

the deficit in equal proportions. A similar provision applies where Insurance Committees extend sanatorium benefit to the dependants of insured persons. In both these cases the council of any borough or urban or rural district may agree with the county council to refund to the latter the whole or part of any expenditure incurred by it in respect of such borough or district. (Sections 3, 15 (7 and 8), 17, and 23.)

[22] *National Insurance Act.*—The Act provides that where it is alleged by the Insurance Commissioners, by an approved society, or by an Insurance Committee that the sickness which has taken place among any insured persons is excessive, and that the excess is due to the conditions or nature of employment of such persons, or to bad housing or insanitary conditions in any locality, or to an insufficient or contaminated water supply, or to the neglect on the part of any person or authority to observe or enforce the provisions of any Act relating to the health of workers in factories, workshops, mines, quarries, or

Sickness Insurance

"local" funds existing for various trades or kinds of undertakings to charge differential rates in the case of such trades or kinds of undertakings as were attended by a considerable diversity of risk to health. This option did not apply, however, to individual undertakings, and experience showed that the limitation thus imposed was open to objection. At the same time the objection was weakened by the fact that if the conditions of an individual undertaking were specially unhealthy the employer could be required to have his own sickness fund. The principal defect of this arrangement was that where higher contributions were charged because of high sickness risk two-thirds of the extra cost (following the general

other industries, or relating to public health, or the housing of the working classes, or any regulations made under any such Act, or to observe or enforce any public health precautions, the Commissioners or the society or committee making such allegation may send to the person or authority alleged to be in default a claim for the payment of the amount of any extra expenditure alleged to have been incurred by reason of such cause as aforesaid, and if an agreement is not arrived at may apply to the Home Office or the Local Government Board, as the case may be, for an inquiry.

Should it be proved to the satisfaction of the person holding the inquiry that the amount of such sickness has during a period of not less than three years before the date of the inquiry, or if there has been an outbreak of any epidemic, endemic, or infectious disease, during any less period, been in excess of the average expectation of sickness by more than 10 per cent., and that such excess was in whole or in part due to any cause specified above, the amount of any extra expenditure found by the person holding the inquiry to have been incurred by any societies or committees will be charged to those found to be responsible. (Section 63.)

Social Insurance in Germany

principle of contribution) fell upon the workpeople. The law as amended makes it possible to charge the whole cost of excessive sickness to the employer. It is provided that the sickness contributions may be graduated in the case both of entire trades and of individual occupations, and that individual employers may be charged more where the risk of sickness is "considerably higher than the average."

IV. The Benefits.

(i) *Under the Old Law.*—Hitherto two scales of benefits have been recognised by the law—the minimum benefits granted by the parochial authorities, and the wider scale prescribed in the case of the local, factory, Guild, and other funds. Bearing in mind a widespread tendency to draw statistical comparisons wherever possible, it seems desirable to specify these scales of benefits, though now altered in some respects, inasmuch as past contributions and expenditure have been based upon them. The minimum benefits comprised :—

1. Free medical attendance (including free medicine, spectacles, trusses, &c.) during sickness.

2. In the case of inability to earn a livelihood, sick pay from the fourth day of sickness in the form of a daily payment (Sundays and holidays excluded) equal to one-half of the local wages of common day labour and payable for a maximum period of 26 weeks (prior to 1904 the period was 13 weeks). (Medical assistance might also be given to the members of the families of insured persons in consideration of extra contributions.)

3. Instead of medical attendance and sickness pay treatment might be given in a hospital. If a person thus

48

Sickness Insurance

treated had relatives for whose support he or she was responsible, an allowance equal to one-half of the amount ordinarily payable to the patient was made to them.

The benefits provided by the local and other funds exceeded those given by the parochial authorities both in number and value. Sickness pay was calculated according to the average daily wages of the class of workers to which the insured person belonged, up to a maximum of 4s. or 5s., as might be decided, instead of being based on the customary local rate of common day labour. The minimum benefits were the following :—

1. Medical attendance and medicine.

2. Sickness pay from the fourth day for 26 weeks of inability to earn a livelihood.

3. Maternity benefit, equal to the sickness pay, for six weeks following childbirth, provided the insured person had been a member of the fund for at least six months during the year preceding her confinement.

4. In the case of death, an amount equal to twenty times the amount of the average daily wages was paid.

Further benefits were permissive, and included the following :—

5. Sickness benefit might be extended from 26 to 52 weeks, might be given on the first three days, on Sundays and festivals, and might be increased from one-half to three-quarters of the average wages.

6. Additional curative measures might be provided in case of need.

7. Together with free treatment in a hospital, sickness pay to the extent of half his average wages might be given to a patient if he had relatives dependent upon him, and to the extent of one quarter if he had not.

Social Insurance in Germany

8. For a year after the discontinuance of sick benefit care might be given to convalescents, as by their maintenance in homes.

9. Women approaching confinement who had belonged to their sickness fund for six months might for six weeks receive benefit equal to that claimable after childbirth, as well as free medical attendance and midwifery.

10. Free medical attendance, free medicine, and other remedies might be given to sick members of the family of an insured person who were not liable to insurance.

11. The funeral money might be increased to forty times the average daily wages of the deceased, and the minimum payment be fixed at 50 marks (£2 10s.)

12. On the death of the wife or child of an insured person, should they not be liable to insurance, two-thirds or one half of the usual funeral money respectively might be paid.

The extent to which these permissive benefits were granted depended entirely upon the willingness of workpeople and employers to bear the additional cost.

(ii) *Under the New Law.*—The new law has both generalised and systematised the benefits granted. These are now defined more clearly as follows :—[23]

[23] *National Insurance Act.*—The immediate benefits provided comprise : (a) Medical treatment and attendance, including the provision of proper and sufficient medicines, and such medical and surgical appliances as may be prescribed by regulations to be made by the Insurance Commissioners ("medical benefit"). (b) Treatment in sanatoria or other institutions or otherwise when suffering from tuberculosis, or such other diseases as the Local Government Board with the approval of the Treasury may appoint ("sanatorium benefits");

Sickness Insurance

(*a*) Sickness benefit (*Krankenhilfe*).

(*b*) Maternity benefit (*Wochenhilfe*).

(*c*) Funeral benefit (*Sterbegeld*), and

(*d*) Family benefit (*Familienhilfe*).

(*a*) *Sickness Benefit.*—This implies, as before, care in sickness from the beginning of the same, comprising medical treatment and medicine, with spectacles, trusses, and other "minor remedies," for a maximum of 26 weeks; sickness pay for the same period to the amount of

for this purpose the State is providing £1,500,000, and £1,000,000 will be available annually from the insurance funds for maintenance. (*c*) Sickness pay during inability to work, commencing from the fourth day, and continuing for a period not exceeding 26 weeks ("sickness benefit"). (*d*) In the case of the disease or disablement continuing after the determination of sickness benefit, periodical payments during incapacity to work ("disablement benefit"). (*e*) Payment in the case of the confinement of the wife or, where the child is a posthumous child, of the widow of an insured person, or of any other woman who is an insured person, of thirty shillings ("maternity benefit"). (*f*) A number of "additional benefits" are scheduled, to be granted as the funds of the various societies allow.

Sickness benefit ceases at the age of 70, when contributions cease and old age pensions are claimable; medical and sanatorium benefits continue throughout life. Discretion is given. to approved societies to substitute for sickness and disablement benefits, or either of them, or any part of them, other benefits deemed to be more advantageous to the insured persons concerned, *e.g.*, superannuation allowances to nurses and domestic servants, payable before the old age pensions are claimable. Benefits (*b*) and (*d*) in the above list are part of invalidity insurance in Germany, as to which see Chapter V., pp. 138–142. (Sections 8, 9, and 10, and 4th and 5th Schedules.)

51

Social Insurance in Germany

half the basal wages for every workday during inability to work, dating from the fourth day of sickness, or the day of disablement should that supervene later.[24]

The way in which sickness benefit works out on this method of calculation may be illustrated by the following table showing the usual contributions paid and sickness pay received by workpeople insured in the great groups of "local" and "factory" funds :—[25]

Weekly Wages.	Weekly Sickness Contributions.*	Weekly Sick Pay.
30s.	6⅔d. or 8¼d.†	12s. or 15s.†
27s.	6⅔d. or 7¼d.†	12s. or 13s. 6d.†
24s.	6⅔d.	12s.
20s.	5¼d.	10s
18s.	5d.	9s.
15s.	4¼d.	7s. 6d.
12s.	3¼d.	6s.

* Exclusive of the contribution for invalidity insurance.
† According as the contributions were levied on maximum wages of 4s. or 5s. a day.

[24] *National Insurance Act.*—The words of the Act are: "Periodical payments whilst rendered incapable of work by some specific disease or by bodily or mental disablement of which notice has been given, commencing from the fourth. day after being so rendered incapable of work." (Section 8 (1) (c).)

[25] *National Insurance Act.*—The general scale of sickness benefits· is for men 10s. and for women 7s. 6d. a week for 26 weeks, with a disablement allowance of 5s. a week in each case from the 27th week during the whole period of such disablement up to the age of 70. These rates are reduced, however, in the following cases :—

(a) Men and women over 50 and not over 60 years on entry

Sickness Insurance

In the new law the term " inability to work " takes the place of " inability to earn a livelihood " (*Erwerbsun-fähigkeit*), with a view to defining more clearly what has been understood by the latter term hitherto. . Inability to work is presumed when an insured person is either unable, or unable without risk of worsening his condition, to follow his usual occupation, independently of whether he might be able to do some other kind of work.

Inasmuch as the normal maximum earnings forming the basal wages for the calculation of contributions and money benefits are 5s. a day, or 30s. a week, it follows that the normal maximum rates of sickness pay are 2s. 6d. a day and 15s. a week. Sickness pay may be increased, however, by raising the basal wages rate to 6s. a day by special rule, as already explained, and a

into insurance, unless they have paid 500 contributions when declaring on the fund, sickness benefit of 7s. and 6s. a week respectively for 26 weeks, and disablement benefit in full thereafter ;

(b) Men and women over 60 years on entry into insurance, sickness benefit of 6s. a week for the first 13 weeks and 5s. a week for the second 13 weeks, and disablement benefit in full thereafter ;

(c) Young persons over 16 and not over 21 years, if unmarried, sickness benefit for males 6s. a week for the first 13 weeks, and 5s. a week for the second 13 weeks, and for females 5s. and 4s. a week respectively, with disablement benefit thereafter of 5s. a week for males and 4s. for females; if such young persons are married the full scale of benefits applies.

(d) Married women who continue their insurance receive sickness benefit of 5s. a week for the first 13 weeks and 3s. for the second 13 weeks, with disablement benefit of 3s. a week. (Fourth Schedule, Tables A to D.)

53

Social Insurance in Germany

fund may in the same way increase the pay to three-quarters of the wages assessed to contributions.[26]

Nevertheless, in spite of these permissive benefits, the general scale of sickness benefit falls far below the possible maximum. In 1910 the actual average for all funds was 1s. 3d. a day per day of sickness causing inability to work, equal to 7s. 6d. a week ; the average for the factory funds, which levy the highest contributions and give the most liberal benefits, was 1s. 6d. a day, or 9s. a week ; while at the other end of the scale the parochial funds paid on the average 9d. a day, or 4s. 6d. a week. The rate of sickness pay is apt to be specially low in funds with a predominance of female members. Two Berlin funds paid to their 100,000 female members in 1910 an average of 5s. 9d. per week of sickness causing inability to work.

Other optional provisions favourable to a more liberal treatment of sick persons may be named. A fund is empowered to grant sickness pay on Sundays and holidays, to pay from the first day of incapacity when sickness lasts longer than a week,[27] ends fatally, or is caused by accident during employment, and also to pay half sickness pay to insured persons in hospital who have no dependants.[28]

[26] *National Insurance Act.*—An increase of sickness or disablement benefit is scheduled amongst prospective "additional benefits." (Part II. of 4th Schedule.)

[27] *National Insurance Act.*—Payment of sickness pay for the first three days is scheduled as an "additional benefit." (Part II. of 4th Schedule.)

[28] *National Insurance Act.*—Payments for the personal use of a member who, by reason of being an inmate of a hospital or other institution, is not in receipt of sickness benefit or dis-

54

Sickness Insurance

There is a tendency for sickness funds to reduce or abolish the waiting time. While in 1899 18·0 per cent. of the funds imposed no waiting time, the corresponding percentage in 1910 was 23·9; 1·4 per cent. in 1899 and 2·4 per cent. in 1910 paid from the second day; the proportion which paid after two clear days correspondingly decreased from 80·6 to 73·7 per cent.

Further, a fund is empowered at discretion to grant sickness and medical benefits for a year, to maintain convalescents in homes for a year after the cessation of these benefits, and to provide cripples with the instruments necessary to enable them to work.[29] With his consent an insured person may have his sickness pay reduced by one-fourth and be nursed at home in lieu of the difference.

There are, on the other hand, certain restrictive provisions. Should an insured person receive sickness pay simultaneously from another insurance his society must reduce his pay, so that the total amount may not exceed his average daily earnings, unless the rules provide for no such curtailment or only a partial curtailment.[30]

ablement benefit, are scheduled amongst the " additional benefits.". (Part. II. of 4th Schedule.)

[29] *National Insurance Act.*—The schedule of " additional benefits" includes "allowances to a member during convalescence from some disease or disablement in respect of which sickness benefit or disablement benefit has been payable." (Part II. of 4th Schedule.)

[30] *National Insurance Act.*—Where in the case of any insured person the rate of sickness benefit or disablement benefit (as the case may be) exceeds two-thirds of the usual rate of wages or other remuneration earned by such persons, the rate of such benefit may be reduced to such an extent as the society

Social Insurance in Germany

The rules may also provide that where an insured person has within 12 months received sickness pay or substitutionary benefits for 26 weeks, either successively or in the aggregate, in the event of recurrent sickness during the succeeding 12 months sickness and medical benefits shall be on the normal scale and limited to 13 weeks; but this restriction will not apply should the sickness be due to a new cause.[31]

Although the law does not specifically require sickness funds to provide their members with dental service as a part of medical benefit, their power to do so is implied by a provision permitting them to conclude agreements with dentists if so disposed, and this power is widely exercised by the stronger funds.[32]

As an alternative to medical attendance at home, hospital treatment may be given. Where a member is

---

or committee administering the benefit, with the consent of the Insurance Commissioners, determines; but where such reduction is made provision must be made for the grant of one or more additional benefits of a value equivalent to the reduction. (Section 9 (2).)

[31] *National Insurance Act.*—Where an insured person, having been in receipt of sickness benefit, recovers from the disease or disablement in respect of which he has received such benefit, any subsequent disease or disablement, or a recurrence of the same disease or disablement, is deemed to be a continuation of the previous disease or disablement unless in the meantime at least 12 months have elapsed and 50 weekly contributions have been paid by or in respect of him. The effect of the application of this provision is to reduce the period during which sickness benefit is payable on the higher scale. (Section 8 (5).)

[32] *National Insurance Act.*—Dental care is scheduled as an "additional benefit." (Part II. of 4th Schedule.)

UEBERRUH SANATORIUM FOR CONSUMPTIVES (BELONGING TO THE WURTEMBERG PRISON BOARD) — GENERAL VIEW, WITH SHELTERS

Sickness Insurance

married or has his own household or is a member of
the household of his family, this can only be done with
his consent unless the kind of illness or of treatment
needed makes home treatment inexpedient. Should
a patient so treated in an institution have relatives
dependent upon him, "household money" to the
amount of half the usual sickness pay is given for the
support of the latter. A fund may, however, adopt rules
increasing the household money to the full sickness pay,
and granting to insured persons in hospital who have
no claim to household money one-half of the usual sickness pay for their own use.[33]

[33] *National Insurance Act.*—Approved societies and
Insurance Committees may grant subscriptions or donations
to hospitals and other charitable institutions, or for the
support of district nurses, and also appoint nurses for the
purpose of visiting and nursing insured persons. (Section 21.)
But no payment shall be made on account of sickness,
disablement, or maternity benefit to or in respect of any
person during any period when the person to or in respect
of whom the benefit is payable is an inmate of any workhouse,
hospital, asylum, convalescent home, or infirmary, supported
by any public authority or out of any public funds or by a
charity, or voluntary subscriptions, or of a sanatorium or
similar institution approved under the Act. The sum which
would otherwise have been payable to such person during
such time shall be paid to or applied in whole or in part for
the relief or maintenance of his dependants (if any) in such
manner as the society or committee by which the benefit is
administered, after consultation whenever possible with such
person, thinks fit, or to the institution. (Section 12.) Nevertheless, payments for the "personal use" of the member
whilst undergoing institutional treatment are scheduled
amongst 'additional benefits." (Part II. of 4th Schedule.)

Social Insurance in Germany

Sickness funds may unite for the purpose of erecting and carrying on hospitals of any kind.[34] As a rule, however, they send their patients to the municipal and other public hospitals on terms arranged. Municipal hospitals often accept such patients at less than the cost. The practice of hospital treatment increases from year to year. In 1910 the cost of hospital treatment was 7s. 10½d. per head of all members in the case of the building funds, 5s. 1½d. in the case of the Guild funds, 3s. 7¾d. in the case of the Local funds, 3s. 6d. in the case of the Factory funds, and 3s. 2d. in the case of parochial insurance. The average cost for all funds (excluding those of the miners) was 3s. 5½d., comparing with 2s. 9½d. in 1906 and 1s. 6d. in 1892. In the case of miners' funds the cost averaged 9s. 1½d. in 1910.

(b) *Maternity Benefit.*—Maternity benefit to the amount of the usual sickness pay is payable for eight weeks (at least six of which must follow confinement) to women who have been insured for six months during the year preceding confinement, but the duration of this benefit may be reduced to four weeks in the case of female members of rural funds who do not come under the Industrial Code, *i.e.*, those engaged in agriculture or domestic service.[35]

[34] *National Insurance Act.*—The schedule of "additional benefits" includes "the building or leasing of premises suitable for convalescent homes and the maintenance of such homes." (Part II. of 4th Schedule.)

[35] *National Insurance Act.*—An insured person is not entitled to maternity benefit (30s.) unless and until 26 or in the case of a voluntary contributor 52 weeks have elapsed since entry into insurance, and at least 26 or in the case of a voluntary contributor 52 weekly contributions have been paid by or in respect of such person. (Section 8 (8).)

Sickness Insurance

The duration of this benefit was originally three weeks, following confinement; in 1892 the period was extended to four weeks, and in 1903 to six weeks. Owing to an amendment of the Industrial Code dated December 28, 1908, extending to eight weeks the total period during which women may not be employed prior to and after confinement (of which six weeks must follow confinement), a further extension of maternity benefit to eight weeks was provided for by the Insurance Consolidation Act of 1911.

Confinement does not count as illness, however, hence does not of itself establish a claim to sickness benefits, but if illness occurs sickness pay and medical attendance, with medicine, may be claimed.[36] But confinement and sickness pay are not granted concurrently. Treatment in maternity homes, with claim to half the usual maternity pay where there are dependants, or nursing at home with a similar allowance, may be given in lieu of maternity benefit. Further, the rules of a fund may provide for the giving of surgical and midwife's aid at confinement, either to insured wives or to all insured women who have been members of any fund for at least six months during the year preceding confinement; women who have belonged to their present fund for at least six months may be given full sickness pay for six weeks in the event of disablement due to pregnancy and, at discretion, medical and midwife's service in addition.[37]

[36] *National Insurance Act.*—Medical benefit does not include a right to medical treatment or attendance in respect of a confinement. (Section 8 (6).)

[37] *National Insurance Act.*—The "additional benefits" scheduled include the increase of maternity benefit. (Part II. of 4th Schedule.)

Social Insurance in Germany

Under the new law nursing money to the amount of half thé sickness pay may be given for twelve weeks after confinement as a condition of natural feeding.

Hitherto maternity benefit has not been given on a large scale by the German sickness funds. The total amount expended in this way by all funds in 1910 was £321,650, equal to 5½d. per head of the aggregate membership and 1s. 9d. per head of the female membership.[38] The groups of funds which most systematically grant this benefit are the "local" and factory funds. Their expenditure on maternity benefit in 1910 will be seen from the following table :—

	Maternity Benefit.	Cost per Female Member.	Cost per head of total Membership.
	£	s. d.	d.
Local Funds..	222,102	2 0	7½
Factory Funds	95,716	2 10	7
Guild Funds..	2,179	0 10	2
Mutual Aid Funds	1,221	0 3	0½
State-regulated Mutual Aid Funds	26	0 1	—
Mining Funds	361	0 6½	—

The parochial funds, in which hitherto the lower paid and most necessitous workers have to a large extent been insured, have almost entirely excluded maternity allowances from their benefits, though over half a million females were insured in these funds in 1910.

No general information exists showing either the

[38] *National Insurance Act.*—The maternity benefit is expected to involve the expenditure of £1,500,000 a year.

Sickness Insurance

average duration of maternity benefit, which might hitherto be given for any period from six to twelve weeks according to the rules of the sickness fund, or the average weekly allowance. As the latter is equal to the ordinary sickness pay (*i.e.*, half the wages) claimable in ordinary illness, the weekly maternity benefit shows all the variations characteristic of women's earnings, always with a tendency to a relatively low figure. The following statement shows for seven large urban sickness funds or federations of sickness funds the percentage of female members in receipt of this benefit in 1909 or 1910 and the average sum paid in each case. So far as data exist on the subject they point to a usual average of about 6s. 6d. a week, but this would not be reached in small towns and rural districts.

	Number of Women who received Maternity Benefit.	Percentage of Female Members.	Average Amount Paid.
			s. d.
Leipzig General Fund	3,671	6·4	38 11
Berlin Printers' Fund	410	5·8	59 1
Berlin Tailors' Fund	2,911	5·2	41 6
Dresden General Fund.. ..	2,550	5·0	38 7
Munich General Fund.. ,.	3,469	6·9	40 4
Frankfurt General Fund ..	1,504	5·8	46 6
Berlin General Fund	2,546	5·8	41 4

(c) *Funeral Money.* — The funeral money payable is as before twenty times the amount of the basal wages rate, and it is paid at the death of all insured persons, but also whenever death ensues within a year of the discontinuance of sickness benefit, so long as it is the result of the same illness and the

Social Insurance in Germany

deceased was to the last incapable of working.[39] By rule, however, the funeral money may be increased to forty times the basal wages rate, and the minimum may be fixed at 50 marks. From the funeral money the costs of interment have first to be defrayed, and these are to be paid direct to the undertaker. Any balance remaining is payable to the widow (or widower), children, father, mother, or brothers and sisters (if they formed part of the deceased's household at the time of death) in this order of precedence; in the absence of all these claimants it goes back to the fund.

(d) *Family Benefits.*—"Family benefit" is an additional benefit given when a fund adopts a rule to that effect, and it may include medical attendance for members of an insured person's family not liable to insurance, maternity benefit for wives not liable to insurance, and funeral money on the death of the wife (husband) or child of an insured person, to a maximum of two-thirds or one-half respectively of the amount claimable at the death of such person, but this payment must be reduced by the amount of the funeral money for which the deceased was insured.[40] Supplementary contribu-

[39] *National Insurance Act.*—Funeral benefits are expressly excluded from the purview of the Act. They are not even contemplated as "additional benefits" to be granted as the funds may permit.

[40] *National Insurance Act.*—Medical treatment and attendance for "any persons dependent upon the labour of a member" is scheduled as an "additional benefit." (Part II. of 4th Schedule.) The Act also provides for the sanatorium treatment of uninsured members of an employed contributor's family. (Section 17.)

Sickness Insurance

tions may be levied on the insured persons where family benefits are given.

IV. SPECIAL PROVISIONS.

The rules may make the additional benefits dependent upon a waiting time of not more than six months from commencement of membership, except in the case of members who have for six of the twelve months immediately preceding had a claim to additional benefits from any fund.

All money benefits, except funeral money, are payable at the end of each week.[41]

Should an insured person remove abroad whilst in receipt of benefits the fund may pay him a lump sum in lieu of such benefits. Sick persons residing outside the district served by their fund may receive their benefits from the "general local" fund, a "special local" fund, or the "rural" fund of their place of residence.[42]

[41] *National Insurance Act.*—Approved societies are required to adopt rules, sanctioned by the Insurance Commissioners, dealing with "the manner and time of paying or distributing and mode of calculating benefits." (Section 14 (2).)

[42] *National Insurance Act.*—No insured person is entitled to any benefit while resident either temporarily or permanently outside the United Kingdom unless residing temporarily abroad with the consent of the society or the Insurance Committee, when he may continue to receive sickness or disablement benefit, but a person resident out of the United Kingdom will not be disentitled to maternity benefit in respect of the confinement of his wife if at the time of her confinement she is resident in the United Kingdom. (Section 8 (4).)

CHAPTER III

SICKNESS INSURANCE.—II. SPECIAL OCCUPATIONS, ADMINISTRATION, ETC.

V. TREATMENT OF SPECIAL CLASSES OF INSURED PERSONS, ETC.

SPECIAL provisions apply in the case of the new classes of insured persons brought within the scope of the law of 1911.

In respect of these the law allows, as a rule, a lower scale of contributions, with correspondingly reduced benefits.

Domestic Servants and Agricultural Labourers.—Permissive provisions apply particularly to the case of domestic servants and agricultural labourers.[1] Reduced

---

[1] *National Insurance Act.*—A special provision was introduced in this Act to meet established usages appertaining to agricultural service. The Insurance Commissioners are empowered to schedule classes of employment and localities in which, according to custom, employed persons receive full remuneration during periods of sickness or disablement, and where this custom prevails employers may claim the benefit of a modification of the law. Such an employer will be liable to pay full remuneration to an employee to the extent of six weeks in the aggregate in any one year during disease or

contributions may be charged in respect of such persons engaged on a yearly contract of service who, in virtue of the same, (*a*) have claim to yearly payments under the Insurance Laws equal in value to at least 300 times the sickness pay that would be claimable, or receive when sick wages in money or kind at least equal in value to such sickness pay; and (*b*) have a legal claim to the continuance of these payments or benefits (within the validity of the contract of service) for at least 26 weeks after the occurrence of sickness. In consideration of the foregoing benefits no sickness pay is granted under the law.

An employer may also contract out where he is under legal obligation to afford his servants a provision equivalent to that offered by the Insurance Law. The conditions of such contracting-out are as follows : (1) The employer must pay the full benefits out of his own pocket ; (2) he must give proof of financial stability ; (3) such an arrangement must apply to the whole of his employees

disablement commencing while in his employment, provided that if any such person is engaged for a term of not less than six months certain, the employer shall be liable to pay full remuneration during any period of disease or disablement lasting less than six weeks, and for the first six weeks of any period of disease or disablement lasting more than six weeks, except for any period extending beyond the term of the engagement. In consideration of the approved society being relieved of the payment of sickness benefit to this extent, the weekly contributions of the employer will be reduced by one penny for men and one halfpenny for women, and that of the employed contributor, whether male or female, one penny. The insured person will have the other benefits provided by the Act. (Section 47.)

so far as they are subject to a contract of service running for at least two weeks. The Insurance Office may annul such an arrangement if it has reason to doubt the employer's monetary position. If an employer fails to provide the benefits for which he is liable, the sickness fund will do it in his stead, and charge him with the cost.

Again, in the interest of agriculture the rules of a "rural" fund may reduce the sickness pay for all or certain groups of insured persons during the period October 1st to March 31st, or part thereof, to one quarter of the local rate of wages, reducing the contributions meantime or increasing the sickness pay during the remainder of the year. The same provision holds good in respect of household money.

The old power given to local authorities to require seasonal agricultural labourers, who hired themselves in harvest and other busy times—for example, small holders and others following a more or less regular occupation of their own—to be insured during such times, the cost being shared with them by their employers in the usual ratio, has been abolished.

Domestic Servants.—The law regards domestic servants as following a " special occupation " subject to differential provisions. In general the provisions relating to agricultural labourers apply.[2]

Casual Labourers.—The law defines casual or irregular

---

[2] *National Insurance Act.*—There are two provisions in the Act which are intended to meet the special conditions of domestic service. The first is the provision that where employers elect to make themselves liable for the continuance of wages to employees during the first six weeks of sickness, or for a maximum of six weeks in a year (according to the dura-

Sickness Insurance

employment as employment which is usually limited to less than one week either by its nature or by the contract of service in advance, and workers so employed are in general included, but the Federal Council can exempt at its discretion. The special provisions applying to agricultural labourers, domestic servants, itinerant workers, and out-workers apply generally to workers of this kind.

They are to be insured in the "general local" funds, or, if they are mainly engaged in agricultural work, the "rural" funds of their place of residence, and they are required to report themselves for enrolment. Membership continues during such periods as they may be temporarily unemployed; but if it is clear that unemployment is not merely temporary, insurance will lapse unless preserved by voluntary contributions.[3]

The contributions and benefits of the casual workers are determined by the rules of the fund to which they

tion of the engagement), the contributions of both will be reduced—in the case of male employees by 1d. each, and in the case of female employees by ½d. to the employer and 1d. to the employee. In this case the sick employee will receive no sickness pay during the first six weeks of illness, but claim to the other benefits will not be affected. (Section 17.) Further, in order to meet the needs of domestic servants and other employees whose chances of securing employment greatly decrease with age, it is provided that instead of the normal sickness and disablement benefits provided by the Act other benefits—e.g., early superannuation pensions—may be given. (Section 13.)

[3] *National Insurance Act.*—In the case of trades or businesses of a seasonal nature and subject to periodical fluctuation, where employers systematically employ persons throughout the year and work short time during the season when the trade or business is slack, the Insurance Commis-

Social Insurance in Germany

belong and are carried to a separate account. The insured have to pay their own contributions direct, instead of through their employers. Should a casual worker have failed to pay contributions for more than eight weeks during the 26 weeks immediately preceding illness he will receive only medical benefit with funeral benefit (if necessary) not exceeding 30 marks (£1 10s.); and the same holds good of an insured person who has not been in membership for 26 weeks unless he has contributed in respect of more than one quarter of the period.

The employers' share of the contributions due in respect of casual workers is to be paid by the local authority at the end of each quarter, and this amount may be levied on all the inhabitants of the district served by the fund, or separately on the residents of districts served by local and rural funds respectively; but those inhabitants who habitually employ casual workers for a long time or in large numbers will be liable to a higher assessment. The rules of a fund may provide, with the assent of the local authority and the Higher Insurance Office, that casual workers may be freed from contributions, in which case reduced benefits will be paid.

Itinerant Workers.—Persons in the employment of an itinerant tradesman, so far as they travel about with him, are insured in the rural fund of the place where his licence has been issued. The insured receive the normal benefits.

sioners may by special order reduce the contributions payable by the employers and contributors in the slack periods and increase them proportionately in the busy periods of the year. (Section 50.)

Sickness Insurance

Out-workers. — Out-workers and the middlemen employing them are as a rule insured in the rural fund of their place of work. Both parties pay contributions, and the principals for whom they work are also required to make supplementary payments computed according to their payments to the middlemen for work done, the value of all raw material provided by the same being first, deducted. The rules of the fund prescribe the amount of the contributions payable by the out-workers and middlemen, as well as the benefits to be given. The contributions have to be such that, together with the supplementary payments of the primary employers, they will meet the expenditure incurred from time to time. For the present the levy upon principals will be equal to 2 per cent. of the wages bill, and it is intended that the contributions of the out-workers and middlemen shall yield an equivalent sum. The benefits given will comprise medical attendance and sickness pay.

Apprentices, &c.—In the case of apprentices employed

* *National Insurance Act.*—The provisions relating to out-workers include the exemption from liability to insurance of any person employed within the meaning of the Act who proves that he is "ordinarily or mainly dependent for his livelihood upon some other person" (Section 2 (1)), and more specifically the exemption of "employment as an out-worker where the person so employed is the wife of an insured person and is not wholly or mainly dependent for her livelihood on her earnings in such employment," and "employment in the service of the husband or wife of the employed person." (Part II. of first Schedule.) The Insurance Commissioners may provide for contributions being determined by reference to the work actually done, instead of the duration of work (Third Schedule (10)).

69

without wages no sickness pay will be given, and the contributions will be reduced accordingly.

Seamen.—The law applies to all persons engaged in inland navigation and in dredging operations, but the crews of sea-going ships, to which the provisions of the Seamen's Ordinance of 1872 apply, are expressly exempted from its operation. The provision made by this Ordinance—which corresponds to our own Merchant Shipping Act—is at the sole cost of the shipowners.[5] The Ordinance, which now applies in the form given to it by amendments of June 2, 1902, and May 12,

[5] *Merchant Shipping Act.*—Under this Act the shipowner is bound in every case of hurt or injury or sickness to bear "the expense of providing the necessary surgical and medical advice and attendance and medicine, and also the expense of the maintenance of the master or seaman until he is cured or dies or is returned to a proper return port, and of his conveyance to the port, and in the case of death the expense of his burial." The shipowner is also liable to pay to an incapacitated seaman his full wages until his discharge before the proper authorities. *National Insurance Act.*— The Act provides for the insurance of persons employed in the mercantile marine in a separate fund under conditions adapted to the present liabilities of shipowners under the Merchant Shipping Act. Only British seamen will have the benefit of insurance, though shipowners will be required to contribute in respect of all foreign seamen employed by them. Seamen engaged in the foreign trade will pay 3d. a week and shipowners 2d. (a reduction in each case of 1d.), and four contributions will be counted as five, since such seamen are only employed for four-fifths of the year, while the ordinary contributions will be paid by and in respect of seamen engaged in the home and coasting trade, who will not be insured in the special seamen's fund unless they so choose. (Section 48.)

Sickness Insurance

1904, provides that every seaman (not being a captain
or skipper) is entitled to maintenance and medical care,
in case of sickness or injury during a voyage, at the
cost of the shipowner or other employer, conditionally on
his sailing in a merchant ship entitled to fly the Imperial
flag. The same claim applies to female employees on
board, but not to pilots. The employer's liability covers
sickness of every kind, however sustained, and whether
it occurred during the discharge of duties or otherwise,
subject to the exception that no claim can arise in respect
of a criminal act or if the seaman has broken his contract
without justifiable grounds. A ship's captain may not
leave a sick seaman behind helpless in a foreign country,
but must at least give such security that destitution
cannot supervene within a period of three months. If
a seaman does not sail with his ship by reason of sickness or injury, the shipowner is liable for the costs of
maintenance and treatment for 26 weeks in case of
sickness, and for 13 weeks in case of injury by
accident. If the seaman has sailed, the shipowner's
liability in respect of sickness continues until the
expiration of six months after he left the ship, whether
in a German or a foreign port, and in respect of injury
for the same period unless the seaman left his ship in a
German port or was transferred from a foreign port into
a hospital at home, in which case the period of liability
is reduced to 13 weeks. In no case, however, does the
shipowner's liability for maintenance continue after a
man is cured, whether he be fit to return to work or not,
and he is not liable for maintenance at all in the event
of incapacity to work unaccompanied by sickness. No
wages can be claimed for the time he may be in a

Social Insurance in Germany

hospital, unless he has dependants, in which case the shipowner is liable to pay one quarter of his wages, direct to the relatives, if he so choose. In the event of death during employment, the shipowner is liable to pay the wages until the day of death, and also the costs of burial.

Aliens.—The law makes no distinction between nationals and aliens in regard to contributions or, so long as resident in Germany, to benefits, save as below.[6] Right to sickness benefit is forfeited, however, by foreigners who have been expelled from the Empire after conviction for a penal offence, but a foreigner expelled from one Federal State is not disqualified from receiving benefits if resident in another Federal State.[7] Should a person entitled to benefit have dependants in Germany who are entitled to family benefit, this shall not be withheld from them, notwithstanding that he has been expelled from the country.

VI. System of Administration.

The old law gave self-government to all the sickness funds, with the one exception of parochial insurance,

[6] *National Insurance Act.*—Persons employed within the meaning of the Act include " all persons of either sex, whether British subjects or not, who are engaged in any of the employments specified in Part I. of the first Schedule, not being employment specified (for exemption) in Part II. of that Schedule." (Section 1 (2).) But aliens do not receive the Government grant except under specified conditions. (Section 45.)

[7] In 1910 514 and in 1909 567 foreigners were expelled from Germany after judicial conviction. Expulsions of " undesirable aliens " by the police for political reasons are not included in these figures.

Sickness Insurance

which was administered by the local authorities. The representative bodies were the executive and general meeting, the former elected by the workpeople and employers in the proportion of their contributions, viz., two-thirds and one-third respectively, except in the case of the free mutual aid funds, which were managed altogether by their members, since the employers did not contribute. The rules of a factory fund, which the employer was empowered to draw up after taking the opinion of the workpeople, might stipulate that the chairman of the executive should be either the employer or his representative.

Practical autonomy is the rule under the new law, for the sickness funds, in contrast to the system of Infirmity Insurance, are still administered by an executive and a committee, upon which workpeople and employers are represented in the proportion of two to one respectively. Nevertheless, with a view to breaking down Social Democratic supremacy in the "local" funds—of the results of which complaint had been made in various parts of the country—the provision has been introduced that in the case of these funds the chairman of the executive must be chosen by a majority both of employers and workpeople voting separately; in the event of disagreement after two attempts the Insurance Office nominates provisionally, but the nominee can only be chosen from either group with the consent of a majority of the other.[8]

In the case of the "rural" funds, however, the

[8] *National Insurance Act.*—The approved societies which administer this Act are so far autonomous that it is a condition precedent to approval that a Society's rules must provide to the satisfaction of the Insurance Commissioners for its affairs being subject to "the absolute control of its members being

73

Social Insurance in Germany

principle of self-government is only indirectly recognised. Here the executive is chosen by the local authority, though from among the employees and insured members, in the proportion of one-third and two-thirds respectively, and the chairman is similarly nominated. The factory or works and Guild funds are also managed by executives and committees.

General oversight is exercised by Insurance Offices formed for different localities, as explained later.[9]

insured persons or, if the rules of the society so provide, of its members whether insured persons or not, including provision for the election and removal of the committee of management or other governing body of the society, in the case of a society whose affairs are managed by delegates elected by members, by such delegates, and in other cases in such manner as will secure absolute control by its members." (Section 23 (2).) The benefits claimable by deposit contributors and medical and sanatorium benefits in respect of members of approved societies will be administered by Insurance Committees formed for the districts of county councils and county borough councils. The revenues of these Committees will be derived from four principal sources : (*a*) such sums as the Insurance Commissioners will pay them for the administration of medical and sanatorium benefits in respect of employed contributors and deposit contributors ; (*b*) a payment from the approved societies of one penny per member yearly; (*c*) any contributions which local authorities may decide to make towards the general purposes of the Committees, and (*d*) optional contributions by the local authorities and the Treasury towards the cost of medical benefit and of the sanatorium treatment of the uninsured dependants of insured persons. (Sections 14 to 17.)

[9] *National Insurance Act.*—The supervising authorities are the Insurance Commissioners for the three kingdoms and

Sickness Insurance

In order to show the practical working of the Sickness Insurance Law it will be useful to survey briefly the operations of one of the great federations of sickness funds as carried on in the populous towns. One of the best examples of what can be done under this law by a large central fund, organised so as to embrace an extensive area presenting more or less uniform industrial conditions, is the Leipzig Federation of Sickness Funds (*Ortskrankenkasse*), serving for that town and its vicinity. When the Sickness Insurance Law came into operation in 1884 eighteen "local" funds for different trades and occupations were formed at Leipzig, in addition to the parochial system of insurance, their aggregate membership being then 20,833. A year's operations sufficed to convince the leaders of the working classes that this multiplicity of organisations did not tend to efficiency, and steps were taken to amalgamate them. Accordingly a combined or "general local" fund was established for the urban district of Leipzig and some forty townships lying within a radius of four miles. This fund had in 1910 a membership of 182,898 persons employed in 27,250 undertakings, and was the largest in Germany. It is governed by the general meeting of members and an executive. The general meeting is elected every three years, and consists of 592 persons, two-thirds representing the insured members and one-third representing the contributory employers. The executive consists of nineteen persons, thirteen being members of the fund and six

Wales respectively. For details as to their constitution and jurisdiction see note to p. 174.

Social Insurance in Germany

employers, elected for three years, but subject to the retirement annually of one-third of the whole. In order to facilitate the registration of members, employers are able to notify engagements and discharges at fifty-two addresses in the district, and these notifications are posted each day to the central office, a large and handsome building erected for the purpose in 1896.

The benefits given by the fund exceed in some cases the minimum requirements laid down by the law, and include : (1) free medical treatment from the beginning of illness, with medicine, spectacles, trusses, and other appliances to the maximum value of £3 15s. ; (2) in case of disablement, sickness pay to the extent of 55 per cent. of the wages up to a maximum of 16s. 6d. weekly for thirty-four weeks, dating from the second day ; (3) in lieu of the benefits (1) and (2), treatment in a hospital, clinic, or convalescent home, with pay to relatives during the time to the extent of two-thirds of the amount which would have been claimable by the sick member, but should the latter be unmarried only to the maximum of one-fourth of the ordinary sickness pay ; (4) in maternity cases cash payments equal to the benefit claimable in sickness for two weeks before and six weeks after confinement, subject to the statutory conditions as to duration of membership ; (5) funeral money according to a scale ranging from 12s. in respect of children under 14 years to £5 in respect of persons contributing in the highest wages class; (6) medical treatment and medicine (without appliances) during thirteen weeks of sickness to uninsured members of the household of an insured person, and funeral money in the case of the death of an uninsured wife or child to the extent of £2 and £1 respectively; (7) treatment in a

76

convalescent home. The extent of the additional benefits afforded by the medical treatment of members of households is shown by the fact that in 1910 free medical attendance was given to 79,235 wives, 161,948 children and 7,577 other dependants of members, and funeral pay in respect of 472 wives and 2,484 children of members.

The contributions are levied on a scale which divides the insured into ten wages classes, and at the uniform rate of 4 per cent. of the average wages earned. The workpeople bear two-thirds and the employers one-third of the combined contribution, the money being collected monthly by the central office. Voluntary membership is allowed to certain classes of employees, of course at their own cost.

The contributions and the sickness and funeral benefits paid now range as follows:—

Wages Class.	Average Daily Wages.	Weekly Contribution of		Daily Sickness Pay.	Funeral Money.
		Workman.	Employer.		
I.	5s.	9½d.	4¾d.	2s. 9d.	£5
II.	4s. 6d.	8¾d.	4¼d.	2s. 6d.	£4 10s.
III.	4s.	7¾d.	3¾d.	2s. 2½d.	£4
IV.	3s. 6d.	6¾d.	3¼d.	1s. 11½d.	£3 10s.
V.	3s.	5¾d.	2¾d.	1s. 7¾d.	£3
VI.	2s. 6d.	4¾d.	2½d.	1s. 4½d	£2 10s.
VII.	2s.	3¾d.	2d.	1s. 1¼d.	£2
VIII.	1s. 6d.	2¾d.	1½d.	10¼d.	£1 10s.
IX.	1s.	1¾d.	1d.	6¾d.	£1
X.	7½d.	1¼d.	¾d.	4¼d.	12s.

There were in the service of the fund in 1910 397 doctors, including 130 specialists, and 24 dentists, and the members can make their choice; but if they desire to be visited they must choose one of the doctors nearest

Social Insurance in Germany

to hand. The fund pays to the doctors a capitation fee of 5s. for every member, or 7s. 3d. if members of families are attended, with special fees for specified services, mileage allowances, and postages. The aggregate payment to the doctors in 1910 was £74,500, and averaged about £188. Payment is made quarterly. Sick members are mainly visited by honorary visitors, to the number of over 300, who are assigned to districts, but there are also 20 paid visitors. Sickness pay is paid on Saturdays at the central office and seven branch depôts.

The fund has at its disposal 195 places in three convalescent homes established by a philanthropic Leipzig employer of labour. The members have also the use of several institutions for electrical and other special treatment, two forest resorts (one for each sex) for consumptives, a similar resort for convalescents generally, and a rural resort for persons suffering from nerve troubles, the last belonging to the fund. Great attention is given to the combating of tuberculosis. Not only is it part of the duty of the doctors to advise and treat members who are found to be suffering from this disease, but they are expected to notify the executive of all cases requiring systematic treatment, and these are sent to suitable institutions. In this branch of its work the fund works hand in hand with a large central dispensary for consumptives established at Leipzig in 1906. No extra contribution is required for the special care which the fund gives to consumptive members. By means of an elaborate "case-paper" system the fund is able to keep a continuous record of the health of members.

An idea of the extent of the operations of this fund

Sickness Insurance

may be gained from the fact that in 1910 its revenue amounted to £366,500 and its expenditure to £353,600, while its accumulated funds stood at £216,500 at the end of the year. The cases of sickness amongst members entailing inability to work numbered in that year 75,215, and in respect of them sickness benefit was paid for 1,860,546 days; while medical attendance without sickness pay was given in 212,877 additional cases to members and in 248,760 additional cases to dependants of members. There were maintained in hospitals 8,316 members, besides 1,531 uninsured members of their families; 4,886 members were sent to convalescent homes, baths, and other health resorts; maternity benefit was paid in 3,671 cases, and funeral money in 4,312 cases.

The expenditure per head for the various benefits given was as follows in 1910: Sickness pay, 15s. 10½d.; medical attendance, 8s. 1¾d.; medicine and appliances, 4s. 4½d.; maternity benefit, 9¼d.; funeral money, 10d.; hospital treatment, 3s. 9d.; a total of £1 13s. 9d. per head.

The average payment made by members (exclusive of the employers' contribution) was £1 6s. 5d., or 6d. a week for every man, woman, and young person insured, after allowance for periods of sickness and unemployment in respect of which no contributions were payable.

VIII. The Medical Service.

The most serious controversy to which the working of the Sickness Insurance Law has given rise is the controversy between the funds and the doctors, and it is not likely that the recent revision of the law will end this long-continued feud. Two questions have been uppermost—the question of the method and measure of payment, and that of "free choice of doctors." The old law left both of these questions open, simply stating that funds might at their discretion decide that medical attendance, the supply of medicine, and the "cure and care" of patients should be provided by such doctors, chemists, and hospitals respectively as might be arranged. In the absence of special agreements, it followed implicitly that the official scales of minimum charges, as fixed by the Governments of the various States (and now uniform for the whole country), would apply both in the case of doctors and chemists. It is to be noted that only in the rarest cases do German doctors dispense.[10]

The discretion thus given to the funds has led to a variety of practice. As to the mode of payment, some funds pay the doctor fixed fees per case, based on the official minima, but the great majority adopt the method of capitation fees, payable upon the total membership, and distributed upon different principles, generally in the ratio which the value of the services performed by the individual doctors, as computed according to the official minimum fees, bears to the amount of the aggregate

[10] *National Insurance Act.*—The Act assumes that the principle of separating medical attendance from the dispensing of medicine will be the rule. It is provided that except as may be prescribed by regulations made by the Insurance Commissioners, no arrangement shall be made by an Insurance Committee with a medical practitioner under which he is bound or agrees to supply drugs or medicine to any insured persons. (Section 15 (5) (ii).)

honorarium after deduction of the fees for special services. In other cases (as in Dresden) the capitation fee method of payment is adopted in conjunction with fixed stipends. A free, or at any rate a wide, choice of doctors is usually allowed from an approved panel, to which in the larger towns all practitioners in independent practice as a rule have the right to be admitted. Usually a patient is allowed to change his doctor at every case of illness if he be so disposed, but not during a course of treatment."

" *National Insurance Act.*—The Act prescribes no special method of paying the doctors who may give attendance under arrangements made with them by the Insurance Committees. Yet on the general question of the conditions of service the doctors enjoy important safeguards which are provided by no German insurance legislation. Alike under the German Sickness, Accident, and Invalidity Insurance Laws the doctors deal with the insurance societies and funds direct without representation upon the bodies which they serve. The National Insurance Act secures to the doctors the main principles for which the German doctors have unsuccessfully contended for years.

The doctors will be engaged by the Insurance Committees, which are semi-public bodies formed for counties and county boroughs, since these Committees administer medical and sanatorium benefits. Upon these bodies the doctors will have from three to six direct representatives, according to the aggregate membership. The arrangements for the medical service which are made by the Insurance Committees must be approved by the Insurance Commissioners, of whom one is a medical man. (Section 15.) Another provision requires the Insurance Committees and District Committees to consult the local Medical Committees (where appointed and deemed by the Insurance Commissioners to be representative of the practitioners resident in the locality) on all general questions

Social Insurance in Germany

It has long been customary to conclude written agreements with the doctors or their associations, and this arrangement is now made obligatory by statute; the

affecting the administration of medical benefit, including the arrangements made with medical practitioners giving attendance and treatment to insured persons. (Section 62.)

The arrangements made by the Insurance Committees with the doctors, in accordance with regulations made by the Insurance Commissioners, must secure (a) the preparation and publication of lists of medical practitioners willing to attend and treat persons whose medical benefit is administered by the Committees; (b) a right on the part of any duly qualified medical practitioner to be included in any such list, subject to the power of the Insurance Commissioners to remove his name from the list if satisfied that his continuance on the list would be prejudicial to the efficiency of the medical service of the insured; (c) a right on the part of any insured person of selecting, at such periods as may be prescribed, from the appropriate list the practitioner by whom he wishes to be attended and treated, and, subject to the consent of the practitioner so selected, of being attended and treated by him; (d) the distribution amongst and, so far as practicable, under arrangements made by, the several practitioners whose names are on the lists, of the insured persons who after due notice have failed to make any selection, or have been refused by the practitioner whom they have selected; also (e) the provision of medical attendance and treatment, on the same terms as those arranged with respect to insured persons, to members of any friendly society which becomes an approved society who were such members at the date of the passing of the Act, and who are not entitled to medical benefit under the Act by reason either that they are of the age of sixty-five or upwards at the date of the commencement of the Act, or that being subject to permanent disablement at that date they are not qualified to become insured persons. (Section 15 (1) (2).)

Sickness Insurance

agreements sometimes lay down in great detail the rights and duties of the contracting parties. Some of the large federated sickness funds conclude with local associations of doctors agreements under which the associations undertake and make themselves responsible for the entire medical service required. In such cases all doctors accepting insurance practice sign the general agreement. The funds reserve the right to object to any doctor on the panel.

The average cost of medical attendance and of medicines per head of all persons insured has constantly increased, and was as follows for the years specified (miners' funds excluded) :—

	Medical Attendance.	Medicine and Minor Appliances. [17]
	s. d.	s. d.
1888	2 3¾	1 10¼
1890	2 6¼	2 2
1895	3 1	2 5
1900	3 7½	2 8¾
1905	4 9	3 1¼
1906	4 10¾	3 1
1907	5 2¾	3 3¾
1908	5 6	3 6¼
1909	5 8½	3 6¾
1910	5 10¼	3 8¼

As to these figures it should be noted that they are averages referring to funds of seven kinds, including those which provide exceptionally high scales of benefits. Further, the cost includes attendance to members of

[17] On a moderate estimate 20 per cent. of the expenditure shown in the German official reports under the heading of "medicine, &c.," is on account of items other than medicine.

Social Insurance in Germany

families wherever this is given. It must also be remembered that the sickness funds care for injured persons during the first 13 weeks following accident. As the "local" funds give the most normal benefits, their scale coming midway between the "minimum" benefits given to "parochial" insurers and the liberal scale provided by many of the "factory" funds—which are the funds in which family benefits are most common—the expenditure on medical benefit of these funds is most instructive. Medical attendance and medicine, &c., cost per head of the membership of the "local" funds in the years above named :—

	Medical Attendance.	Medicine and Minor Appliances
	s. d.	s. d.
1888	2 1¾	1 10¾
1890	2 5	2 2¼
1895	2 8¾	2 4
1900	3 3	2 7¾
1905	4 5¼	3 0¼
1906	4 7¼	3 0¼
1907	4 10¾	3 3¼
1908	5 1½	3 6
1909	5 3¼	3 6¼
1910	5 5¼	3 8¼

The Government has consistently refused to side with the medical profession in its demand that the principle of free choice of doctor should apply in every case. In a memorandum which accompanied the first draft of the Insurance Consolidation Bill the Government admitted the fairness of the claim of the funds that local circumstances must determine the question in every given case, and pointed out that if there were no alternative to the plan of "free choice of doctors" the funds would often be unable

Sickness Insurance

to negotiate with the medical profession on equal terms :
" The doctors can take up club practice or not as they
like. On the other hand, the law compels the sickness
funds to provide their members with medical attendance.
The doctors may decline both individually and collectively
to give this attendance. They can strike, but the funds
cannot."

In that Bill the Government endeavoured to find a
modus vivendi which should put an end to the constant
disputes between the sickness funds and the doctors.
The explanatory memorandum already named dealt with
this question in considerable detail. It stated :—

" It is lamentable that for many years keen dissensions
have occurred between the doctors and the sickness
insurance authorities, resulting in many places in bitter
disputes and a state of open conflict. Disputes of this
kind, however, are often prejudicial to the proper
medical care of the sick and lead to serious public injury.
The abuses have reached such proportions that legal
measures were emphatically called for in the most various
quarters as the only practicable course, and in fact it is
no longer possible for the legislative bodies to evade the
duty of seeking a remedy."

Upon the general merits of the question the Government stated :—

" That the introduction of statutory sickness insurance
has in general injured the interests of the medical profession cannot be acknowledged. It is certain that the
doctors as a whole are indebted to this institution for
many benefits, and particularly for an enormously
increased demand for medical assistance and for greater
security for payment. If owing to the large and to some

Social Insurance in Germany

extent excessive influx into the medical profession which has been observable since the introduction of the Sickness Insurance Law the individual doctors have not benefited proportionately, that is not the fault of the Insurance Laws."

It was pointed out, at the same time, that the law had had certain results unfavourable for the medical profession, and one of these had been the exclusion from the purview of general medical practice of large groups of people owing to the widely developed system of the " club doctor."

As a result of conferences between the sickness funds, the doctors, and administrative officials experienced in insurance practice, the Government put forward in the Bill proposals for setting up committees of arbitration and conciliation, to be composed of representatives of the funds and of the medical profession in equal numbers and to be formed for large districts. The committees were to exercise three functions : (a) To lay down general principles which should govern the two parties in the conclusion of contracts ; (b) to act as voluntary courts of conciliation in the event of inability to agree upon the terms of contracts ; and (c) to settle minor disputes of a more personal and individual character arising between the funds and the doctors.

The Government declined, however, to consider the proposal of the practitioners that minimum rates of pay for medical attendance should be laid down by law, and insisted that the whole question of remuneration was one for negotiation between the two parties: " The claim often made by doctors, that payment in every case should be according to services rendered, and that

Sickness Insurance

the minimum charges of the official schedule should be adopted for this purpose, is impracticable. Such a provision, if rigidly carried out, would mean the ruin of many sickness funds. It disregards the existing great diversity in local and economic circumstances, and can only be applied generally in dealing with individual patients, since these in calling in medical assistance are compelled to take into account their own financial resources. Members of a sickness fund, however, have not to consider that aspect of the question, and experience shows that they resort to the doctor for trivial indispositions, and even repeat their consultations to an unnecessary extent in respect of the same illness."

During the consideration of the Consolidation Bill in Committee the whole of the clauses providing for the setting up of machinery of arbitration and conciliation were dropped, and the Bill as passed fell far short of the hopes and expectations of moderate men on both sides. The present law provides that members of sickness funds are always to have the choice of at least two doctors, so long as no considerable extra cost is caused to the fund. If a member agrees to bear the extra expense he may choose any doctor on the fund's recognised list. The rules may provide that a member may only change his doctor during the same illness or during the current business year with permission. Should the medical service suffer owing to the inability of the fund to conclude a contract on reasonable terms with a sufficient number of doctors, or should the doctors not carry out a contract, the fund may be allowed to pay to sick members an amount not exceeding two-thirds of the average amount of sickness pay in lieu of medical attendance.[13]

The more the sickness funds have been compelled to make hard bargains with the doctors and their associations, the more they have endeavoured to make the doctors responsible for the economical use of their money. It is, of course, in the power of the doctors to save the sickness funds much unnecessary expenditure, as, for example, in the following ways: (a) The strict oversight of patients with a view to detecting and rejecting the malingerer. The rules of the Frankfurt local fund state : "The doctors are bound, consistently with a conscientious treatment of the sick, to guard the rights and interests of the fund, as by resisting all cases of deception with care and firmness, and notifying the same to the fund, together with persons who wilfully retard or prevent recovery." The Leipzig doctors' agreement requires recognised practitioners to exercise great care that the money of the fund is not wasted, and if negligence is brought home to them they may find their salaries reduced. The officers of the

[13] *National Insurance Act.*—If the Insurance Commissioners are satisfied that the practitioners included in any list are not such as to secure an adequate medical service in any area, they may dispense with the necessity of the adoption of such system as aforesaid as respects that area, and authorise the Insurance Committee to make such other arrangements as the Commissioners may approve, or the Commissioners may themselves make such arrangements as they think fit, or may suspend the right to medical benefit in respect of any insured persons in the area for such period as they think fit, and pay to each such person a sum equal to the estimated cost of his medical benefit during that period. (Section 15 (2) (r).)

Sickness Insurance

fund keep sickness statistics for each doctor separately, and if the general average duration of sickness is exceeded it is the duty of the doctors' committee to inquire into the reason. Where a doctor is found to have shown negligence a deduction may be made from his share of the honorarium paid for medical service. In extreme cases a defaulting doctor may be deprived of his appointment. It is, indeed, an essential feature of the Leipzig medical service system that the doctors' committee examines all doctors' accounts with a view to discovering whether unnecessary expense has been caused owing to negligence or any other reason. (*b*) Economy in the ordering of medicines. Some sickness funds found that patients were often receiving prescriptions for twice or thrice as much medicine as was needful. They now require the doctors to prescribe just as much medicine as is necessary, and no more. The Frankfurt rules state: " If a doctor injures the fund by repeated transgression of the rules as to economical prescriptions a deduction may be made from the fee payable to the doctors' association." (*c*) Before a doctor orders the removal of a patient to a hospital (except in urgent cases) he is required to obtain the consent of the fund, since hospital treatment invariably means larger expense.

The controversy with the doctors has had a counterpart in an even more acute struggle with the chemists as to the terms and conditions for the supply of medicine, drugs, and other remedies. All that the law says as to the pharmacy service is that sickness funds may at their option conclude agreements with special chemists—other local chemists being able to come in if disposed—and prohibit their members from

Social Insurance in Germany

obtaining medicines elsewhere, except in urgent cases, unless at their own expense.[14] Here, again, the sickness funds have been hampered by the fact that in Germany a pharmacy is a monopoly business which can be established only by Government permission, that the law prescribes a long schedule of medicines which can only be procured from the chemist, and that for these medicines the Government fixes the prices chargeable.

[14] *National Insurance Act.*—The Insurance Committees, which administer medical benefit, are required to make provision for the supply of proper and sufficient drugs and medicines and prescribed appliances to insured persons in accordance with regulations made by the Insurance Commissioners, which shall provide for the arrangements made being subject to the approval of the Insurance Commissioners, and being such as to enable injured persons to obtain from any persons, firms, or bodies corporate with whom arrangements have been made such drugs, medicines, and appliances if ordered by the medical practitioner by whom they are attended, and shall require the adoption by every Insurance Committee of such a system as will secure the preparation and publication of lists of persons, firms, and bodies corporate who have agreed to supply drugs, medicines, and appliances to insured persons according to a scale of prices fixed by the Committee, and a right on the part of the same to be included in any such lists. Nevertheless, if the Insurance Commissioners are satisfied that the scale of prices fixed by the Committee is reasonable, but that the persons, firms, or bodies corporate included in any list are not such as to secure an adequate and convenient supply of drugs, medicines, and appliances in any area, they may dispense with the necessity of the adoption of such system as aforesaid as respects that area and authorise the Committee to make such other arrangements as the Commissioners may approve. (Section 15 (5).)

Sickness Insurance

Various methods of exclusive trading have been tried, and unsuccessful endeavours have been made to set up central dispensaries, with the result that the funds have in general arrived at a tacit understanding that, under the conditions prevailing in Germany, the pharmacy service offering the greatest guarantee of efficiency, and, given proper safeguards, probably of economy, is one based on collective local agreements with the chemists or their organisations, providing for preferential terms, and giving the members of the contracting funds the same free choice which they usually exercise in relation to medical practitioners.

Year.	Average Number of Persons Insured.	Percentage of Population.
1885	4,670,959	10·0
1886	4,911,212	10·5
1887	5,220,782	11·0
1888	5,790,431	12·0
1889	6,557,336	13·5
1890	7,018,183	14·3
1891	7,312,958	14·8
1892	7,427,699	14·8
1893	7,574,912	14·9
1894	7,756,686	15·1
1895	8,005,797	15·4
1896	8,413,049	16·0
1897	8,865,685	16·6
1898	9,325,722	17·1
1899	9,742,259	17·6
1900	10,159,155	18·1
1901	10,319,561	18·1
1902	10,529,160	18·2
1903	10,909,288	18·6
1904	11,418,446	19·2
1905	11,903,794	19·7
1906	12,451,183	20·4
1907	12,945,212	20·9
1908	13,189,599	20·9
1909	13,385,290	21·5
1910	13,954,973	21·5

Social Insurance in Germany

IX. Statistics of Growth and Operations.

The steady growth of the German system of sickness insurance since 1885 will be seen from the table on the previous page, showing for successive years the average numbers of persons insured together with the percentages of the population they formed.

Of 23,188 funds in existence in 1910 (the miners' funds excluded), 22,341, among which were all the parochial funds, restricted benefits to 26 weeks, 249 gave it for 26 to 39 weeks inclusive, 585 for 39 to 52 weeks, and 13 longer than 52 weeks. The proportion of wages given by the various funds (the registered funds excluded, since they are not subject to statutory limits) in sickness pay in 1910 was 50 per cent. in the case of 88·1 per cent. of all funds, from 50 per cent. to 66⅔ per cent. inclusive in 9·8 per cent., and from 66⅔ per cent. to 75 per cent. inclusive in 2·1 per cent. of the funds. The proportions in which the various funds gave these money benefits were as follows :—

Funds.	50 per cent. of Wages.	Over 50 per cent. to 66⅔ per cent. of Wages, inclusive.	Over 66⅔ per cent. to 75 per cent. of Wages, inclusive.
	Per Cent.	Per Cent.	Per Cent.
arochial	99·8	0·1	0·1
Local	83·0	14·6	2·4
Factory	79·8	16·2	4·0
Building	95·6	2·2	2·2
Guild	79·2	17·0	3·8

In 1910 the percentages of wages represented by the

Sickness Insurance

HOW THE CLASSES OF FUNDS HAVE VARIED DURING THE SIX YEARS 1905-1910.

	Parochial.	Local.	Factory.	Building.	Guild.	Registered Benefit.	State Regulated benefit.	Mining.	Total.
1905	8,333	4,740	7,774	44	710	1,364	162	173	23,300
1906	8,366	4,741	7,823	46	744	1,339	155	168	23,382
1907	8,290	4,757	7,914	41	761	1,319	151	168	23,400
1908	8,237	4,768	7,954	42	784	1,310	145	170	23,410
1909	8,254	4,775	7,974	45	901	1,286	144	168	23,149
1910	8,217	4,752	7,957	46	818	1,262	136	166	23,354

MEMBERSHIP AT THE END OF EACH OF THE ABOVE YEARS.

Funds.	1905.	1906.	1907.	1908.	1909.	1910.
Parochial	1,434,697	1,445,883	1,475,489	1,496,606	1,538,469	1,572,698
Local	5,470,141	5,804,587	5,915,114	6,020,224	6,347,374	6,722,490
Factory	2,876,580	3,025,790	3,146,386	3,059,752	3,148,602	3,282,293
Building	20,403	11,383	15,232	15,651	13,805	13,806
Guild	245,340	236,198	240,687	247,921	271,925	290,196
Registered benefit	856,290	878,068	893,330	899,255	887,625	929,390
State regulated benefit	36,819	36,015	36,168	35,434	36,646	35,969
Mining *	719,318	761,795	806,276	865,505	884,513	985,598

* Average membership.

Social Insurance in Germany

combined contributions levied were as follows in the
several groups of insurance funds :—

Funds.	1½ and under.	Over 1½-2.	Over 2-3.	Over 3-4½.	Over 4½-6.
	Per Cent.	Per Cent.	Per Cent.	Per Cent.	Per Cent.
Parochial ..	50·3	24·6	25·1	—	—
Local ..	1·3	9·0	53·1	34·7	1·9
Factory ..	6·7	12·1	51·6	27·0	2·6
Building ..	8·7	—	63·1	15·2	13·0
Guild ..	7·3	22·7	47·2	21·4	1·4
Together ..	20·0	16·6	41·8	18·2	1·4

The cases and days of sickness in respect of which
benefit was paid or treatment given have been as follows
for all funds together :—

Year.	Cases of Sickness.	Days of Sickness.
1885	1,956,635	27,864,226
1886	1,874,302	28,962,927
1887	1,895,040	29,590,454
1888	1,923,554	32,116,110
1889	2,211,617	36,155,685
1890	2,627,124	42,002,835
1891	2,616,433	43,948,953
1892	2,699,091	46,405,474
1893	3,037,372	50,120,082
1894	2,719,175	47,380,530
1895	2,943,159	50,301,640
1896	3,001,684	51,461,851
1897	3,220,802	55,577,087
1898	3,262,194	57,347,993
1899	3,780,811	65,198,471
1900	4,023,421	70,146,991
1901	3,983,898	72,446,146
1902	3,930,639	73,124,529
1903	4,177,280	77,603,490
1904	4,642,679	90,051,510

[*Table continued on next page.*

Sickness Insurance

Year.	Cases of Sickness.	Days of Sickness
1905	4,848,610	94,715,219
1906	4,831,108	91,573,327
1907	5,106,076	101,883,006
1908	5,701,180	111,921,654
1909	5,561,006	112,190,311
1910	5,704,429	113,459,544
1885 to 1910 (26 years)	92,582,319	1,679,553,045

An analysis of the returns of sickness shows that cases of sickness are more numerous amongst males than females, but that the average duration of sickness is longer amongst females. This will be seen from the following tables. The first shows for a series of years the number of cases of sickness entailing inability to work (hence carrying sickness pay) per 100 members of all sickness funds except those for miners :—

Year.	Male Members.	Female Members.
1898	35·3	30·6
1903	38·3	33·0
1904	40·9	35·4
1905	41·4	35·0
1906	39·4	33·4
1907	42·7	35·6
1908	44·3	36·6
1909	42·2	35·2
1910	41·3	35·7

The Imperial Statistical Office, which publishes the annual statistics of the sickness funds, comments upon these figures : " The explanation of the greater frequency of sickness amongst men may be explained in part by the higher average age of the male labouring population and the fact that the number of cases of sickness increases

Social Insurance in Germany

with age, while male workers are more liable to accident, and the conditions of their employment are apt to be severer than in the case of women."

In comparing the following figures, showing the number of days' sickness carrying sickness pay or hospital treatment per 100 members, it is necessary to bear in mind that the duration of benefits was by an amending law of 1903 extended from 13 to 26 weeks. The effect of this change will be seen in the returns from 1904 forward :—

AVERAGE NUMBER OF DAYS' SICKNESS PER 100 MEMBERS.

Year	Male Members.	Female Members.
1900	659·1	670·0
1901	696·5	674·5
1902	687·6	670·8
1903	695·3	720·4
1904	762·1	822·9
1905	775·9	821·9
1906	729·6	804·7
1907	789·7	833·1
1908	836·6	860·7
1909	820·8	835·5
1910	781·0	853·2

The same disparity is shown by the comparison on p. 97 of the average duration of all cases of sickness causing inability to work for males and females in the same years.

The editor's explanation of this disparity is as follows: "Since 1904 the number of days' sickness has increased regularly and largely amongst women. Here the influence of the law of 1903 (increasing the duration of benefits from 13 to 26 weeks) has made itself felt. As women suffer more from long illnesses than men, the extension of the duration of benefits has specially benefited them."

96

Sickness Insurance

AVERAGE NUMBER OF DAYS PER CASE OF SICKNESS.

Year.	Male Members.	Female Members
1900	17·0	20·1
1901	17·8	20·9
1902	18·2	21·3
1903	18·1	21·9
1904	18·7	23·2
1905	18·7	23·5
1906	18·5	24·1
1907	18·5	23·4
1908	18·9	23·5
1909	19·4	23·8
1910	18·0	23·9

The aggregate costs of sickness, inclusive of money benefits and medical care of all kinds, but exclusive of administration, have been as follows (all funds, including those for miners) :—

Year.	Marks.	Year.	Marks.
1885	52,758,868	1899	159,170,508
1886	59,001,876	1900	174,012,063
1887	61,217,418	1901	182,368,109
1888	67,917,540	1902	186,042,373
1889	77,609,952	1903	200,795,839
1890	91,733,381	1904	235,620,162
1891	97,938,723	1905	255,803,589
1892	103,983,397	1906	266,553,033
1893	112,115,146	1907	301,296,469
1894	109,263,892	1908	329,311,015
1895	115,031,824	1909	337,644,505
1896	119,899,974	1910	355,732,905
1897	131,715,503	1885 to	
1898	140,029,447	1910 (26 years)	4,345,550,532

The expenditure of all funds per member on the principal kinds of benefit and the total expenditure on all benefits were as follows in 1910 :—

Funds.	Medical Treatment.	Medicine, &c.	Hospital & other Institutional Treatm't.	Sickness Pay.	Miscellaneous Benefits *	Total.
	Marks.	Marks.	Marks.	Marks.	Marks.	Marks.
Parochial	4·18	2·20	3·15	4·06	0·01	13·60
Local	5·44	3·69	3·64	10·41	1·23	21·41
Factory	7·88	4·81	3·50	13·42	1·49	31·10
Building	7·07	3·34	7·87	11·60	0·54	30·42
Guild	5·26	2·96	5·42	8·78	0·62	23·04
Registered Mutual Aid	4·93	4·69	1·96	11·70	0·68	21·96
State Mutual Aid ..	4·27	3·10	1·73	7·67	1·24	18·01
All the above Funds..	5·85	3·69	3·47	10·40	1·08	24·49
Mining..	5·83	4·58	9·14	19·77	1·10	40·32

* Funeral money, maternity pay, and care for convalescents.

The proportions of the total cost of sickness benefits of all kinds which fell to money payments and to medical benefits of all kinds in 1910 were as follows :—

Funds.	Sickness, Maternity, and Funeral Pay.	Medical Benefits of all kinds.
	Per cent.	Per cent.
Parochial	29·93	70·07
Local	47·58	52·42
Factory	47·89	52·11
Building	39·90	60·10
Guild	40·77	59·23
Registered Mutual Aid ..	56·36	43·64
State Mutual Aid	49·43	50·57
Mining	51·85	48·15

Sickness Insurance

The contributions of employers and workpeople respectively in 1910 were as follows :—

Funds.	Contributions of Employers.	Contributions of Workpeople.
	Marks.	Marks.
Parochial	7,542,758	15,096,911
Local	64,620,347	131,371.376
Factory	34,880,095	70,492,644
Building	188,215	377,887
Guild	2,773,023	5,634,818
Registered Aid	—	23,917,881
State Aid	—	691,210
Mining	19,828,249	20,519,971
Totals ..	129,832,687	268,132,701

The total ordinary income of all funds in 1910 was 421,251,652 marks, and the ordinary expenditure was 388,102,927 marks, showing a surplus of 33,102,927 marks. There was an excess of income in the case of 66·0 per cent. or two-thirds of the funds. The numbers and percentages of funds with an excess or a deficit respectively were as follows (the miners' funds being excluded) :—

Funds.	Funds with Excess of Income.		Funds with Excess of Expenditure.	
	No.	Per cent.	No.	Per cent.
Parochial	5,028	61·2	3,189	38·8
Local	3,575	75·2	1,177	24·8
Factory	5,199	65·3	2,758	34·7
Building	27	58·7	19	41·3
Guild	567	69·3	251	30·7
Registered Aid ..	818	64·8	444	35·2
State Aid	87	64·0	49	86·0

Social Insurance in Germany

The costs of administration in 1910 amounted to 22,018,748 marks, equal to 5·2 per cent. of the ordinary revenue and 5·7 per cent. of the ordinary expenditure. The ratios were as follows in the case of the various groups of funds:—

Funds.	Per cent. of Ordinary Revenue.	Per cent. of Ordinary Expenditure.
Local	7·9	8·5
Factory	0·7	0·8
Building	1·1	1·2
Guild	9·3	10·3
Mutual Aid..	10·1	10·9
Miners	3·8	4·2

The low percentages in the case of the factory and Guild funds are due to the fact that the cost of their bookkeeping falls on the employers.

The Imperial Statistical Office regards as "financially sound" such funds as place to reserve each year an amount equal to 10 per cent. of the contributions. In 1910 11,073 out of 23,188 statutory funds, or 47·8 per cent., had a surplus which enabled them to pass at least this sum to reserve. The ratio of solvent and insolvent funds according to this standard was as follows in 1910 and 1909:—

Funds.	Solvent.		Insolvent.	
	1910.	1909.	1910.	1909.
Parochial	50·1	49·2	49·0	50·8
Local	44·8	38·8	55·2	61·2
Factory	47·3	45·3	52·7	54·7
Building	47·8	37·8	52·2	62·2
Guild	48·8	43·9	51·2	56·1
Registered Aid ..	40·3	35·8	59·7	64·2
State Aid	41·9	31·2	58·1	68·8

Sickness Insurance

In all groups there had been an increase in the number of the solvent funds as compared with the preceding year.

The total accumulated funds at the end of 1910 amounted to 318,573,507 marks.

CHAPTER IV

ACCIDENT INSURANCE

THE first compulsory Accident Insurance Law (disregarding the Employers' Liability Act of 1871) was that of July 6, 1884 (operative from October 1, 1885) relating to mines, shipbuilding yards, factories, and to roofers, stonemasons, and well-sinkers. New laws and amendments to existing ones extended liability to insurance successively to the inland transport trades, including railway, canal, and river undertakings, and the postal and telegraph systems; to naval and military establishments; agriculture and forestry; to certain works of construction; to the shipping trade and sea-fisheries; and to prisoners.

The last revision of this legislation is contained in the Insurance Consolidation Act of 1911, which extended accident insurance to a few additional trades and occupations, including inland fisheries, and made foremen, technical employees, and works officials insurable where their yearly earnings are below 5,000 marks (£250), instead of 3,000 marks (£150), as formerly; in the case of marine insurance this extension applies also to *entrepreneurs*.[1] Manual workers are liable to insurance irrespective of the amount of their wages.

[1] *Workmen's Compensation Act.*—The term workman within the meaning of the Act does not include any person employed

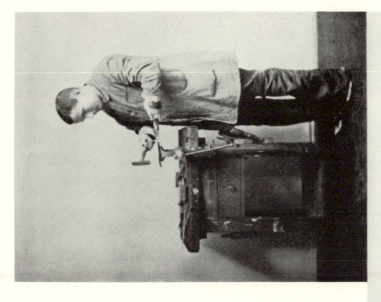

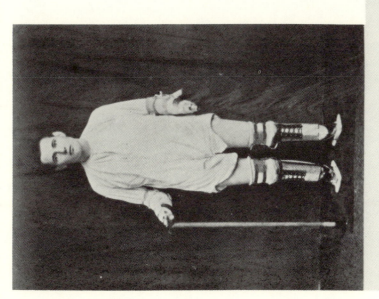

MAN-MENDING UNDER THE ACCIDENT INSURANCE LAW.

I.—INJURED WORKMAN PROVIDED WITH ARTIFICIAL ARMS AND LEGS.

II.—THE SAME IN THE WORKSHOP.

Accident Insurance

The trades and undertakings now brought under the law are specified as follows :—

1. Mines, salt works, ore-dressing works, quarries, and pits.

2. Factories, shipbuilding yards, smelting works, pharmacies, industrial breweries, and tanneries.

3. Building-yards; undertakings in which building, decorators', stonemasons', fitting, smiths', and well-sinking works are executed, with stone-breaking and building works of a non-industrial character.

4. Chimney-sweeping, window cleaning, butchering, and bathing establishments.

5. All undertakings connected with the railway, post, and telegraph services, and those of the naval and military administrations.

otherwise than by way of manual labour whose remuneration exceeds £250 a year or a person whose employment is of a casual nature, and who is employed otherwise than for the purpose of the employer's trade or business, or a member of a police force, or an out-worker, or a member of an employer's family dwelling in his house; but subject to the foregoing exceptions it includes any person who has entered into or works under a contract of service or apprenticeship with an employer, whether by way of manual labour, clerical work, or otherwise, and whether the contract is expressed or implied, is oral or in writing. (Section 13.) The Act also applies to masters, seamen, and apprentices to the sea service, and apprentices in the sea-fishing service, provided they are workmen within the meaning of the Act, and are members of the crew of any ship registered in the United Kingdom or of any other British ship or vessel of which the owner or manager has his principal place of business in the United Kingdom. (Section 7.)

6. Inland navigation, rafting, ferries, towing, inland fisheries, pisciculture, and ice-getting (so far as carried on as an industry or by State, communal, or other public authorities), dredging, the keeping of vessels in inland waters.

7. Carrying trade, posting and livery stables if carried on as an industry, the keeping of conveyances drawn by horse or mechanical power and of horses for riding.

8. Warehousing and storage businesses.

9. The trades of goods-packing and loading, lighterage, weighing, measuring, &c.

10. Undertakings engaged in the transportation of persons or goods, and lumbering carried on by way of commerce if not on a small scale.

11. All undertakings engaged in the handling of goods subject to the condition last stated.

Factories within the meaning of the law are defined as undertakings which manufacture or prepare objects as an industry, and in so doing employ regularly at least ten workpeople, which manufacture explosives or produce or distribute electric power, which use (other than temporarily) boilers or motors, and other undertakings regarded as factories by the Imperial Insurance Office.

All workpeople, assistants, journeymen, and apprentices engaged in these undertakings, and also all works officials, foremen, and technical employees whose yearly earnings do not exceed £250, are liable to insurance.

All agricultural undertakings are similarly liable to compulsory insurance, and while it is left to the Imperial Insurance Office to decide what are to be regarded as

Accident Insurance

such in case of uncertainty, the following auxiliary works are specially included: improvements to agricultural buildings; land improvements and reclamation; road, dyke, drainage, and similar agricultural works; also horticulture, park and garden works, not being of an ordinary domestic nature, cemeteries, and finally undertakings dependent on agriculture engaged in the manufacture of agricultural products or the supply of agricultural needs, so long as they do not come under the industrial section of the law.

The handicrafts and small trades, the home industries, and commercial undertakings are still outside this system of compulsory insurance, but with these exceptions virtually all wage earners engaged in industrial employments are included.

A discretionary power is given to the executive authorities to extend obligatory insurance to *entrepreneurs* whose yearly earnings do not exceed 3,000 marks (£150) or who do not regularly employ more than two workmen, to outworkers carrying on the trades specified above (pp. 103 and 104), also to works officials with earnings above 5,000 marks (£250), and voluntary insurance at their own expense is allowed to certain classes of persons.

Contracting-out is not allowed.[2]

[2] *Workmen's Compensation Act.*—An employer and his workmen may jointly contract out of the Act where it is proved to the satisfaction of the Registrar of Friendly Societies that the workmen have the benefit of a scheme of compensation or insurance, providing scales of compensation not less favourable to them and to their dependants than the corresponding scales contained in the Act, and that a majority

Social Insurance in Germany

Further, the Federal Council is empowered to extend accident insurance to occupational diseases on the principle of the British Workmen's Compensation Act.[3]

The following provisions apply to industrial insurance, but in the main also to agriculture. The provisions relating to marine insurance differ in various points.

I. ORGANISATION AND ADMINISTRATION.

Insurance is effected on the mutual principle and on a trade basis.[4] For this purpose employers are combined in Mutual Associations (*Berufsgenossenschaften*) covering in some cases whole trades and in others (for example, the engineering, textile, wood, and building

of the workmen are in favour of such substitutionary scheme. (Section 3.)

[3] *Workmen's Compensation Act.*—The Act schedules six "industrial diseases" in respect of which compensation is payable as in the case of accident under conditions laid down, and it empowers the Home Secretary to make orders for extending this provision to other diseases and other processes. (Section 8.)

[4] *Workmen's Compensation Act.*—The principle of mutual insurance is encouraged by the provision that where a mutual trade insurance company or society for insuring against the risks under the Act has been established for an industry and a majority of the employers engaged in the industry are insured against such risks in the company or society, and the company or society consents, the Secretary of State may by Provisional Order require all employers in that industry to insure in the company or society upon the terms and conditions and subject to the exceptions to be set forth in the Order. The same obligation may be applied to the employers of a particular locality or class. (Section 8 (7).)

Accident Insurance

trades, and agriculture) wide areas of the country. Where the geographical or industrial limits of a Mutual Association are too wide for efficient centralised management, it may be divided into "sections." In most matters a section is autonomous—it may, for instance, fix the compensation payable for injuries sustained—but on the larger questions it is subordinate to the main organisation.

In the case of State and communal undertakings executive boards (*Ausführungsbehörde*) appointed by the authorities to which the undertakings belong, discharge the functions of the Mutual Associations.

A small group of Insurance Institutes, which deal with only 0·5 per cent. of all accidents compensated, completes the machinery by which insurance is carried out.

The various organisations which administered the Accident Insurance Laws in 1910 comprised :—

66 Industrial Mutual Associations of employers,
14 Insurance Institutes,
48 Agricultural Mutual Associations of employers,
210 State Executive Boards, and
336 Provincial and Communal Executive Boards.

The 66 industrial Mutual Associations comprised 322 sections, and the 48 agricultural Mutual Associations comprised 593 sections, and in the service of the combined Associations were 1,161 members of central executives, 5,838 members of sectional executives, 26,646 confidential agents, 4,470 administrative officials, and 385 technical supervisory officials. The Industrial Associations represented the following groups of industries and trades: Building trades, 12 Associations; textile

Social Insurance in Germany

trades, 8; iron and steel trades, 8; wood trades, 4; inland navigation, 3; railways and tramways, metals, paper-making and manufacturing, 2 each; and one Association each in the case of the mining, stone-quarrying, musical instrument, sugar, gas and water works, leather, milling, food-stuffs, fine mechanism and electro-technical, glass, earthenware, brick, chemical, butchering, dairy, distilling and starch, brewing and malting, tobacco, clothing, excavation, printing, smith, chimney-sweeping, warehousing, carting, and shipping trades.

The average numbers of persons insured by the various Mutual Associations and Executive Authorities (including Insurance Institutes in the case of Building Works and Marine Insurance), with the numbers of undertakings affiliated, were as follows in 1909 :—

Insurance Authorities.	No. of such Authorities.	No. of Under-takings.	Average No. of Persons Insured.
Industry—			
1. Mutual Associations ..	64	704,284	9,009,411
2. State authorities ..	63	—	562,053
Building Works—			
1. Mutual Associations ..	1	19,161	293,252
2. State authorities ..	79	—	57,748
3. Communal authorities	336	—	109,558
4. Insurance Institutes ,..	13	—	85,430
Marine—			
1. Mutual Associations ..	1	1,654	79,215
2. State authorities ..	13	—	973
3. Insurance Institutes ..	1	—	—
Agriculture and Forestry—			
1. Mutual Associations ..	48	5,434,100	17,179,000
2. State authorities ..	55	—	262,362

The total number of workpeople shown as insured is 27,639,002, but from this number 3,400,000 have to be

Accident Insurance

deducted on account of duplications in the case of agriculture, reducing the total to something under twenty-four millions, a little over 60 per cent. being males. Exactitude cannot be claimed, however, for the figures for the agricultural Mutual Associations, since owing to the difficulty of computing the average membership, the figures of the last census of occupations (1907) are accepted, and " the returns of the Mutual Associations are almost always less than these figures." [5]

The Mutual Associations are, as a rule, formed by the employers themselves, and such an Association serves for all employers whose undertakings belong to the branch of trade concerned and which have their seats in the district of the Association. The employers determine their own regulations and procedure within the provisions of the law. Each Association has an honorary executive, committees, and general meeting, with the requisite staff of paid officials. Under the law prior to its revision in 1911 courts of arbitration for the settlement of disputes regarding claims were formed by the employers and workpeople, a Government official acting as president, with right of appeal to the Imperial Insurance Office; but these bodies have given place to the Higher Insurance Offices. The workpeople have a voice in the issue of regulations for the prevention of accidents, but for practical purposes the Mutual Associations are entirely managed by the employers.

The procedure in the case of accident is as follows: Within three days of hearing of an accident which causes

[5] " Amtliche Nachrichten des Reichsversicherungsamts " (January 10, 1912, p. 3), from which these and the later figures are taken.

death or injury entailing disablement for more than three days, the employer or his representative must notify the fact to the local police authority and his Mutual Association, and the former holds an inquiry as soon as possible whenever the injuries have been fatal or are likely to give rise to compensation.[6]   The police must notify the injured person, or his relatives in case of death, also the Mutual Association, the Sickness Fund, the employer concerned, and the Insurance Office of the district, and all these may take part in or be represented at the inquiry.   If a Mutual Association is not satisfied with the ascertained facts of an accident it may require evidence to be taken (on oath if necessary) by the Insurance Office or the local court of summary jurisdiction.

Compensation takes the form of pensions.   The executive of the Mutual Association or one of its sections fixes the amount to be paid in case either of injury or death, and notifies its decision, with reasons for the same, to the injured person or his representatives, who may call for an inquiry by the Insurance Office, and may formally appeal first to the Higher Insurance Office, and then, under certain circumstances, to the Imperial Insurance

[6] *Workmen's Compensation Act.*—Proceedings for the recovery of compensation for injury are not maintainable unless notice of the accident has been given " as soon as practicable after the happening thereof and before the workman has voluntarily left the employment in which he was injured," and unless the claim for compensation has been made within six months from the occurrence of the accident, or in case of death within six months from the time of death.   But the time condition is waived if failure to observe it was due to mistake, absence from the United Kingdom, or other reasonable cause. (Section 2.)

Accident Insurance

Office.[7] Should it be impossible to determine whether a pension will be permanent, the amount may be fixed for two years and then reconsidered.

II. FORM AND MEASURE OF COMPENSATION.

In order that it may establish title to compensation an accident must directly or indirectly arise out of the injured person's occupation ; accidents arising on the way to or from work are only recognised if occurring on premises belonging to or serving the purposes of the undertaking, or if the injured person is at the time engaged in his employer's service. Accidents due to negligence are compensated if they occur on the employer's premises and in the course of work, but no compensation can be claimed if an injury was caused intentionally, and if the accident occurred as a result of a criminal act, compensation may be altogether or partially withheld.[8]

[7] *Workmen's Compensation Act.*—If any question arises in any proceedings under the Act as to the liability to pay compensation under the Act, or as to the amount or duration of such compensation, and the question be not settled by agreement, it shall be settled by arbitration according to rules prescribed in the second schedule to the Act. (Section 1 (3).)

[8] *Workmen's Compensation Act.*—The definition of liability is " If in any employment personal injury by accident arising out of and in the course of the employment is caused," &c. (Section 1 (1).) If the injury was caused by the personal negligence or wilful act of the employer or some person for whose act or default he is responsible, nothing in the Act shall

Social Insurance in Germany

Benefits during the First Thirteen Weeks.—For the first thirteen weeks the benefits claimable by injured persons are those provided by the Sickness Insurance Act, and in the case of most workpeople the cost falls mainly upon the sickness funds.[9] From the beginning of the fifth week after the occurrence of an accident until the expiration of the thirteenth week, however, the sum payable to a disabled person by the sickness fund must amount to at least two-thirds of the wages adopted as the basis for the calculation of benefits, and the difference between this sum and the lower benefit fixed by statute or rule is refunded to the sickness fund by the Mutual Association or, under certain circumstances, by the employer in whose undertaking the accident occurred). If injured persons are not insured against sickness the entire sickness benefit for the first thirteen weeks falls upon the employer. After the lapse of thirteen weeks the

affect any civil liability of the employer, and the workman may at his option take proceedings under the Act or independently. If it is proved that the injury to a workman was attributable to serious and wilful misconduct on his part, compensation in respect of such injury shall be disallowed unless the injury results in death or serious and permanent disablement. (Section 1 (2*b* and *c*).) Further, the employer is not liable under the Act in respect of any injury which does not disable the workman for a period of at least one week from earning full wages at the work at which he was employed. (Section 1 (2*a*).)

[9] Dr. Zacher estimates that the cost of care for injured persons during the first thirteen weeks of disablement is equal to 6⅜ per cent. of the total costs of sickness, and that in this way the workpeople bear 8 per cent. of the cost of accident insurance.

Accident Insurance

Mutual Associations must take over full responsibility, and under certain circumstances they do so earlier.

Special provisions apply to agriculture, merchant shipping, inland navigation, and building works. Before sickness insurance was extended to agricultural labourers the cost of accident insurance during the first thirteen weeks fell upon the local authorities; but since 1911 these authorities are relieved of the greater part of this liability.

Inasmuch as some time may elapse before pensions to injured persons can be fixed on the basis of medical testimony, the sickness fund may continue to act in the place of the Mutual Association, at the latter's expense, for a second thirteen weeks.

Pensions in Case of Injury.—In addition to continued medical treatment, should it be necessary, the injured man receives after the first thirteen weeks a pension equal to two-thirds of his yearly earnings in case of total disability and proportionately less in case of partial disability, or treatment may be given in a hospital with a grant to dependants to the amount of the annuities which would be due to them in the event of the death of the injured person.[10] The latter's assent to such treat-

---

[10] *Workmen's Compensation Act.*—The compensation payable for injury is as follows : Where total or partial incapacity for work results from the injury a weekly payment during incapacity not exceeding 50 per cent. of the workman's average weekly earnings during the previous twelve months, if he has been so long employed, but if not, then for any less period during which he has been in the employment of the same employer, such weekly payment not to exceed £1. Should the incapacity last less than two weeks, however, no compensation

Social Insurance in Germany

ment is necessary in the case of a person who is married or who lives with a member of his family, unless the injury is of such a kind as to need treatment which cannot be given at home, unless the disease is infectious, unless the injured person has repeatedly disregarded medical orders, or unless his condition requires constant observation. In cases of institutional treatment a grant of money may also be made if necessary.

The earnings which are taken as the basis of computation in fixing compensation are those of the preceding year, but above 1,800 marks (£90)—until 1912 1,500 marks (£75)—one-third only is counted. Should the injured man have worked a complete year prior to the accident the year's earnings are taken at 300 times the average daily earnings, though less or more days are counted according to the particular mode of working; should he not have been employed a full year the average of the days actually worked is taken, and for the rest of the term of 300 days the full daily earnings of similar workpeople are accepted, should they be ascertainable, otherwise the man's own rate. In the event of employment in the undertaking concerned being very inter-

is payable for the first week; and in the case of the total incapacity of a workman under 21 years at the date of injury and whose average weekly earnings are less than 20s., 100 per cent. shall be substituted for 50 per cent. of his average weekly earnings, but the weekly payment may in no case exceed 10s. (First Schedule, Section 1 (b).)

Where any weekly payment has been continued for not less than six months the liability therefor may be redeemed by the payment of a lump sum on conditions prescribed. (First Schedule, Section 17.)

Accident Insurance

mittent, the wages for the number of days short of 300 are to be those of adult day-labourers in the locality. In any case the minimum basis is 300 times the last-named rate."

Should an injured man be so helpless that he has to depend on outside care and nursing, the pension for total disablement must be adequate to his needs and may be increased to the full yearly wages, and a partial pension may be increased to the same extent where a man is unable to find employment owing to accident. Compensation is awarded for accidents irrespective of the time during which the injured person has been employed; there is no "waiting time," as in the case of the Infirmity Insurance Law.

In measuring the degree of disablement suffered the man's earning capacity at the time of the accident is considered; hence if at the time of fixing a pension a man's capacity was reduced by 80 per cent., but it had already been reduced by 30 per cent. before the accident

" *Workmen's Compensation Act.*—Average weekly earnings are to be computed " in such manner as is best calculated to give the rate per week at which the workman was being remunerated." Where by reason of the shortness of time during which the workman has been in the employment of his employer, or the casual nature of his employment, or the terms of the employment, it is impracticable at the date of the accident to compute the rate of remuneration, regard may be had to the average weekly amount which, during the twelve months previous to the accident, was being earned by a person in the same grade employed at the same work by the same employer, or, if there is no such person so employed, by a person in the same grade employed in the same class of employment in the same district. (First Schedule, Section 2.)

occurred, a 56 per cent. reduction is all that can be attributed to the accident and is liable to be compensated.

In course of time the Mutual Associations have arrived at a general understanding as to the degrees of disablement which should be compensated in the case of well-defined injuries, and the following are illustrations of compensation actually awarded in different trades :—

Loss of right hand	66⅔	per cent. of full pension.
Loss of right arm	75	„ „
Loss of left forearm	66⅔	„ „
Blindness in both eyes	100	„ „
Loss of one eye	50	„ „
Loss of foot	75	„ „
Loss of left leg	70	„ „
Loss of left thumb	30	„ „

During the first two years after an accident the condition of the injured man may be reconsidered at any time, unless a permanent pension has been legally assigned to him during this period, in which case and after the first two years such reconsideration can only take place after intervals of at least a year, except by agreement. In the event of any change having occurred in the degree of disablement the pension may be proportionately readjusted.[12]

[12] *Workmen's Compensation Act.*—Any workman receiving weekly payments under the Act " shall if so required by the employer from time to time submit himself for examination by a duly qualified medical practitioner provided and paid by the employer. If the workman refuses to submit himself to such examination or in any way obstructs the same, his right to such weekly payments shall be suspended until such examination has taken place," &c. Further, " any weekly payment may be reviewed at the request either of the employer or of

Accident Insurance

Compensation in the event of Death.—In case of death funeral money is paid equal to one-fifteenth of the yearly earnings, with a minimum of 50 marks (£2 10s.), and pensions are granted to the widow until her death or remarriage, and to the orphans under 15 years of age (but to an illegitimate child only if the deceased was legally liable for its maintenance) to the amount of 20 per cent. of the deceased's yearly earnings as above calculated to each, but to a maximum of 60 per cent. altogether.[13]

the workman, and on such review may be ended, diminished, or increased, subject to the statutory maximum, and the amount of payment shall in default of agreement be settled by arbitration under the Act. (Second Schedule, Sections 14 and 16.)

[13] *Workmen's Compensation Act.*—Where death results from the injury there are three scales of compensation—(a) if the workman leaves any dependants wholly dependent upon his earnings a sum equal to his earnings in the employment of the same employer during the three years next preceding the injury, or £150, whichever of these sums is the larger, but not exceeding £300 in any case, any sums already paid under the Act being first deducted; if the workman has been employed by the said employer for a less period than three years the amount of his earnings during the three years shall be deemed to be 156 times his average weekly wages during the period of his actual employment with the said employer; (b) if the workman leaves only dependants partially dependant upon his earnings, such sum, not exceeding in any case the amount payable as above, as may be agreed upon, or in default of agreement as may be determined on arbitration under the Act to be reasonable and proportionate to the injury to the said dependants; and (c) if he leaves no dependants, the reasonable expenses of medical attendance and burial, not exceeding £10. (First Schedule, Section 1.)

Social Insurance in Germany

Pensions are also paid to necessitous parents or grand-parents, and to necessitous grandchildren under 15 years, in so far as the deceased supported them wholly or mainly, the amount being here 20 per cent. of the earnings in the aggregate for relatives in the ascending line and the same for the grandchildren, but in any case the total must not exceed 60 per cent.[14] Thus 18,651 survivors of persons fatally injured, to whom pensions were paid for the first time in 1910, included 5,956 widows and widowers, 12,416 children and grandchildren, and 279 relatives in the ascending line.

As to women, it is to be noted that the provisions as to orphans' pensions apply equally to the children of an unmarried woman killed by an accident as a result of employment. Further, in the event of a fatal accident to a wife who has wholly or mainly supported her family owing to the husband's disablement, a pension equal to one-fifth of her yearly earnings is paid during

[14] *Workmen's Compensation Act.*—The item "dependants" within the meaning of the Act means such members of the workman's family as were wholly or in part dependent upon the earnings of the workman at the time of his death, or would but for the incapacity due to the accident have been so dependent, and where the workman, being the parent or grandparent of an illegitimate child, leaves such a child so dependent upon his earnings, or, being an illegitimate child, leaves a parent or grandparent so dependent upon his earnings, it includes such an illegitimate child and parent or grandparent respectively. "Member of a family" means wife or husband, father, mother, grandfather, grandmother, stepfather, stepmother, son, daughter, grandson, grand-daughter, stepson, stepdaughter, brother, sister, half-brother, and half-sister. (Section 13.)

need to the husband until his death or remarriage, and to each child under 15 years.

Neither a widow nor a widower has any claim if the marriage took place after the accident, but in the case of a widow the Mutual Association may at discretion grant a pension.

Lump-sum Payments.—Lump-sum payments are the rare exception. Compensation may be so compounded for in the case of (*a*) a widow remarrying, who receives three-fifths of the amount of her late husband's yearly earnings; (*b*) a lump sum may also be paid at discretion, and with his or her consent, in the case of a recipient of a partial pension of 15 per cent. of a full pension or less; and (*c*) in the case of a foreign workman leaving Germany, who with his consent is given three times the yearly pension in settlement of all claims, or the full capital value of his pension without his consent. Upon the subject of lump-sum payments, the Imperial Insurance Office says:—

" The system of social insurance against accident and infirmity would have failed of its object had not the method of pension been preferred. Only in this way is it possible to provide adequately against need and to secure to people of small means, during loss of earning capacity caused by accident or infirmity, a care which cannot be sacrificed owing to improvident conduct or misfortune, as may easily happen where compensation takes the form—so largely favoured by private insurance—of a lump-sum payment.[15] [16]

[15] " Das Reichsversicherungsamt und die deutsche Arbeiterversicherung " (*Festschrift*), 1910, p. 88.

[16] *Workman's Compensation Act.*—A safeguard against the

Social Insurance in Germany

In 1909 the discretionary power to grant compensation in a lump sum where the diminished incapacity does not exceed 15 per cent. was exercised in 5,405 cases, out of a total of 139,070 cases in which compensation was paid for the 'first time; the sum so paid being 1,791,980 marks (£89,599)—giving an average of 331½ marks (£16 11s. 6d.)—out of a total compensation bill of 161,332,900 marks (£8,066,645).

Pensions Liable to Suspension.—Pensions are suspended in the case of German subjects who go abroad to live and omit to notify their addresses to the Mutual Association affected and to present themselves to a German consul or such other authority as may be prescribed; [17] also of German subjects judicially convicted

[17] unwise use of the lump-sum compensation provided for in case of death by this Act is contained in the provision that "the payment in the case of death shall, unless otherwise ordered as hereinafter provided, be paid into the County Court, and any sum so paid into court shall, subject to rules of court and the provisions of this schedule, be invested, applied, or otherwise dealt with by the court in such manner as the court in its discretion thinks fit for the benefit of the person entitled thereto under this Act." (First Schedule, Section 5.)

[17] *Workmen's Compensation Act.*—If a workman receiving a weekly payment ceases to reside in the United Kingdom he shall cease to be entitled to receive any weekly payment unless the medical referee certifies that the incapacity resulting from the injury is likely to be of a permanent nature; in the latter case he shall be entitled to receive quarterly the amount of the weekly payments accruing due during the preceding quarter, so long as he proves, in such manner as may be prescribed, his identity and the continuance of the incapacity in respect of which the weekly payment is payable. (First Schedule, Section 18.)

Accident Insurance

during the period of detention in a prison or a place of correction; but in the latter case the pension is paid to the dependants, if any.

Pensions due to foreigners are suspended so long as they reside abroad of their free will, and so long as they are expelled from the Empire on conviction of a penal offence or from a federal State if not resident in another federal State. The Federal Council is empowered, however, to annul these provisions in the case of subjects of States whose legislation affords Germans and their survivors a corresponding provision. Should expulsion arise otherwise than as a result of judicial conviction the same provisions apply as to German subjects living abroad. Nevertheless, a foreigner entitled to pension who ceases to reside ordinarily in Germany may, with his consent, be paid a lump sum equal to three times the yearly pension in settlement of all claims, or without his consent the full capital value of his yearly pension.

The relatives of a foreigner who were not ordinarily residing in Germany at the time of a fatal accident have no claim to pensions, but the Federal Council is empowered to annul this provision in the case of the subjects of countries whose legislation affords to the relatives of Germans killed by accident a provision corresponding to that offered by this law.

As a rule, pensions are paid in advance monthly, except where the annual amount is 60 marks or less, when they are paid quarterly, and in all cases payment is made through the Post Office. The Post Office used also to advance the pensions, being repaid at the end of the year, but since January 1, 1910, the insurance organisa-

Social Insurance in Germany

tions have provided the Post Office in advance with the sums necessary. A law of July 15, 1909, converted the amount advanced by the Post Office in that year for the compensation of insured persons into a floating debt, bearing interest at 3½ per cent. from July 1, 1910, and redeemable at the rate of 3½ per cent. plus the interest saved each year, two-fifths both of the interest and the repayments falling on the Empire, but this has been repealed by the Consolidation Act.

Assessment of Employers to the Cost.—With the exception of the expenditure incidental to the first thirteen weeks, the employers alone bear the costs of insurance, and their liabilities are met in the form of yearly assessments to cover the requirements of the year, a method which avoids the costly device of great accumulations of capital, to the great relief of employers. In the case of the Mutual Association for works of excavation, however, the contributions must cover the capital value of the pensions for which the Association has become liable in the preceding year. Reserves have in all cases to be formed to meet contingencies, though in accordance with the scale laid down the contributions to the reserve fund steadily diminish.

The assessments are calculated on the amount of wages and salaries paid, and according to a fixed schedule of risks, but all such amount of wage or salary as exceeds 1,800 marks (£90) a year is counted to the extent of one-third only, in consequence of the corresponding limitation in fixing the basis of compensation.

Regulations for the Prevention of Accidents.—One of the most important functions of the Mutual Associations is the issue and enforcement of regulations for the

122

prevention of accidents. These regulations must be approved by the Imperial Insurance Office, and apply to the whole or a part of the district for which an Association is formed or to special branches of industry or kinds of undertakings, and if they are not observed the defaulting employers may be fined as much as 1,000 marks. An employer so penalised may appeal against a decision of his Association to the Higher Insurance Office, the decisions of which are final.[18]

Before regulations of this kind are issued the opinion of the workpeople's representatives must be taken regarding them; but on the other hand when they are once in force the workpeople are liable to punishment like the employers for neglect to observe them. The Insurance Consolidation Act of 1911 has made more stringent the provisions as to the issue, execution, and supervision of regulations for the prevention of accidents, and these provisions have been extended to marine insurance. The Mutual Associations may appoint officials to watch the observance of these regulations, and in general to inspect the undertakings of insured firms

[18] The preventive and deterrent effect of this method of penalising negligent employers brings into relief the advantage of obligatory insurance on the mutual principle as compared with insurance through private adventure companies. The only pressure which the commercial company can exert upon its clients in the direction of minimising accident risk is to offer lower premiums to undertakings in which special precautions are enforced. The efficacy of this method of preventing accidents is limited, however, to the extent that insurance companies are ready to underbid each other in the competition for business.

Social Insurance in Germany

with a view to their assessment in the proper danger classes, and of verifying their returns of workpeople and wages. The Associations and the execution of the law generally are subject to the Imperial Insurance Office.

The Industrial Mutual Associations alone expended in 1910 no less than £110,300 in measures of various kinds for the prevention of accidents. An admirable object-lesson in this preventive work is afforded by the " permanent exhibition of contrivances for the prevention of accidents " which has been formed at Charlottenburg. The Mutual Associations had not long been in existence before they made a collection of these contrivances for the use of their members, and it was exhibited in various parts of the country. In 1900, however, the Government granted money for the formation of a permanent collection on a larger scale and for its housing in a special building. This building was erected at Charlottenburg, and on its completion in 1903 it was placed under the Imperial Ministry for the Interior. The main hall occupies an area of 2,160 square yards, and has a gallery with about half this area. The floor is occupied by machines in operation supplied with contrivances for the prevention of accidents, while in the gallery is a multitude of appliances which cannot conveniently, or do not need to be, shown in motion. Other apparatus of the same kind is exhibited outside. Most of the contrivances have been given or lent to the exhibition by various Mutual Associations formed under the Accident Insurance Laws.

A special department of the exhibition is devoted to industrial hygiene, the objects here shown comprising

APPARATUS FOR KNITTING.

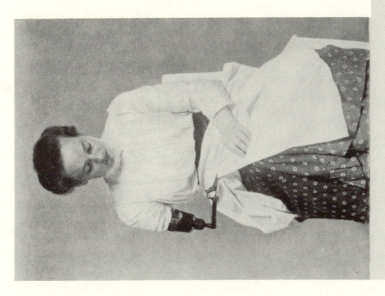

APPARATUS FOR SEWING.

Accident Insurance

scientific apparatus for testing air, anatomical preparations, representations of injuries caused to health by industrial processes, contrivances for ventilating workrooms and keeping them free from dust and gases, washing and bathing arrangements, illustrations of factory dressing- and dining-rooms, and the like. Most objects are shown in full size, and where this is not possible accurate models are used. The practical value of the exhibition is increased owing to the fact that only apparatus actually in use is shown, all out-of-date contrivances being promptly discarded in favour of the most modern improvements.

III. OPERATIONS UNDER THE LAW.

The accident insurance legislation has now been in force for twenty-seven years. During the first quarter of a century compensation was paid to over two million injured persons, as follows :—

Years.	Injured Persons.	Years.	Injured Persons.
1885	268	1898	98,023
1886	10,540	1899	106,036
1887	17,102	1900	107,654
1888	21,236	1901	117,336
1889	31,449	1902	121,284
1890	42,038	1903	129,375
1891	51,209	1904	137,673
1892	55,654	1905	141,121
1893	62,729	1906	139,726
1894	69,619	1907	144,703
1895	75,527	1908	142,965
1896	86,403	1909	139,070
1897	92,326		
		Total ..	2,141,066

Social Insurance in Germany

During the same years compensation was paid to the aggregate amount of 1,803,900,000 marks, divided as follows :—

	Marks.
Pensions to injured persons	1,302,000,000
,, survivors	322,600,000
,, relatives	18,300,000
Lump-sum compensation to injured persons (natives) ..	12,300,000
,, ,, widows ..	12,100,000
,, ,, foreigners ..	3,900,000
Funeral money	10,400,000
Care during waiting time	10,500,000
Curative treatment	44,600,000
Institutional treatment	67,200,000

The compensation paid in the various years was as follows :—

Year.	Marks.	Year.	Marks.
1886	1,915,366	1898	71,108,729
1887	5,932,930	1899	78,680,633
1888	9,681,447	1900	86,649,946
1889	14,464,303	1901	98,555,869
1890	20,315,320	1902	107,443,326
1891	26,426,377	1903	117,246,500
1892	32,340,178	1904	126,641,740
1893	38,163,770	1905	135,437,933
1894	44,281,736	1906	142,436,864
1895	50,125,782	1907	150,325,292
1896	57,154,398	1908	157,062,870
1897	63,973,548	1909	161,332,900

The number of accidents notified in 1910 was 672,961, and the number for which compensation was paid for the first time was 132,064, 8,857 having fatal result and 1,072 causing complete permanent incapacity.

The total expenditure of that year was 227,821,118 marks (£11,391,055), including compensation of various

Accident Insurance

kinds to the amount of 163,326,820 marks (£8,166,311) ; the care of injured persons during the statutory waiting time cost 1,091,149 marks (£54,707), and the costs of administration were 16,550,030 marks (£827,501).

The amount put to reserve during the year 1910 was 18,796,191 marks, or £939,809.

The accumulated reserves of the industrial Mutual Associations at the end of the year 1910 amounted to 288,407,693 marks (£14,420,385), and of the agricultural Mutual Associations to 17,498,824 marks (£874,941), or together 305,906,517 marks, or £15,295,326.

CHAPTER V

INVALIDITY, OLD AGE, AND SURVIVOR PENSIONS

LEGISLATION introducing obligatory insurance against invalidity and old age completed the trio of insurance laws operative in Germany until the present year (1912).

The Insurance Consolidation Law of 1911 enlarged the scope of this measure by adding provision for pensions to the survivors (widows, widowers, and orphans) of insured persons in receipt of or entitled to invalidity pensions.

The obligation to be insured extends to the great majority of the wage-earning class of both sexes, as well as to other classes of persons from the age of 16 to that of 70 years;[1] at the latter age exemption may be obtained on application. The law specifies the following as liable to insurance:—

1. Workpeople (*e.g.*, in factories and workshops, mines, transport undertakings, agriculture, &c.), assistants, journeymen, apprentices, servants.

2. Works officials, foremen, and other employees in a similar higher position, if their employment is their principal occupation.

3. Shop and chemists' assistants and apprentices.

[1] *National Insurance Act.*—For conditions and scope of insurance under this Act, see Chapter II., Sickness Insurance, p. 25, note 2.

Invalidity and Old Age Pensions

4. Members of theatrical companies and orchestras, regardless of the artistic value of their performances.

5. Teachers and tutors.

6. The crews of German sea-going vessels and vessels engaged in inland navigation.

The condition of insurance is that employment must be for remuneration, and in Classes 2 to 5 there is a wages limit of 2,000 marks (£100). Manual workers are insured irrespective of earnings. Persons receiving only free maintenance are exempted from obligatory insurance.

Out-workers still remain outside the obligatory provisions of the law, but by resolution of the Federal Council they may be brought in, and already the out-workers engaged in the tobacco and textile trades have been included.

Power is also reserved to the Federal Council to include small *entrepreneurs* working without assistants or with only one.

Another class of persons excluded are those whose earning capacity is permanently reduced owing to age, sickness, or other infirmity to less than one-third of the wages earned in the same locality by persons in the same position, of normal capacity and healthy in body and mind.

State and local officials, teachers and tutors in public schools, and employees of insurance authorities created or recognised by the law are not liable to be insured so long as they enjoy, by the conditions of their employment, a claim to pensions equal to the minima provided by the law.

Several classes of persons otherwise liable to insurance may be exempted at their own request, viz., persons who in the course of the calendar year perform paid labour only at definite seasons during not more than 12 weeks or not more than 50 days altogether, and during the rest of the year maintain themselves independently or work without remuneration; also persons who are temporarily occupying a position which is preparatory to entrance into a non-insurable employment.

The Federal Council is also empowered to exempt from insurance against invalidity foreigners who are allowed by the authorities to reside in Germany for a definite period only, but the employer may be required to pay the usual contributions in respect of such persons.

On the other hand, other classes of persons who are not formally included are allowed to insure voluntarily so long as they have not completed their fortieth year. Such are works officials, foremen, shop assistants, teachers and tutors, and ships' captains, so far as their salaries exceed £100 but fall below £150, also independent *entrepreneurs* who do not regularly employ more than two workpeople liable to insurance, casual workers, persons employed only in return for board and lodging, and those who cease to follow an insurable employment.

The number of persons insured under the law in 1909 was 15,444,300, 10,707,100, or 69 per cent., being males, and 4,737,000, or 31 per cent., females. Some 600,000 persons were voluntarily insured.

It will be convenient to consider in order the three questions—(i) Organisation and Administration, (ii) the Contributions, (iii), (iv), (v) the Benefits Given, and (vi) Scope of Operations

(i) ORGANISATION AND ADMINISTRATION.

The organisation and the administration of this system of insurance are distinctly bureaucratic in character. The

Invalidity and Old Age Pensions

great majority of the administrative bodies are known as Insurance Institutions (*Versicherungsanstalten*), described in the following pages as Pension Boards.[2] They are organised by the Governments of the various States independently, being formed either for large local government areas (as in the case of Berlin), for divisions of a State, or for an entire State or combination of States. Each Board is directed by an Executive, at the head of which is a permanent president, assisted by other paid officials, appointed by the State or communal authority, according to the organisation of the Board, and representatives of the employers and workpeople in equal numbers. There is also a committee, which must consist of at least five representatives of the employers and five of the insured workpeople, the chairman being the president of the Executive. Only persons directly affected by the law can be elected on these bodies, and their offices are honorary, except that mere out-of-pocket expenses are paid, including loss of work in the case of workpeople.

It is the duty of local Insurance Offices [3] to receive and examine claims for pensions, to examine proposals to withdraw pensions, and to consider cases in which medical treatment is desirable, with a view to staving off invalidity, and they report the results of all such inquiries to the Pension Board concerned. The actual pensions awarded are fixed by the Executive of the Pension Board.

[2] *National Insurance Act.*—Administration is by approved societies of insured persons, as explained in Chapter II., Sickness Insurance, p. 35, note 9.

[3] See Chapter VI., on the Insurance Consolidation Act, for the constitution of these and other supervisory authorities, pp. 174–176.

Social Insurance in Germany

Should a claim for pension be refused, appeal is allowed to the Higher Insurance Office, and similar appeal may be made against the amount of a pension granted and the date of its commencement. In some cases a right of appeal is given to the Imperial Insurance Office.

The only exceptions to this bureaucratic form of administration are certain Superannuation Funds approved by the Federal Council on condition of their providing benefits equivalent to those provided by the law.[4]

In 1910 there were in existence 31 territorial Pension Boards and 10 Superannuation Funds for special classes of insured persons. The former group included 13 Boards for Prussia, 8 for Bavaria, 1 each for Saxony, Wurtemberg, Baden, Hesse, Mecklenburg, the Thuringian States, Oldenburg, Brunswick, the Hanse Cities, and Alsace-Lorraine. The Superannuation Funds were : One for the workpeople engaged on the Prussian and Hessian State Railways, four for the miners (*Knappschaften*), one for the Bavarian State Railways, Post and Telegraphs, one for the Saxon State Railways, one for the Baden State Railways and saltworks, one for the railways of Alsace-Lorraine, and the invalids', widows', and orphans' insurance fund of the Trade Association for seamen.

The whole system of insurance is under the superintendence of the Imperial Insurance Office, except that some of the States have separate Insurance Offices for their own territories and the miners' and railway funds are under the respective State authorities.[5]

[4] *National Insurance Act.*—The nearest corresponding provision of this Act is that authorising employers' superannuation or other provident funds to become approved societies on complying with certain conditions. (Section 25.)

[5] *National Insurance Act.*—The corresponding authorities

Invalidity and Old Age Pensions

(ii) The Contributions.[6]

The bodies which administer the law have two main sources of income—contributions by the insured workpeople and their employers (in equal amounts) and a yearly addition to every pension from the Imperial Treasury.

For the fixing of the contributions the insured are divided into five wages classes according to their yearly earnings as ascertained by different methods. These classes are :—

Class I.—Persons in receipt of wages not exceeding 350 marks (£17 10s., or 6s. 9d. weekly).

Class II.—Persons in receipt of wages from 350 marks to 550 marks (£17 10s. to £27 10s., or 6s. 9d. to 10s. 7d. weekly).

Class III.—Persons in receipt of wages from 550 marks to 850 marks (£27 10s. to £42 10s., or 10s. 7d. to 16s. 4d. weekly).

Class IV.—Persons in receipt of wages from 850 marks to 1,150 marks (£42 10s. to £57 10s., or 16s. 4d. to 22s. 1d. weekly).

Class V.—Persons in receipt of wages exceeding 1,150 marks (£57 10s., or 22s. 1d. weekly).

The wages class to which an insured person belongs is determined by a system of averages.

The methods of computation are as follows: (a) In the case of members of sickness funds, 300 times the base wage adopted for the calculation of contributions and sickness benefit; (b) in the case of seamen, such average amount as may be fixed by the Imperial Chancellor;

---

under this Act are the Insurance Commissioners for the three Kingdoms and Wales respectively. (Sections 57, 80–82.) See Chapter VII., on the Insurance Consolidation Act, p. 174, note 8.

[6] *National Insurance Act.*—For the rates of contribution (covering both sickness and disablement insurance) under this Act see Chapter II., Sickness Insurance, pp. 44, 45, note 19.

(c) in other cases, unless the Higher Insurance Office decides differently for special branches of industry, 300 times the local daily rate of common labour. Agri-·cultural works officials fall into the third class, and teachers and tutors into the fourth, where they do not prove yearly earnings exceeding 850 and 1,150 marks respectively.

The Consolidation Law left the wages classes as before, while modifying the basis upon which average wages are computed.

The contributions payable in the five wages classes are fixed by the Federal Council for ten years at once.[7] The contributions must be so calculated that on average they cover the capital value of the pensions and the other expenditure of the Pension Boards. In all cases the pensions bear a certain proportion to the contributions made. At the end of each decennial period the Imperial Insurance Office determines whether the basis of insurance is actuarially sound ; and according as the contributions are found insufficient or excessive, they may be increased or reduced.

---

[7] *National Insurance Act.*—Approved Societies must submit to valuation every three years ; if a surplus is shown the benefits may be increased, if a deficit they may be reduced, or a special levy may be made. (Sections 36 and 37.) Societies. with branches and affiliated small societies are required to pool a portion of their contingent surpluses. (Sections 39 and 40.) The rules of an approved society, not being a society with branches, may provide for the separate valuation of its male and female sections, and for separate procedure in the case of surplus or deficit respectively. (Section 41.)

Invalidity and Old Age Pensions

The following table shows the scale of weekly joint contributions: (a) Under the law prior to the revision of 1911 (old law), and (b) under the Consolidation Act, adding survivor pensions (new law), the nearest English equivalents down to farthings being given :—

Wages Class.	(a) Old Law	(b) New Law.
	Pfennige.	Pfennige.
I.	14 = 1¾d.	16 = 2d.
II.	20 = 2½d.	24 = 3d.
III.	24 = 3d.	32 = 3¾d.
IV.	30 = 3½d.	40 = 4¾d.
V.	36 = 4¼d.	48 = 5¾d.

As the workers and the employers share the contributions equally, the payments of each are now approximately 1d., 1½d., 2d., 2½d., and 3d. respectively for the different wages classes.

It is optional for an insured person to insure himself in a higher class than that to which he is assigned, but he must bear the whole of the extra cost himself, unless the employer voluntarily agrees to pay on the higher scale.

For every week in which an insured person is employed in an occupation liable to insurance (called a "contributory week") a contribution has to be paid on the foregoing scale, the week being reckoned from Monday.

The double contributions are paid in the first instance by the employer, who is entitled to deduct the workman's share at the next pay-day. Should he neglect to deduct it then he may do so on the following payment, but not later, except for the purpose of paying up arrears which have accumulated owing to no fault of his own.

An employer is liable for a week's contribution of every worker whom he employs on Monday. If a person works for more than one employer during the week, the one who first employed him is, as a rule, liable for the week's contribution.

The Pension Board has discretion to allow employers to pay over the contributions at other intervals than the ordinary pay days, and insured persons may pay direct to the Pension Board if they please, and claim back from their employers one-half the contributions, but this is seldom done.

An employed person forfeits right to such portion of an invalidity pension as is represented by contributions which his employer has neglected to pay on his behalf, except in so far as arrears may still be paid up, but he has a right to proceed in the civil courts for the recovery of damages sustained. On the other hand, the law deals severely with the defaulting employer. Wilful omission to report persons liable to insurance against invalidity or to pay promptly the contributions due is punishable by the Pension Board with a fine not exceeding 300 marks, and in the latter case the offender may be required also to pay up to three times the amount of the arrears. An employer who wilfully retains contributions which he has deducted from his workpeople's wages may be imprisoned and in addition fined up to a maximum of 3,000 marks; where extenuating circumstances are shown he may be let off with a fine.

Invalidity and Old Age Pensions

Contributions are not payable by the insured during military service, mobilisation, and sickness causing incapacity to work; nevertheless, such periods count as "contributory weeks" in the second wages class.

Two methods of payment are recognised by the law —payment by means of stamps and payment in cash. The former method is the more general. Stamps are issued separately by every Pension Board for every wages class, and for one, two, or thirteen weeks together; they are sold at all post offices, and at other accredited agencies. The stamps are affixed to a receipt card, containing spaces for stamps for at least 52 contributory weeks. When a card is full, it is handed in to the Pension Board and a new one is issued. Stamps have to be affixed as a rule on each pay day, or where there is no periodical pay day at the latest at the end of employment, but the Pension Boards may vary this rule according to the circumstances of individual firms. All stamps must be cancelled as from the latest day for which they pay.

Cash payments are made to the funds to which the miners and the employees of most State railway administrations belong; in the case of the Marine Insurance Fund both methods are adopted.

On a limited scale the plan of collecting the contributions is followed, in virtue of a provision which empowers the supreme administrative authority to require the contributions of all persons liable to insurance, or certain classes of them, to be collected by statutory sickness funds, including those of the miners, or by special pay offices established for the purpose by the Insurance Offices, or by the local government authorities.

Social Insurance in Germany

The collection of contributions has been introduced chiefly in Saxony, Wurtemberg, Hesse, the Thuringian States, Brunswick, the Hanse Cities, and the Rhenish province of Prussia.

(iii) The Benefits Granted.

The benefits provided by the measure as extended are five, viz. :—

(*a*) Old age pensions, claimable at 70.

(*b*) Invalidity pensions.

(*c*) Survivor pensions (from 1912).

(*d*) Gratuities to widows and orphans (from 1912).

(*e*) Sanatorium and other institutional and curative treatment, the direct purpose of which is to defer claims for invalidity pensions.[8]

(*a*) *Old Age Pensions.*—An insured person who reaches the age of 70 years obtains an old age pension, whether able to work or not ; in this case the pension is simply an increase to his income.[9] Should he continue to be employed and to pay his contributions he will be able in case of permanent infirmity to exchange the old age

---

[8] *National Insurance Act.*—The comparable benefits under this Act are the disablement allowance of 5s., payable during the entire period of incapacity to work (following 26 weeks of sickness benefit) until age 70, and sanatorium benefit, which may be extended to the dependants of insured persons. (Sections 8 (1), (*b*) and (*d*), 16, and 17, as explained in Chapter III., Sickness Insurance, pp. 50, 51, note 23.)

[9] *National Insurance Act.*—Permanent disablement benefit ceases at the age of 70, when old age pensions of equivalent amount (5s.) are claimable, under certain conditions as to income, under the Old Age Pensions Act of 1908. (Section 8 (3).)

138

pension for an invalidity pension, should it be larger, but both pensions cannot be held concurrently.

(b) *Invalidity Pensions.*—The old law made invalidity pensions dependent upon permanent inability to earn a livelihood (*Erwerbsunfähigkeit*), and in the clause exempting such persons from insurance defined that condition as follows :—

"Those persons whose inability to earn a livelihood is, in consequence of age, sickness, or other infirmity, permanently reduced to less than one-third. This is to be assumed when they are no longer able by an activity, corresponding to their powers and capacity, such as might be expected of them having regard to their training and past occupation, to earn one-third of the sum usually earned by physically and mentally healthy persons of the same kind with a similar training in the same locality." [10]

This definition is retained by the Consolidation Act, but the term "permanent inability to earn a livelihood" is dropped, and it is provided that "An insured person who is permanently invalid in consequence of sickness or other infirmity receives an invalidity pension regardless of age." It has been laid down that a workman (*e.g.*, a miner) who may be incapacitated from following his own calling cannot claim a pension so long as he is able to work at another occupation.

Provisional pensions, called sickness pensions, are

---

[10] *National Insurance Act.*—The Act provides for the payment to insured persons, after the cessation of sickness benefit, of disablement benefit, "whilst rendered incapable of work" by such specific disease or bodily or mental disablement as qualified for sickness benefit. (Section 8 (1).)

Social Insurance in Germany

payable to those who are not permanently invalid, but have been in receipt of sickness benefit for 26 weeks continuously, or are invalid after the discontinuance of sickness pay (having exhausted their statutory claims under the Sickness Insurance Law), for the further term of such invalidity.

Incapacity which has been intentionally or culpably caused disqualifies for a pension ; and if caused by the commission of an indictable offence it may be wholly or partially refused or be paid to the family of the insured person. To take an example, injury caused by attempted suicide may be held to disqualify.

Incapacity occasioned by an accident only justifies a claim to an invalidity pension in so far as such pension would exceed the pension due under the Accident Insurance Law.

Before any of the foregoing pensions can be claimed a "waiting time" must be observed. This is 1,200 contributory weeks in the case of old age pensions, and 200 contributory weeks when at least 100 contributions have been paid (otherwise 500 contributory weeks) in the case of invalidity pensions.[11] Special conditions apply to voluntary insurance. Periods of military service and of sickness entailing incapacity (not exceeding a year), and certified by a statutory sickness fund, count as contributory weeks without any payments, though not in the latter case

[11] *National Insurance Act.*—No insured person is entitled to disablement benefit unless and until 104 weeks have elapsed since his entry into insurance and at least 104 weekly contributions have been paid by or in respect of him. (Section 8 (8) (c).)

BEELITZ SANATORIUM (BELONGING TO THE BERLIN PENSION BOARD)—PAVILIONS, SHELTERS, AND PROMENADES.

if the sickness has been caused intentionally or culpably.

(c) and (d). *Survivor Pensions and Gratuities.*—These are payable to the widows (or widowers), if infirm, and orphans of insured persons whether these have been in receipt of invalidity pensions or not.

(e) *Sanatorium Benefit.*—The curative work undertaken by the Pension Boards has of late years become a very important part of their work. It is fully described in the chapter dealing with the crusade against consumption.[12] The Pension Boards are also

---

[12] *National Insurance Act.*—In aid of the establishment of a sufficient number of sanatoria, &c., a State grant of one and a half million pounds has been made, and this sum will be distributed by the Local Government Board between England, Wales, Scotland, and Ireland, in proportion to their relative populations in 1911. (Section 64 (1).) Grants may be made to local government authorities or to other bodies undertaking the provision of such institutions, and contributions towards their maintenance may be made by the Insurance Committees out of the funds available for sanatorium benefit in consideration of their affording treatment to such persons as may be recommended by the Committees. (Section 64 (4).)

The sums payable to the Insurance Committees for defraying the expenses of sanatorium benefit are 1s. 3d. in respect of each insured person resident in the county or county borough for which the Committee is formed, payable out of the funds out of which benefits are payable under the Act, and 1d. in respect of each such member payable out of moneys provided by Parliament The Insurance Commissioners are empowered, however, to retain the whole or any part of the sums provided by Parliament and to apply it to research work. (Section 16 (2).)

The Insurance Committee for any county or county borough

empowered, with the sanction of the supervising authorities, to adopt general measures for preventing premature invalidity, and for promoting the health of the insured population. Such measures are the provision and support of curative institutions of all kinds, the encouragement of Building Societies, the holding of popular health lectures, the publication of health literature, &c.[13]

(iv) Value and Calculation of Pensions.

The pensions and other money benefits given under the law consist of a fixed State (Imperial) subsidy and a contribution from the funds of the Pension Boards. The State subsidy amounts in the case of invalidity, old age, widows', and widowers' pensions to 50 marks (£2 10s.) yearly, in the case of orphans' pensions to

may, if it thinks fit, extend sanatorium benefit to the dependants of insured persons, and if in any year the amount available for defraying the expenses of sanatorium benefit is insufficient to meet the estimated expenditure on sanatorium benefit for insured persons and such dependants the Treasury and the council of the county or county borough concerned may agree to defray the deficit in equal proportions. The council of any borough or urban district may agree with the County Council to refund to the latter the whole or part of any expenditure incurred by it in respect of such borough or urban district. (Sections 17 and 22.)

[13] *National Insurance Act.*—The powers of Insurance Committees include, besides the administration of medical and sanatorium benefits, the institution of inquiries as to the health of insured persons, and provision for the giving of lectures and the publication of information on health questions. (Section 60 (1).)

Invalidity and Old Age Pensions

25 marks (£1 5s.) yearly, in the case of widows' money a single payment of 50 marks, and in the case of an orphan's dowry 16⅔ marks (16s. 8d.). The contribution of the Pension Board depends upon the number and value of the contributions which have been paid, counting thereto the weeks of sickness or military service which rank for contributory purposes.

(a) *Old Age Pensions.*—These are made up of fixed contributions by the Pension Boards and the Imperial Treasury, graduated as follows according to the wages class in which the insured persons have contributed:—

Wages Class.	Paid by the Fund.	Paid by the Imperial Treasury.	Total.
	Marks.	Marks.	Marks.
I.	60	50	110
II.	90	50	140
III.	120	50	170
IV.	150	50	200
V.	180	50	230

If contributions have been paid in different wages classes the average pension corresponding to these contributions is given. If there have been more than 1,200 contributory weeks, the 1,200 contributions in the highest wages classes are taken as the basis, and the pension is calculated accordingly.

(b) *Invalidity Pensions.*—The invalidity pension is made up of three distinct elements. (a) The first is a fixed basal sum, which is different for each wages class. (b) The second is an accretion or supplement dependent

Social Insurance in Germany

upon the number of contributory weeks shown at the time the pension is claimed. Both these constituents in the pension are paid by the Pension Board. (c) The third is the uniform State subsidy of £2 10s. per annum.

The basal amount of the pension is calculated on the assumption that at least 500 weekly contributions have been paid, but should that number not have been reached it is made up by imputed contributions in the lowest wages class, and if more than 500 contributions have been made, those on the higher scales are counted. The rates of the accretions also differ according to the wages class, and are multiplied by the number of weeks of contribution. The contributory parts of an invalidity pension are accordingly made up as follows in the case of a person insured for 500 weeks :—

Wages class.	(a) Basal amount. Pfennige.	(b) Accretion. Pfennige.
I.	12	3
II.	14	6
III.	16 } × 500	8 } × 500
IV.	18	10
V.	20	12

In illustrating the invalidity pensions which may be claimed under the law, it will be advisable to take several hypothetical periods of contribution. It should be stated, however, that in the case of persons who have been insured for a short time only the pensions claimable give excessive weight to the State grant, while in the case of pensions claimable at a distant date, when the

Invalidity and Old Age Pensions

full benefit of insurance is felt, it is impossible to allow for possible increases in the rates of contribution.

Assuming a basis of 500 weeks' (say ten years') contributions, the pensions claimable in the five wages classes will be as follows :—

Wages Class.	Basal Amount.	Accretion.	State Subsidy.	Total.
	Marks.	Marks.	Marks.	Marks.
I.	60*	15†	50	125 (£6 5s. or 2s. 5d. a week)
II.	70	30	50	150 (£7 10s. or 2s. 11d. a week)
III.	80	40	50	170 (£8 10s. or 3s. 3d. a week)
IV.	90	50	50	190 (£9 10s. or 3s. 8d. a week)
V.	100	60	50	210 (£10 10s. or 4s. a week)

* That is, 500 times 12 pfennige, and so on according to the foregoing scale.
† That is, 500 times 3 pfennige, and so on according to the foregoing scale.

The pensions which will accrue in respect of what the German Government calls an " average period of working capacity," which it estimates at 1,763 weeks of contributions, or, roughly, 34 years, will be as follows :—

Wages Class.	Yearly Pension.	Weekly Pension.
	Marks.	
I.	163 or £8 3s.	3s. 1d.
II.	226 or £11 6s.	4s. 4d.
III.	271 or £13 11s.	5s. 2d.
IV.	317 or £15 17s.	6s. 1d.
V.	362 or £18 2s.	6s. 11d.

Social Insurance in Germany

The following are the pensions which would be claimable by persons uninterruptedly insured from the age of 16 years, and becoming invalid at a period mid-way between the attainment of the necessary waiting time (*i.e.*, after 4 years of insurance) and the time of maximum benefit—say, at the age of 45 years, assuming 50 contributions a year:—

Wages Class.	Yearly Pension.	Weekly Pension.
	Marks.	
I.	168·50 or £8 8s. 6d.	3s. 2d.
II.	237 or £11 17s.	4s. 7d.
III.	286 or £14 6s.	5s. 6d.
IV.	335 or £16 15s.	6s. 5d.
V.	384 or £19 4s.	7s. 6d.

When contributions have been paid regularly for 50 years, the pensions which will be claimable will be £9 5s. or 3s. 6d. a week in the lowest wages class, £13 10s. or 5s. 2d. a week in the second class, £16 10s. or 6s. 4d. a week in the third class, £19 10s. or 7s. 6d. a week in the fourth class, and £22 10s. or 8s. 8d. a week in the highest class. As these pensions presuppose unbroken contributions, they represent, of course, impossible maxima.

The average value of the pensions granted increases by several shillings yearly, and is now 176·93 marks, or £8 16s. 11d. (3s. 5d a week), in the case of invalidity pensions, comparing with 113¼ marks or £5 13s. 6d. (2s. 2d. a week) in 1891; 164·31 marks or £8 4s. 4d.

Invalidity and Old Age Pensions

(3s. 2d. a week) in the case of old age pensions, comparing with 121 marks or £6 4s. (2s. 5d. a week) in 1891; and 175·74 marks or £8 15s. 9d. (3s. 5d. a week) in the case of provisional sickness pensions, comparing with 147·73 marks or £7 7s. 8¾d. (2s. 10d. a week) in 1900.

Further, the opportunity is afforded to insured persons of supplementing their old age and invalidity pensions by voluntary contributions of a minimum amount of 1s. at convenient times. For every supplementary contribution of 1s. so made the insurer will, on his claim to pension maturing, receive the sum of 2 pfennige (¼d.) for every year that has elapsed since the contribution was paid. If the supplementary pension should not exceed 60 marks (£3), the beneficiary may require its commutation into a lump-sum payment.

The way in which these supplementary contributions will materialise may be shown as follows, on the assumption that 500 supplementary contributions were made during the years 1912–1920 and that the invalidity pension matured in the following year :—

Year.	Amount of Contributions.	No. of Years since Date of Contributions.	Addition to Pension.
	Marks.		Pfennige. Marks.
1912	20	8	$20 \times 2 \times 8 = 3·40$
1913	10	7	$10 \times 2 \times 7 = 1·40$
1914	40	6	$40 \times 2 \times 6 = 4·89$
1915	25	5	$25 \times 2 \times 5 = 2·50$
1916	100	4	$100 \times 2 \times 4 = 8·00$
1917	50	·3	$50 \times 2 \times 3 = 3·00$
1918	100	2	$100 \times 2 \times 2 = 4·00$
1919	155	1	$155 \times 2 \times 1 = 3·10$
1920	—	—	—
			30·20

Social Insurance in Germany

An insured person who for a period of thirty years affixed to his card an extra shilling stamp every month would in the event of invalidity receive a supplementary pension of about £6.

Pensions payable to members of a recognised superannuation fund are calculated upon the same basis. Here, too, such contributory time as is represented by periods of military service and of sickness counts to the second wages class in fixing a pension.

Under the amended law of 1911, should the invalid pensioner have children under 15 years his pension is increased for each such child by one-tenth, to a maximum of 50 per cent. additional.[14]

Should the condition of an invalid pensioner change so that he can no longer be regarded as incapable of earning his livelihood, the pension may be discontinued, and should there be reason to suppose that a pensioner would regain capacity by undergoing a course of medical treatment, he may be required to agree to this on pain of forfeiting his pension wholly or partially.

On the application of a pensioner, a Pension Board may give him maintenance in an infirmary or other institution instead of paying him a pension; such arrangement holding good for three months at a time.

(c) *Widows' and Orphans' Pensions.*—The benefits provided under the new scheme of "survivor insur-

[14] *National Insurance Act.*—One of the "additional benefits" scheduled is the increase of sickness benefit or disablement benefit in the case either of all members of the society or of such of them as have any children or any specified number of children wholly or in part dependent upon them. (Part II. of 4th Schedule.)

Invalidity and Old Age Pensions

ance" are pensions for the widows, widowers, and orphans of insured persons, widows' money, and dowries for orphans.[15] The pensions are only payable if the insured had at the time of death fulfilled the requisite waiting time and retained his expectation or contingent claim, and the other benefits if in addition the widow had fulfilled these conditions. Pensions are payable as follows: (a) On the death of her husband a pension to the widow if she is permanently invalid or has been uninterruptedly invalid for 26 weeks for the period of such invalidity, the same definition of invalidity as above being applied here; (b) on the death of an insured father pensions to children under 15 years born in wedlock; (c) to the fatherless children of an insured woman, whether legitimate or not, up to the same age; (d) pensions to a widower and orphans, in case of need, on the

[15] *National Insurance Act.*—The only provisions in this Act corresponding in any way to the benefits conferred upon widows of insured persons under the Invalidity Insurance Act are those dealing with women who cease to be employed contributors owing to marriage. Such a woman may elect to become a voluntary contributor, paying 3d. a week and receiving medical benefit, and also, on a reduced scale, sickness and disablement benefits. Failing voluntary membership, she is suspended from receiving the ordinary benefits provided by the Act during the life of her husband, but she is allowed to draw upon two-thirds of her transfer value according to a special scale of benefits until such sum is exhausted, the remainder of this transfer value going to a suspense account for the purpose of keeping up her insurance until her husband's death. If on the death of her husband she again becomes an employed contributor, she enters at once into full insurance, without liability to pay up arrears. (Section 44.)

149

death of the insured wife of a man unable to work, provided she has been the sole or chief support of the family. If an insured person leaves behind orphan grand-children under 15 years who were wholly or mainly dependent upon him, they have an equal claim to orphans' pensions so long as in need.

Should a widow receive no survivor pension owing to the fact that she is in receipt of, or by virtue of her own contributions has a claim to, a larger invalidity pension, she receives on the death of her husband a single payment in the form of " widow's money " and dowry money for each child on its reaching the age of 15 years.

These survivor pensions are calculated on much the same basis as the invalidity and old age pensions. In addition to the Government a subsidy of 50 marks yearly given in the case of widows' pensions, and 25 marks in the case of orphans' pensions, the Pension Board contributes in the former case 3/10ths of the basal amount and the rates of accretion of the invalidity pension which the breadwinner received at the time of his death or would have received in the event of invalidity ; where there is one orphan the Pension Board contributes 3/20ths and for each additional orphan 1/40th of these two amounts, with the proviso that the survivor pensions together may not exceed one and a half times the said invalidity pension. Orphans' pensions alone may not exceed the amount of the invalidity pension. Dependent grandchildren have a claim to pensions as orphans in so far as the maximum sum payable is not claimed by the children.

The amount of the " widow's money " is equal to twelve

Invalidity and Old Age Pensions

monthly instalments of the widow's pension and that
of the orphans' dowry to eight monthly instalments of
the orphans' pension, the Imperial Government adding
50 marks (£2 10s.) in the former case and 16⅔ marks
(16s. 8d.) in the latter.

Several provisions are introduced in favour of persons
newly insured under the law, and particularly of widows
and orphans entitled to pensions. It is provided that
until December 31, 1930, contributions paid towards
invalidity pensions shall count in reducing the waiting
time qualifying for survivor pensions (200 weeks if the
insured person has paid 100 contributions, otherwise 500
weeks), but from that date only contributions paid after
January 1, 1912, will be counted. Where 500 contributions (the number upon which the "basal amount"
forming one of the three elements in an invalidity pension
is calculated) have not been paid since January 1, 1912,
the deficiency will be made up out of the highest contributions paid prior to that date; and if 500 contributions
have not been made altogether the balance will be made
up by "imputing" the missing contributions on the
lowest scale. On the other hand, the accretions counted
in calculating a survivor's pension are only those in
respect of contributions paid by the deceased persons
after January 1, 1912.

The following illustration will show how the amounts
of survivors' pensions are arrived at. Assuming that the
breadwinner had paid 700 contributions in the third wages
class (yearly wages of between £27 10s. and £42 10s., or
10s. 7d. to 16s. 4d. weekly), 50 of these falling after
January 1, 1912, the basal amount of his invalidity
pension would be 500 × 16 pfennige or 80 marks (£4).

Social Insurance in Germany

A widow's pension would be 3/10ths of this sum (24 marks) plus 3/10ths of the accretions to the 15 contributions paid from January 1, 1912 (*i.e.*, 15 × 8 pfennige) or 36 pfennige, rounded off to 40 pfennige, plus the State supplement of 50 marks, or together 74·40 marks, equal to 6s. 2d. a month. An orphan's pension would be 3/20ths of the basal amount and of the accretions as above, making 12·20 marks, with the State supplement of 25 marks, or together 37·20 marks, equal to 3s. 1d. a month.

An invalidity or old age pension is withheld or curtailed in the case of a person in receipt of an accident pension in so far as the two together would exceed seven and a half times the basal sum payable towards such invalidity pension, and survivors' pensions are also subject to a certain curtailment when accident pensions are received.[16]

A pension is also suspended so long as the person entitled to it (*a*) is in prison for more than a month, or is detained in a house of correction, when it is paid to his dependants if any ; (*b*) usually resides abroad of his free will, but in this case if the person is a foreigner

---

[16] *National Insurance Act.*—Where an injured person had received or recovered, or is entitled to receive or recover, compensation or damages under statute in respect of injury or disease no sickness benefit or disablement benefit shall be paid to him in respect of that injury or disease should any weekly sum or the weekly value of any lump sum paid or payable by way of compensation or damages be equal to or greater than the benefit otherwise payable to such person under the Act, and where any such weekly sum or the weekly value of any such lump sum is less than the benefit in question, such part

Invalidity and Old Age Pensions

a lump sum is payable to the amount of three times the yearly pension or one and a half times in the case of an orphan's pension ; or (c) if a foreigner is expelled from the country on conviction of a criminal offence or is similarly expelled from any federal State unless he resides in another federal State.[17] The Federal Council has power to annul the suspension in (b) in the case of countries whose legislation gives to Germans and their survivors corresponding provision. When a foreigner is expelled from the country without conviction (e.g., expulsion by the police authorities on account of political agitation) his claims may be commuted by a lump-sum payment with his consent.

Local authorities may, with the sanction of the higher

only of the benefit shall be paid as, together with the weekly sum or the weekly value of the lump sum, will be equal to the benefit. (Section 11 (1) (a).)

[17] *National Insurance Act.*—Under this Act misdemeanour will be dealt with by the rules of the approved societies, as is now the case with the Friendly Societies, under a provision authorising approved societies, with the consent of the Insurance Commissioners, to apply existing or make new rules "with regard to the . . . suspension of benefits," &c. (Section 14 (2).)

Permanent or temporary residence outside the United Kingdom disqualifies for benefit, unless such residence abroad is approved by the approved society or Insurance Committee concerned, in which case sickness and disablement benefits may be given. But a person resident out of the United Kingdom will not be disentitled to maternity benefit in respect of the confinement of his wife if at the time of her confinement she was resident in the United Kingdom. (Section 8 (4).)

administrative authorities, adopt by-laws providing that pensions may up to two-thirds be paid in kind in the case of pensioners resident in the district when they or the persons supporting them, being agricultural labourers, are paid in kind by local custom and agree to accept such substitutionary payment. In the case of orphans' pensions the consent of the legal guardian and the court of wards is also necessary. Inebriates may under certain conditions be paid the whole amount of their pensions in kind.

The Invalidity Insurance Law does not affect the liability of communes and Poor Law Unions in regard to the maintenance of destitute persons or any other existing legal, statutory, or contractual liability for the care of old, sick, and incapacitated or destitute persons. When, however, a commune or Poor Law Union gives relief to destitute persons in respect of a period for which they have a claim to invalidity or old age pensions, the partial refund of such relief from the pensions due may be required.[18]

Under the old law half the amount of the contributions paid for insured persons were returnable under certain circumstances, viz. :—

1. Women who married before pensions had been assigned to them, provided contributions had been paid for at least 200 weeks before marriage, such return of contributions being in settlement of all claims.

[18] For a fuller discussion of the relationships between the Insurance and Poor Laws see the chapter on "The Insurance Consolidation Act" (pp. 170–172).

Invalidity and Old Age Pensions

2. Insured persons who had sustained an accident causing permanent incapacity in the sense of this law, and had no claim to an invalidity pension.

3. The contributions of the insured were also returned to the widow or legitimate children under 15 years of male persons for whom contributions had been paid for at least 200 weeks, yet who had died before pensions had been assigned to them. Should an insured person have claimed a pension and died before receiving it, the claim might be pursued, and the pension be claimed up to the time of such decease, by the widow or widower or next of kin.

4. The same right was reserved to the children under 15 years in respect of a widow or wife deserted by her husband for whom contributions had been paid for at least 200 weeks.

Thus in 1910 contributions were returned in 147,291 cases of marriage, in 494 cases of accident, and in 37,923 cases of death to an average amount of 40·27 marks (£2 0s. 3d.), 98·62 marks (£4 18s. 7d.), and 100·30 marks (£5 0s. 3d.) respectively.

Now that survivor pensions have been introduced these refunds of contributions have been discontinued.

(v) LAPSES AND ARREARS.

The question of arrears under the Invalidity Insurance Laws has a twofold importance for the insurer, viz., (a) as affecting the validity of a contingent claim (*Anwart-schaft*) to pension, and (b) as affecting the value of such pension in so far as the value is determined by the number and amount of the contributions paid.[19]

As has been explained, a contingent claim to pension is created in the first instance by the payment of at least 100 contributions in respect of employment entailing liability to insurance during a " waiting time " of 200 contributory weeks ; but in other cases the waiting time is 500 weeks. This condition is lightened owing to the fact that persons in regular employment are allowed to count as " contributory weeks " all periods of military service and of certified temporary incapacity due to illness (in the latter case to a maximum of one year and provided the illness was continuous).

A contingent claim thus created is preserved by the payment of contributions in the ordinary way, but it lapses temporarily unless during two years dating from the issue of the insurer's receipt card contributions have been paid for at least 20 (in the case of voluntary insurers 40) contributory weeks. Such payments are not conditional upon employment. Here, again, periods of military service and sickness, and also of unemployment during which the insured person has been in receipt of an accident, invalidity, or old age pension, count as contributory weeks. The condition as to 20 contributions being paid within two years is fulfilled if the insurer, whatever his previous contributions may have been, pays on the lowest scale, viz., 16 pfennige or 2d. (for, if unemployed, he must pay the total contribution himself), so that the contingent claim may be

[19] *National Insurance Act.*—For explanation of the provisions of the Act relating to waiting times and arrears, see Chapter II., " Sickness Insurance," pp. 32 and 41, notes.

Invalidity and Old Age Pensions

kept valid for two years of unemployment at a cost of 3s. 4d.

A contingent claim which has lapsed may be revived by resumption of an insurable employment or renewal of insurance by voluntary contributions, and the observance of a new waiting time of 200 contributory weeks, but should disablement occur in the meantime there is no claim to pension. It has been ruled by the Imperial Insurance Office, however, that it is not necessary that the 100 contributions establishing a fresh contingent claim must necessarily fall to the new waiting time of 200 weeks; contributions belonging to a previous waiting time which have provisionally become invalid are revived by new payments and reduce the necessary 100 contributions proportionately.

Should the insured person, on resuming insurable employment or renewing his insurance by voluntary contributions, have reached the age of 60 years, his contingent claim is only revived if before its lapse he had used at least 1,000 stamps (of any denomination). If an insured person is 40 years old the claim is only revived by voluntary contributions if before its lapse he had used at least 500 stamps and observed a waiting time of 500 contributory weeks.

It is, nevertheless, provided that contributions in arrear can only be paid up within two years unless they have been withheld owing to an undetermined dispute or for other reasons for which those concerned are not to blame, in which case they may be paid up and counted for a period of four years after becoming due. Voluntary contributions and contributions for a higher wages class than that to which the insurer properly belongs may not be paid up for a longer period than one year, nor may such contributions be paid retrospectively after the occurrence of invalidity or during invalidity.

While, however, actual forfeiture of claim to pension may occur under certain circumstances, the usual result of broken insurance is simply to decrease two of the three component parts of the pension, viz., the basal sum, which presupposes a minimum of 500 contributions, and the accretions, which depend absolutely upon the aggregate number of payments made.

Of the 2,471,265 pensions granted up to December 31, 1910, 75·4 per cent. were on account of invalidity, 20 per cent. were on account of old age, and 4·6 per cent. on account of sickness, ending in most cases in permanent disablement. On January 1, 1911, 1,034,060 pensions were in force, viz., 918,760 invalidity, 98,335 old age, and 16,965 provisional sickness pensions.[20]

The new invalidity pensions granted in 1910 fell to the following ages :—

Age.	Number of Pensions.	Age.	Number of Pensions.
20 to 24	3,154	50 to 54	10,810
25 to 29	5,262	55 to 59	14,180
30 to 34	5,430	60 to 64	21,408
34 to 39	5,591	65 to 69	21,087
40 to 44	6,182	70 and over	13,866
45 to 49	7,725		114,755

[20] The number of old age pensions in force in the United Kingdom on the 31st of March, 1910, in virtue of the Old Age Pensions Act of 1908, was 699,352, of which 638,147, or 91 per cent., were for 5s. a week.

Invalidity and Old Age Pensions

(vi) SCOPE OF OPERATIONS.

The following have been the numbers of pensions granted and the aggregates paid in each year since the law came into force:—

Year	Invalidity New Pensions	Invalidity Total Paid	Temporary Sickness New Pensions	Temporary Sickness Total Paid	Old Age New Pensions	Old Age Total Paid	Aggregate Pensions Granted
1891	31	—	—	—	132,926	—	132,957
1892	17,784	—	—	—	42,128	—	59,312
1893	35,177	—	—	—	81,083	—	66,260
1894	47,385	—	—	—	33,871	—	81,256
1895	55,983	—	—	—	30,144	—	86,127
1896	64,450	—	—	—	25,953	—	90,403
1897	75,746	237,416	—	—	22,320	226,275	98,066
1898	84,781	295,640	—	—	19,525	223,169	104,306
1899	96,665	361,564	—	—	17,320	218,649	113,935
1900	125,717	450,056	6,677	6,677	19,852	214,985	152,246
1901	130,482	535,817	7,632	12,750	14,849	203,921	152,963
1902	142,789	689,704	8,733	17,433	12,885	192,335	164,404
1903	152,882	727,724	9,216	21,361	12,430	190,980	174,528
1904	140,099	903,232	10,458	24,644	11,936	168,556	162,486
1905	122,868	857,923	11,861	28,846	10,692	156,158	145,421
1906	110,969	891,730	12,421	32,561	10,666	144,766	134,056
1907	112,220	926,795	11,527	33,624	10,813	136,416	134,500
1908	116,852	958,844	11,951	32,032	10,996	127,873	139,789
1909	115,264	983,350	12,716	31,803	11,003	119,640	138,983
1910	114,679	—	12,263	—	11,612	—	138,554
Totals..	1,862,816		115,455		492,994		2,471,265

Social Insurance in Germany

The official returns do not classify as to sex.

Invalidity pensions are no longer granted with as free a hand as formerly. After the amendment of the Invalidity Insurance Law in 1899, there was a very large increase in the number of invalidity pensions granted from year to year. The total number of such pensions granted in 1895 was 55,983, but it rose to 125,737 in 1900, to 130,482 in 1901, 142,789 in 1902, and 152,882 (the high-water mark) in 1903. As a consequence the Government directed the Imperial Insurance Office to send Commissioners to those Pension Board districts whose returns showed an abnormal increase in pensions granted, with a view to ascertaining the causes, stiffening the system of control, and generally " hardening the hearts " of the authorities. A more elaborate system of inspection was introduced—the number of inspectors being largely increased—and the administration of the law, which had hitherto been, perhaps, unduly indulgent, was made more exact. The immediate result of the new and more rigid spirit of administration was a great decrease in the number of pensions granted. In the first year after the Government took action the decreases in pensions granted in four representative Pension Board districts were 25, 36, 37, and 49 per cent. Taking nine Pension Board districts which were visited by Government commissioners during the years 1901–5 the number of pensions granted in 1906 as compared with the year preceding inspection showed a reduction of 39·2 per cent. To-day some Pension Boards are granting yearly only from one-half to two-thirds the number of pensions granted eight or ten years ago, in spite of a large increase in the number of persons insured.

Invalidity and Old Age Pensions

The payments made by the 41 Pension Boards and Funds on account of pensions and return of contributions have been as follows since the law came into operation :—

Year.	Pensions.	Return of Contributions.
	Marks.	Marks.
1891	15,299,133	—
1892	22,363,970	—
1893	27,912,706	—
1894	34,451,412	—
1895	41,829,540	219,345
1896	48,171,309	1,975,248
1897	54,617,290	3,390,931
1898	61,813,195	4,497,478
1899	69,194,022	5,446,147
1900	80,448,760	6,616,721
1901	90,977,029	6,925,166
1902	103,884,218	7,131,097
1903	117,147,657	7,555,523
1904	128,849,097	7,858,169
1905	136,904,031	8,171,548
1906	142,972,601	8,436,367
1907	147,593,320	8,854,889
1908	152,691,477	9,237,034
1909	158,265,664	9,420,433
1910	163,997,252	9,430,086
1891 to 1910 (20 years.)	1,799,873,683	105,169,182

Of the aggregate sum of 1,799,373,683 marks paid in pensions, 1,159,614,213 marks were borne by the Insurance organisations, and 639,759,471 marks by the Empire (2,024,408 marks being on account of contributions payable during periods of military service).

The total revenue of the Pension Boards and other executive authorities from contributions in 1910 was

180,624,699 marks, being 90,312,349 marks each for employers and workpeople.

Their expenditure on pensions, independently of the supplements added by the Imperial Treasury, was 111,449,217 marks; and they returned contributions to the amount of 9,429,933 marks. The cost of curative measures, including the concurrent support of relatives (viz., 2,039,219 marks), but after the deduction of 5,833,251 marks refunded by sickness and accident insurance organisations and other persons liable, was 21,102,167 marks. The total cost of the maintenance of patients in infirmaries was 1,216,406 marks, reduced by 367,677 marks deducted from the patients' pensions and 77,947 marks contributed from other sources, making the net expenditure under this head, 770,782 marks.

The costs of administration were 21,367,298 marks, equal to nearly 12 per cent. of the revenue from contributions and 13 per cent. of the total expenditure. In relation to the whole of the year's receipts these costs formed 8·4 per cent. in 1910, being 8·3 per cent. in the case of the Pension Boards, and 8·9 per cent. in the case of the recognised Pension Funds, ratios comparing with 6·4, 6·6, and 4·9 per cent. respectively in 1900; the increase in the interval has been constant.

The expenditure charged to administration includes the cost of determining claims to pensions, of courts of arbitration, of collecting contributions, of supervision, as well as of general management, but it excludes all expenditure of the Imperial Insurance Office, the other State Central Offices, and public authorities.

The total costs of administration for all the Pension Offices and other executive bodies formed the following

Invalidity and Old Age Pensions

percentages of (a) income, (b) contributions, and (c) expenditure in the years named:—

Year.	Per Cent. of Income.	Per Cent. of Contributions.	Per Cent. of Expenditure.
1900	6·4	7·8	13·7
1901	6·4	7·9	13·0
1902	6·8	8·4	12·4
1903	6·9	8·6	11·8
1904	7·1	8·9	11·7
1905	7·2	9·1	11·7
1906	7·4	9·3	11·7
1907	7·5	—	—
1908	7·8	9·9	12·2
1909	8·1	10·4	12·5

After allowing for appreciations and depreciations of securities and real estate, the gross revenue of the year was 254,351,458 marks, and the gross expenditure, similarly adjusted, was 166,304,097 marks, showing a credit balance of 88,047,361 marks. The credit balances for the last ten years have been as follows:—

Year.	Marks.	Year.	Marks.
1900	83,097,211	1906	80,985,431
1901	83,403,129	1907	85,542,018
1902	78,315,351	1908	85,542,965
1903	76,803,474	1909	84,500,765
1904	76,184,464	1910	88,047,361
1905	77,134,732		

At the close of the year 1910 the net assets of the

Social Insurance in Germany

whole of the Pension Boards and other executive bodies amounted to 1,662,158,740 marks, in addition to 6,666,869 marks, the book value of the movable property. Of the accumulated funds 1 7 per cent. was in cash, 93·2 per cent. (1,549,213,509 marks) was invested in securities and loans, and 5·1 per cent. (85,013,983 marks) was invested in real estate.

The officials and others engaged by the various Pension Boards, &c., included in 1910 323 members of Executives, 4,008 other paid officials of all kinds, 628 members of Committees, 168 assessors of pension agencies, 13,222 assessors attached to the local administrative authorities, 124 courts of arbitration, 2,363 stamp agencies, and 1,729 persons employed in sanatoria of all kinds.

CHAPTER VI

THE INSURANCE CONSOLIDATION ACT

THE most important revision of the Insurance Laws yet undertaken is that embodied in the Insurance Consolidation Act of 1911, which codifies the various laws, extends the scope of two of them, and reorganises the supervisory authorities and the machinery for the settlement of disputes. After the leading proposals of the Government had been before the country for some time, the Bill on the subject was introduced in the Imperial Diet early in 1910. In due time it was referred to a Committee consisting of 28 members; the second and third readings took place in May, 1911, and it became law on July 19th. The law came into operation at once in so far as related to the measures necessary for its execution; the portion relating to invalidity and survivor insurance came into force on January 1, 1912, and it was provided that the remaining provisions should be applied as might be expedient in virtue of Imperial decrees, issued with the assent of the Federal Council.

The law is divided into six books. The first deals generally with the organisation of the three insurance systems and the insurance authorities, and contains various provisions common to all three systems. The

Social Insurance in Germany

second, third, and fourth books deal respectively with sickness, accident, and invalidity and survivor insurance in the order of their historical origin, the book on accident insurance being divided into three parts, devoted to industrial, agricultural, and marine insurance respectively. The fifth and sixth books contain the regulations governing the reciprocal relations between the several insurance systems and the procedure to be adopted in adjudication, arbitration, &c.

In so far as the Consolidation Act modifies the scope and general operation of the sickness, accident, and invalidity insurance laws as they existed up to 1911, its provisions have already been explained sufficiently in the chapters dealing separately with these laws. In the present chapter certain important provisions which apply to the entire system of working-class insurance will be summarised and the broad lines upon which supervision will henceforth be exercised by outside authorities be indicated.

Scheduled Rates of Wages.—For the purpose of calculating benefits and contributions under certain portions of the Act local rates of wages for day labour ("the usual local daily rates of remuneration for common day labour") are to be scheduled by the Higher Insurance Offices for each district of an Insurance Office. This must be done for insured persons of both sexes (*a*) under 16 years, (*b*) from 16 to 21 years, (*c*) over 21 years. Separate rates may permissively be ascertained for young people from 14 to 16 years and for children under 14 years. Each local rate must be uniform for the district of the Insurance Office, and represent the average for the entire district, but an exception may be made when the wages differ greatly in various localities or in town and country. These rates must be fixed simultaneously for the whole Empire, and the first rates will be in force until December 31, 1914, a revision taking place thereafter every four years ; changes which may be made in the interval continue in force only until the next general computation. Before the "local wage" is scheduled the executives of the Pension Offices of the territory to which the districts belong must be heard, and the Insurance Office must give its opinion after consulting the local authorities and the executives of the sickness insurance funds affected.

Payments in Kind.—Remuneration within the meaning of the Act includes, besides salary or wages, shares of profits and payments in kind made to the insured in lieu of or in addition to salary or wages by the employer or a third person.

The value of payments in kind will be computed according to local prices by the Insurance Offices.

Approved Practitioners.—Medical and dental treatment is defined in all cases as treatment by certificated doctors or dental surgeons ; auxiliary treatment by other persons (*e.g.*, baths, services of midwives, nurses, *masseuses*, &c.) can only be given when ordered by the doctor, except in urgent cases.[1]

---

[1] *National Insurance Act.*—"Every Insurance Committee shall for the purpose of administering medical benefit make arrangements with only qualified medical practitioners," &c. (Section 15 (1).) Similarly, the regulations of the Insurance Commissioners shall prohibit arrangements for the dispensing of medicines being made with persons other than "persons, firms, or bodies corporate entitled to carry on the business of

Social Insurance in Germany

Benefits to Inebriates.—Benefits in kind must be given, wholly or partially, to inebriates on the proposal of the local authority or Poor Law Union of the district, and these benefits may take the form of special institutional treatment.

Investment of Reserve Funds.—Reserves must be invested in trustee securities as approved by law, in mortgage deeds of German mortgage banks scheduled in Class I. by the Imperial Bank, but also, with the approval of the Supreme Administrative Authorities, in loans to local authorities.[2]

a chemist and druggist under the provisions of the Pharmacy Act, 1868, as amended by the Poisons and Pharmacy Act, 1908, who undertake that all medicines supplied by them to insured persons shall be dispensed either by or under the direct supervision of a registered pharmacist or by a person who, for three years immediately prior to the passing of this Act, has acted as a dispenser to a duly qualified medical practitioner or a public institution"; but nothing in the Act shall interfere with the rights and privileges conferred by the Apothecaries Act, 1815, upon any person qualified under that Act to act as an assistant to any apothecary in compounding and dispensing medicines. (Section 15 (5).)

[2] *National Insurance Act.*—The Insurance Commissioners will receive the contributions of employers and insured persons in the first instance, and will credit to each approved society the contributions paid by or in respect of the members of the society after deducting the amounts retainable therefrom for discharging the liabilities of the Insurance Commissioners in respect of reserve values. On carrying any sum to the credit of a society in the investment account, they will pay over to the society for investment, or, at the request of the society, retain for investment on behalf of the society, four-sevenths, or, so far as the sums are attributable to

168

The Insurance Consolidation Act

Obligation to serve on Committees, &c.—The law requires an employer to serve on managing bodies when elected on pain of a fine not exceeding £25, unless he is 60 years old, has more than four legitimate children under age, suffers from sickness or infirmity, employs only domestic servants, or discharges certain specified public duties. Further, members of an executive who shirk their duties may be fined up to £2 10s. on a first cause of complaint, and £15 on a repetition (or £5 in the case of a sickness insurance fund).

Non-Assignment of Benefits.—Benefits can only be pledged or assigned in order to meet advances lawfully made by employers or insurance authorities· on the strength of claims upon the latter, demands for repayments due to Communal and Poor Law authorities, claims on account of costs of maintenance for which

women, one-half, of the amount so credited to the society. Approved societies will be required to invest sums paid to them for investment in any securities in which trustees are for the time being by law empowered to invest trust funds, or in any stocks, mortgages, or other securities issued by any local authority within the meaning of the Local Loans Act, 1875, and charged on any rates levied by or on the order or precept of such authority, or in any other securities for the time being approved by the Insurance Commissioners. (Section 56.)

Amounts available for investment by the Insurance Commissioners are to be paid over to the National Debt Commissioners and to be invested by them, in accordance with regulations made by the Treasury, in any securities authorised by Parliament as investments for Savings Bank funds ; but preference shall be given to local loans for the purpose of advances for the erection of dwellings under the Housing of the Working Classes Acts 1890 to 1909. (Section 54 (3).)

Social Insurance in Germany

the insured person is legally liable, and arrears of insurance contributions going back for a period not exceeding three months. The Insurance Office of the district may sanction exceptions to this rule.[3]

Relation to Poor Law Authorities.—The law, in all its branches, leaves untouched the legal duties of Communes and Poor Law Unions relative to the relief of destitute persons.[4] Should a Commune or a Poor Law

[3] *National Insurance Act.*—Every assignment of or charge on, and every agreement to assign or change, benefits conferred by the Act is void; and in the case of the bankruptcy of any person entitled to such benefits the latter shall not pass to his creditors. (Section 111.) Further, insured persons are also protected during sickness against distress or execution upon their goods, and ejectment on account of non-payment of rent where the medical practitioner in attendance certifies that such process would endanger their life, but appeal against such medical certificate is allowed to the county court registrar, and a certificate may only be issued for a week at once, and for a month in the aggregate, unless security for the debt be not provided on demand, but in no case for longer than three months in the aggregate. (Section 68.)

[4] *National Insurance Act.*—In granting outdoor relief to a person in receipt of or entitled to receive any benefit under this Act, a Board of Guardians may not take into consideration any such benefit, except so far as it exceeds five shillings a week. (Section 109.)

No payment is made on account of sickness, disablement, or maternity benefit to or in respect of any person during any period when the person is an inmate of *any workhouse, hospital, asylum, convalescent home, or infirmary supported by a public authority*, by public funds, or by a charity or voluntary subscriptions, or of a sanatorium or similar institution approved under the Act; but the sum which would otherwise have been

The Insurance Consolidation Act

Union, in fulfilment of its legal obligation, relieve a destitute person during a period in respect of which he could claim benefits under the Insurance Law, it can only recover up to the sum of such claim as specified below (*a, b,* and *c*). But a Commune or Poor Law Union may only claim to be reimbursed for the benefits given by a sickness fund if it has given relief by reason of a sickness entitling the person relieved to a claim upon the fund. The refunds from a sickness fund are recoverable as follows :—

(*a*) Costs of interment of a deceased person may be recovered from the funeral money payable in respect of him.

(*b*) Relief in sickness in the form of medical attendance or hospital treatment may be recovered from the accepted money value of benefits of these kinds, viz., in each case three-eighths of the wages taken as the basis of cash benefits.

(*c*) Other relief may be recovered from the corresponding sickness insurance benefits. Maintenance in hospital is reckoned at one-half of the wages taken as the basis of cash benefits.

A Commune or Poor Law Union may only recover from the benefits payable under the Accident Insurance Law if relief has been given by reason of an accident. Here, again, costs of interment come out of the funeral money; costs of medical and hospital treatment, reckoned

payable will be paid to, or applied in whole or in part for the relief or maintenance of, the person's dependants if any, and in the absence of dependants it will by arrangement be paid in whole or part to *the institution of which the person is an inmate.* (Section 12.)

Social Insurance in Germany

according to the actual costs incurred, are recoverable from the corresponding benefits given by the insurance authority concerned; and other relief is recoverable from the accident pensions, but to a maximum of one-half of the pension for the time to which the relief refers. Refunds from benefits granted under the Invalidity Insurance Law can only be claimed from the pensions.

A Commune or Poor Law Union can claim a refund when the destitute person who has a claim to an invalidity, old age, or survivor pension dies without having advanced his claim to such pension.

Aliens and Foreign Legislation.—The relationship of the several Insurance Laws to the corresponding legislation of other countries is laid down more definitely than hitherto.[5] The three systems of insurance make no distinction between nationals and foreigners except in the matter of residence abroad while in receipt of benefits.[6]

It is provided, however, that in so far as other States have introduced a provision corresponding to that made

---

[5] For the treatment of foreigners under the Sickness Insurance Law see Chapter III., p. 72; under the Accident Insurance Law, Chapter IV., p. 121; and under the Invalidity Insurance Law; Chapter V., p. 154.

[6] *National Insurance Act.*—Aliens aged 17 and upwards are not entitled to State aid on behalf of the benefits offered by the Act, and in their case the benefits will be proportionately reduced; but this disqualification does not apply to aliens who on May 4, 1911, were members of societies approved under the Act and had then been resident in the United Kingdom for five years or upwards or to persons transferred to an approved society or the Post Office fund in pursuance of an arrangement with the Government of any foreign State. (Section 45.)

The Insurance Consolidation Act

by the Imperial insurance legislation the Imperial Chancellor may, with the assent of the Federal Council, conclude reciprocal arrangements with any other State, determining to what extent provision shall be regulated by the Consolidation Law or according to the measures of that other State in the case of undertakings carrying on operations in both countries and in the case of insured persons who are temporarily employed within the territory of such other State.[7] Similarly, and on a reciprocal basis, modifications of the law may be applied in the insurance of subjects of a foreign State, and the operation of the provision made by one State may be facilitated in the other. In agreements of this kind the employer's liability to contribute created by the Consolidation Act can neither be modified nor abolished. In order to meet cases where German subjects are prejudiced by differential treatment it is provided that the Imperial Chancellor may, with the assent of the Federal Council, exercise the right of retaliation as against the subjects of a foreign State and their heirs and assigns.

Supervisory Authorities, Courts of Arbitration, &c.—

[7] *National Insurance Act.*—Provision is made for the transfer of insured persons no longer permanently resident in the United Kingdom to corresponding societies or institutions in a British possession or a foreign country approved by the Insurance Commissioners, providing such societies or institutions give corresponding rights to any of their members residing in the United Kingdom. (Section 32.)

Emigrants not so transferred may be allowed to continue their membership of the home society and receive benefits independently of the Act if they have been in membership for five years at the time of ceasing to reside in the United Kingdom. (Section 33.)

173

Social Insurance in Germany

Henceforth the supervisory authorities will be the Insurance Offices, which are local bodies and represent the lowest instance, the Higher Insurance Offices, the Imperial Insurance Office, and the State Insurance Offices, where such are established.[8] These bodies

[8] *National Insurance Act.*—The analogy offered by the supervisory bodies created under this Act is remote, owing to the very wide powers of self-regulation secured to the executive societies and committees. The central authority in each of the three kingdoms and in Wales is a body of Insurance Commissioners, of whom one must be a duly qualified medical practitioner who has had personal experience of general practice. The most important functions of the Commissioners are the issue and approval of regulations, the control of finance (including the collection and investment of funds, the distribution to the executive societies and committees of the amounts due to them for the payment of benefits, &c.), and adjudication in certain classes of disputes. (Sections 57, 80–83.)

The Commissioners will be assisted by an Advisory Committee appointed by themselves for the purpose of giving them advice and assistance in connexion with the making and altering of regulations. This committee is to consist of representatives of associations of employers and approved societies, of duly qualified medical practitioners who have personal experience of general practice, and of such other persons as the Commissioners may appoint, of whom two at least shall be women. (Section 58.)

Provision is made for the determination by the Insurance Commissioners of questions as to the interpretation of the law; but disputes between approved societies or their branches and members, between approved societies and their branches, and between branches of approved societies, with internal questions generally, will be decided by the rules of the approved societies, with right of appeal to the Insurance Commissioners. (Sections 27 and 67.)

take over all the duties which have hitherto fallen upon the State and local government authorities in regard to legal decisions, and most of those relating to administration which have been exercised by the same authorities, though certain of the latter remain to the Federal Council, the Imperial Chancellor, the higher administrative bodies, the local police authorities, &c. In general, disputes occurring in connexion with the administration of the Insurance Laws are settled by the Insurance and Higher Insurance Offices respectively, according to the degree of importance, with right of appeal in some cases from the first to the second instance, and in others to the Imperial Insurance Office.

Insurance Offices.—The principal function of these offices is to exercise oversight over the sickness funds and the general administration of the Sickness Insurance Law. The miners' funds, however, will continue under the supervisory authorities created by the mining laws of the several States. The Insurance Offices will, as a rule, consist of departments for workmen's insurance formed by all the lower administrative bodies, *i.e.*, the municipal or communal (local government) authorities in the larger towns and the sub-prefects (*Landräte*) in the smaller towns and rural communes.[9] The supreme

[9] *National Insurance Act.*—A semi-public position is occupied by the Insurance Committees formed for counties and county boroughs, for the administration of medical and sanatorium benefits in the case of all insured persons, and all benefits in the case of deposit contributors (Sections 14, 15, and 16), inasmuch as they come into direct contact with the local authorities, and serve as channels through which these may contribute out of the rates towards the objects of the Act. (Section 17.) An Insurance Committee may consist of from

Social Insurance in Germany

administrative authority can decide, however, that several local government districts shall combine to form an Insurance Office, and in States in which there is only one Higher Insurance Office, or in which it is not possible to form insurance departments in connexion with the local government bodies, the Insurance Offices may be constituted as independent authorities. The president of the lower administrative authority (*i.e.*, the mayor or sub-prefect in town or country respectively) becomes *ex officio* the president of the Insurance Office, and the members have to include one or more permanent insurance experts. Much of the business of the Insurance Offices will be transacted by the president or the permanent experts, who will act as his deputies, but in a number of cases representatives (men only) of the employers or employed (to the minimum number of twelve—six of each) will be called in as assessors. These assessors will be elected by the executives of the sickness insurance funds, employers and employed each choosing their peers, but it is provided that one-half in each case shall consist of persons

40 to 80 members, of whom three-fifths shall be representatives of the insured persons and deposit contributors, one-fifth appointed by the council of the county or county borough concerned (two at least of these being women), two members appointed by the doctors, one, two (if the committee is 60 or upwards), or three (if the committee numbers 80) doctors appointed by the council of the county or county borough, and the remaining members appointed by the Insurance Commissioners, one at least being a doctor and two at least women. Where a county or county borough bears any part of the cost of medical or sanatorium benefit, the county may be given a larger representation at the expense of the representation of insured persons. (Section 59.)

176

The Insurance Consolidation Act

who take part in the administration of accident insurance. The representative members of an Insurance Office are not paid, but they receive out-of-pocket expenses and recompense for lost time. The cost of an Insurance Office is borne by the local authority when it is formed in connexion with such authority, and when otherwise by the Federal State concerned. Besides supervising the execution of the Sickness Insurance Law, the Insurance Offices will discharge all such duties as are imposed upon the local administrative authority by the several Insurance Laws, and they may be called upon to act as intelligence departments in insurance matters.

Higher Insurance Offices.—The Higher Insurance Offices take the place of the courts of arbitration formed under the Accident and Invalidity Insurance Laws, but the Mutual Associations formed under the first of these laws and the Pension Boards formed under the second are placed under the oversight of the Imperial or State Insurance Offices. As a rule a Higher Insurance Office will be formed for the district of every higher administrative authority—*i.e.*, the district administered by a Government President or Governor—either as part of an existing State authority or as an independent authority. At the head will be a director with a permanent deputy ; and besides other permanent officials there will be at least forty assessors, chosen in equal numbers by the employers and employed. Of the employers' assessors, one-half will be elected by the employers on the executive of the Pension Board affected, and one-half by the executives of the agricultural Mutual Associations (and one other Mutual Association to be named), formed under the Accident Insurance Law ; the representatives of the insured will

Social Insurance in Germany

be chosen by their spokesmen in the Insurance Offices of the district. A Higher Insurance Office will have one or more chambers of award and also executive chambers, consisting of permanent members and assessors. The Government President supervises the Office and is responsible for providing the necessary staff and buildings, and the costs of administration fall upon the State affected. A fee is payable for every decision sought by an insurance society or fund.

Imperial and State Insurance Offices.—The highest authority for awards, decisions, and supervision is still the Imperial Insurance Office (*Reichsversicherungsamt*), the organisation of which remains much as hitherto; but the number of non-established members has been increased to 32, 8 elected by the Federal Council and 12 each by the employers and the insured. The existing State Insurance Offices (*Landesversicherungsämter*) will continue in those cases where such an Office comprises at least four Higher Insurance Offices.

The functions of the Imperial Insurance Office call for more detailed notice. While the several systems of insurance have been organised and administered independently of each other from the first, it was foreseen that the interests of efficiency required the creation of an organisation that would serve to some extent to co-ordinate their work. The Imperial Insurance Office has held the several insurance systems together in such a degree of unity as their different purposes have allowed. Created by the Accident Insurance Law of 1884, the Imperial Insurance Office was entrusted with important duties under both this law and the later Invalidity Insurance Law. It has not hitherto exercised formal

The Insurance Consolidation Act

supervision over the sickness funds, but the law of 1911 confers upon it certain supreme judicial and supervisory powers in relation thereto. Already it has come to be regarded as the supreme authority, under the Federal Council and the Government, on insurance law and procedure for the entire Empire. Nevertheless, the functions of the department in regard to accident and invalidity insurance are restricted owing to the large powers conferred upon the State Insurance Offices which the various Governments are allowed to establish for the federal areas. Such State Offices have been formed for Bavaria, Saxony, Wurtemberg, Baden, Hesse, Mecklenburg-Schwerin, Mecklenburg-Strelitz, and Reuss (older line).

Out of small beginnings the Imperial Insurance Office has developed to such proportions and importance that it may now be almost regarded as the Imperial Ministry for Social Insurance. It has exerted very wide powers and a most wholesome influence in the administration of all the insurance laws; it has served as the final court of appeal under these laws; it has had to prepare, issue, or approve regulations of various kinds, including those promulgated in the name of the Federal Council and those for the prevention of accidents; and through all it has consistently and successfully endeavoured to hold the balance between employers and workpeople fairly, to smooth away the difficulties which have constantly arisen, and to commend the Insurance Laws to the confidence and approval of the nation at large. From year to year the duties and responsibilities of this department have increased, until it now forms the main artery of the entire insurance system. The Imperial Insurance Office has its seat in Berlin in a large block of buildings

Social Insurance in Germany

which was erected for the purpose at a cost (including the site) of some £160,000, and has been in use since 1894.

In 1910, before the reorganisation necessitated by the new law, the department consisted of 75 members, including the President.[10] Of these members six were nominated by the Federal Council and were not permanent; two were directors of the Invalidity and Accident Insurance divisions respectively; 23 were presidents of senates; and 40 were permanent officials engaged in different capacities; and there were nine assistants. Further, 99 assessors, all of them judges in State service, were engaged for legal business. The elected and honorary members of the department included two employers and two workpeople under the Industrial, Agricultural, and Marine Accident Insurance Laws respectively, with deputies in each case. Election to these honorary positions has hitherto been for five years. The unestablished members of the department and the judges have hitherto received a payment of 1,500 marks (£75) per annum ; and the deputies have received 18 marks per day as required, with travelling expenses where they lived out of Berlin. The permanent staff of the department, including minor employees of all grades, numbered nearly 300 in 1910, and there were in addition over 100 assistants and employees not on the establishment. In order that the officials and the honorary members of the various committees and courts of arbitration connected with the Imperial Insurance Office may

[10] Dr. Tonio Bödiker from 1884 to 1897 ; Privy Councillor Otto Gaebel from 1897 to 1906 ; Dr. Paul Kaufmann from 1906 to the present.

The Insurance Consolidation Act

be better fitted to deal with the difficulties which arise in the course of their work, the department arranges for the holding of periodical lectures on technical subjects by professors of medicine and surgery and practising physicians.

CHAPTER VII

THE CRUSADE AGAINST DISEASE

IMPORTANT though the general relief work of the Insurance organisations has been—in the cure and maintenance of the sick, in the treatment of injuries and the awarding of liberal compensation to the victims of accident, and in the permanent provision made for the aged and the infirm—still more notable in many ways, and perhaps more salutary in its ultimate effects, is their preventive work as illustrated by the systematic crusade against disease which has been carried on with increasing energy during the past fifteen years. For, after all, what the self-reliant workman values more highly than distress benefits is a fair and full use of his faculties. What he wants is not sickness pay but a healthy life ; not accident compensation, but sound limbs and unimpaired energies ; not infirmity pensions, but the opportunity and the power to follow his employment as long as possible. Hence in the development of a preventative crusade against disease, the Pension Boards have been conscious throughout of the good will and confidence of the working classes. Not long ago the leading German labour newspaper, the *Vorwärts*, wrote : " The prophylactic part of the Infirmity Insurance Law is for the working classes its most important part,"

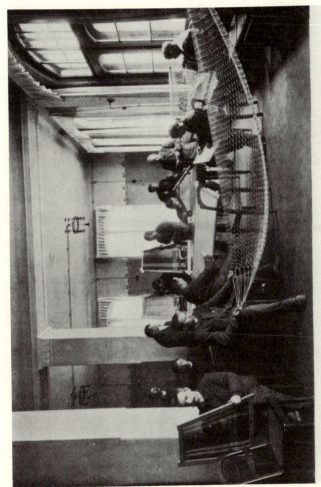

BEELITZ SANATORIUM (BELONGING TO THE BERLIN PENSION BOARD)—A WORKROOM.

The Crusade against Disease

and the same thing holds good *pari passu* of the other Insurance Laws. Commenting lately (January 13, 1912) upon the curative work done in 1911 by the Berlin Pension Board, which expended no less than 28 per cent. of its revenue upon measures of a more or less directly prophylactic order, the same journal said: "By this expenditure it has achieved more good for society at large than by all its invalidity and old age pensions." It is not too much to say, indeed, that this enlightened crusade—in which the Pension Boards of the industrial centres of the Empire have particularly distinguished themselves—constitutes so far the peculiar distinction of the German Insurance system.

Here, again, the provision afforded by the Sickness Insurance Societies forms a substantial basis for the whole scheme of curative measures. The members of these societies are served not only by the ordinary practitioners of their choice, but by specialists for all sorts of diseases. Often the most costly methods both of surgery and medicine are applied without stint, and hospital and other institutional treatment is given where desirable; in short, whatever is necessary to restore and safeguard health is done, and the question of expense is often a secondary consideration. Convalescents are sent in large numbers to special homes, seaside and country health resorts, baths, &c., maintenance there being granted if necessary for as long as twelve months. Further, some of the societies do an important prophylactic work by the inspection of the dwellings of their members, with a view to remedying unhygienic conditions, by instruction in the form of lectures and literature on questions of personal health and sanitation,

Social Insurance in Germany

and in other ways. The popular lectures, given in public halls or at trade union headquarters, are regarded as one of the most effective ways of securing the co-operation of the working classes in the crusade against disease. The Central Committee of the Sick Funds of Berlin, which devotes great attention to this subject, arranges for regular courses of lectures to be given by prominent medical practitioners in all parts of the city on the causes, symptoms, treatment, and prevention of various diseases to which men and women respectively are particularly prone.

Hitherto the Sickness Funds have engaged in this preventive and educational work on their own initiative and responsibility, for the existing law did not formally confer upon them powers of the kind. The Consolidation Act just passed, however, expressly authorises them to adopt the measures which seem to them expedient in order to protect the health of their members, and there is no doubt that the new powers will be extensively exercised. The Berlin " Local " Sickness Fund for Commercial Employees has been specially active in this matter for some years—particularly in the investigation of the sanitary conditions of the dwellings occupied by sick members — and in a paper on " The Prophylactic Tasks of the Sickness Funds," read at the last annual conference of the " Local " Sick Funds of Germany, the president of this fund stated: " Now that the Consolidation Law recognises our long-continued efforts and pressure to the extent that the adoption of measures of a general kind for the prevention of sickness amongst our members is expressly permitted, it is expedient that we should take stock of the vast field which is thus

The Crusade against Disease

opened up to us. There can be no doubt amongst us that directly the Government concedes us the far-going rights referred to, it will be our endeavour to make extensive and beneficent use of them in the interest of our members."

Similarly the Mutual Associations formed under the Accident Insurance Laws, in addition to their systematic endeavours to lessen risk to life and limb, arrange for instruction in first-aid (providing the necessary appliances), and do their utmost to discourage amongst the working classes personal habits prejudicial to health. These Associations are empowered to provide hospitals, convalescent homes, &c., and some of them have done so ; witness the hospitals for miners at Halle and Bochum, for wood-workers at Neu Rahnsdorf, near Berlin, for the building trades at Stötteritz, near Leipzig, and for iron workers, quarry workers, &c., at Strassburg. Of the remedial work of the Mutual Associations, Professor Rieder, of Bonn, said recently : " The duration and cost of treatment of injured persons are secondary considerations. The best that can be done for their restoration is only good enough." The activity shown by the Mutual Associations in the prevention of accidents in factory, workshop, and mine, to which reference has been made already, is hardly secondary in importance to their positive measures for the relief of suffering and want.

But the efforts of the Sickness and Accident Insurance organisations in the domain of prophylaxis are quite subsidiary to those of the Pension Boards. The splendid work done in this field by these bodies owes its justification and efficiency to a provision of the Invalidity Insurance Law which sets forth "that

Social Insurance in Germany

if an insured person should be ill in such a way that incapacity to earn a livelihood may be apprehended as the result, the Pension Board may require him to undergo medical treatment," which treatment may take place in a hospital or a convalescent home. Nevertheless, the patient's consent to hospital or institutional treatment is necessary should he be married, have a household of his own, or be a member of the household of his family. Should an insured person become incapacitated owing to sickness, the usual pension may for a time be wholly or partially refused, if he has without justification declined to submit to the medical treatment prescribed by the Pension Board. But where institutional treatment takes place, the benefit to which the insured may be entitled under the Sickness Insurance Law must be paid by the Pension Board, which must compensate his family, if dependent upon him, to the extent of half the usual sickness pay or one quarter of the wages of common day labour, according as he was insured against sickness or not. A further provision allows a Board to treat persons already in receipt of pensions, should there be reason to hope that thereby their ability to work may be restored. If a Pension Board treats persons whose infirmity is due to accident, the Mutual Associations liable under the Accident Insurance Law have to bear the costs of the treatment given. Meantime, the Pension Board is required here also, within variable limits, to contribute towards the maintenance of the patient's family and others dependent upon him, even though he be not liable to sickness insurance.

For a long time the wide powers thus invested in the Pension Boards were exercised very sparingly—perhaps

The Crusade against Disease

from want of due appreciation of their importance—but of late years they have been put to generous use. In 1891 these Boards expended less than £20 in curative treatment, but in 1910 over a million and a quarter pounds, or about 10 per cent. of their total revenue. In incurring this expenditure they know that they are doing the best for the workers and the best for the insurance funds : the former are preserved in health and earning capacity ; the latter are protected against heavy permanent demands. The diseases most frequently treated are pulmonary tuberculosis, rheumatism, gout, heart disease, lung diseases of a tuberculous nature, anæmia, venereal diseases, and alcoholism. The Pension Boards have hitherto had an entirely free hand both as to the mode of treatment adopted and its duration. Among the various institutions used are hospitals and clinics, consumptive sanatoria, outdoor air cures, convalescent homes, forest health resorts, day recreation grounds, orthopædic and medico-mechanical institutions, baths (sea, mineral, sulphur, &c.), and private nursing homes. During the fifteen years 1895-1910 the Boards built or acquired out of their own resources an imposing array of 74 sanatoria, hospitals, and convalescent homes ; additions are made every year, and the number added during the last six years was 34. The importance of these institutions may be judged from the following figures :—

Accommodation—7,493 beds (5,000 for men and 2,493 for women).
Area of ground covered—3,834 acres.
Cost of land, buildings, and equipment—£3,280,960.
Cost of maintenance and administration in 1910—£525,100.
Number of patients admitted in 1910- 46,336 (32,275 men and 14,061 women).

Social Insurance in Germany

Of these institutions, which are equipped in the most perfect manner, Privy Councillor Bielefeldt, Director of the Pension Board for the Hanse Cities, truly says that they "could never have been called into existence and have remained efficient had it not been for the Pension Boards, which provided the necessary funds." Several of the Boards have gone so far as to establish rural labour colonies, in which convalescent workmen are enabled to follow their old occupations or learn new ones under conditions favourable to health.

Nevertheless, the institutions named form but a small proportion of the curative agencies in the direct service of the Pension Boards. In 1910 the principal institutions used were as follows :—

	For Pulmonary Tuberculosis.	For other Diseases.
Hospitals and Infirmaries ..	207	67
Sanatoria and Open-air Cures ..	152	102
Convalescent Homes	25	102
Baths	25	193

The list of all German institutions of these kinds at the disposal of the working classes would make a far larger total.

The first table on the next page shows the numbers of persons who, under the care of the Pension Boards, underwent a systematic course of treatment during the 14 years 1897–1910.

Of those treated for pulmonary consumption in 1910, 31,508 were men and 15,209 women ; the corresponding

The Crusade against Disease

Year	For Pulmonary Tuberculosis.	For other Diseases.	Totals.
1897	3,374	7,190	10,564
1898	4,937	8,821	13,758
1899	7,759	12,280	20,039
1900	11,150	16,277	27,427
1901	14,757	17,953	32,710
1902	16,516	19,433	35,949
1903	20,171	23,422	43,593
1904	23,511	25,980	49,491
1905	26,834	29,586	56,420
1906	31,375	35,508	66,883
1907	32,543	41,480	74,023
1908	39,340	47,650	86,990
1909	42,940	58,218	101,158
1910	46,717	67,593	114,310
Totals ..	321,924	411,391	733,315

numbers of those treated for other diseases were 38,025
and 29,568. The grand totals of men and women treated
during the whole period were 472,803 and 260,512 respectively, or, together, 733,315.

Those treated in institutions during 1910 numbered
83,610, made up as follows :— .

	For Pulmonary Tuberculosis.	For other Diseases.	Total.
Hospitals, &c.	907	15,937	16,844
Sanatoria and Open-air Cures	38,944	2,701	41,645
Convalescent Homes ..	1,539	7,336	8,875
Baths	4,193	11,316	15,509
Private Cure, &c... ..	26	711	737
Totals	45,609	38,001	83,610

Social Insurance in Germany

In 1910 677 persons (including only 7 women) were treated for dipsomania, and 25,260 for teeth diseases.

The expenditure of the Pension Boards upon curative measures has increased as follows since 1897 :—

Year.	Number of Persons treated for all Diseases	Total Cost of Treatment.	Portion of Total Cost representing Relief to Relatives.	Portion of Total Cost refunded by other Insurance Authorities, Communes, &c.
		Marks.	Marks.	Marks.
1897	10,564	2,011,149	50,254	179,273
1898	13,759	2,769,330	95,202	304,537
1899	20,039	4,056,975	176,415	496,003
1900	27,427	6,210,720	506,773	948,059
1901	32,710	7,912,220	732,160	1,239,681
1902	35,919	9,056,211	916,274	1,397,035
1903	43,593	11,501,205	1,202,260	1,805,262
1904	49,491	12,735,081	1,429,877	2,410,664
1905	56,420	14,448,005	1,692,936	2,820,930
1906	66,883	16,660,445	2,050,364	3,300,464
1907	74,023	17,951,706	2,121,537	8,588,688
1908	86,990	21,625,883	2,706,506	4,368,454
1909	101,158	24,275,577	3,221,957	4,948,044
1910	114,310	26,935,418	2,039,219	5,833,251
Total	733,315	178,152,955	18,941,733	33,640,345

It is the contention of the Pension Boards that the enormous increase in expenditure on this head which has taken place during the years covered by the return must be attributed less to an increase of disease than to the extension of the scope of the Boards' work—the inclusion of larger classes of persons [1] and of additional

[1] Between the years 1897 and 1910 the number of persons insured against sickness increased from 8,865,685 to 13,954,973, and the number insured against infirmity and old age increased from 11,813,300 to 15,444,300 (1909)

The Crusade against Disease

diseases in their scheme of operations, as well as to an increasingly bold use of the knowledge and methods which science has brought to light. In regard to tuberculosis in particular, the recognition of the fact that this disease, if taken in an early stage, often yields to curative treatment has encouraged the Pension Boards to spend money and effort freely. Incidentally the perfecting of the statistics of disease has shown the need for a resolute crusade against tuberculosis in its various forms. A classification, according to 28 diseases, of 315,089 persons to whom pensions were granted between 1895 to 1899 showed that tuberculosis took the third place as a cause of infirmity with men, and the second place with women. Of all male workers in the mining and smelting industries and the building trades who became infirm by the age of 35 years more than one-half, and between the ages of 20 and 24 nearly two-thirds, were found to suffer from tuberculosis. In the case of females engaged in the same occupations nearly one-half (47 per cent.) became infirm owing to tuberculosis between the ages of 25 and 29 years, and 37 per cent. between the ages of 30 and 34 years. Even among agricultural labourers over 37 per cent. of all pensioners between the ages of 20 and 24 years became infirm from the same cause.

The average cost per head of systematic treatment for pulmonary consumption in 1910 was 381·86 marks, or 5·22 marks per day with an average treatment of 73 days; the cost for men was 404·36 marks, or 5·75 marks per day for 70 days, and for women 336 marks, or 4·25 marks per day for 79 days. The cost per head for persons suffering from other diseases (lupus excluded) was 213·09 marks, being 236·50 marks for men and 180·32 marks for

Social Insurance in Germany

women, or 4·69, 5·21, and 3·97 marks per day respectively, with an average of 45 days in each case.

It would appear that the curative treatment given to women is throughout longer than that deemed to be necessary in the case of men. The number of days' treatment in each case was as follows in the years named :—

AVERAGE NUMBER OF DAYS' TREATMENT.

Year.	(a) Tuberculosis.		(b) Other Diseases.	
	Males.	Females.	Males.	Females.
1897	73	87	52	56
1900	72	80	49	52
1905	73	79	46	47
1906	72	80	44	46
1907	71	81	44	47
1908	71	78	45	47
1909	70	80	46	47
1910	70	79	45	45

In 1897 the net expenditure of the Pension Boards (after the deduction of all repayments from other insurance authorities) on curative work of all kinds formed 1·6 per cent. of their revenue from contributions and 3·4 per cent. of the sum of all pensions paid ; in 1910 the proportions were 10·7 and 12·8 per cent. respectively. In 1897 9 persons per 10,000 of all liable to insurance against infirmity were treated ; in 1910 78 per 10,000.

Furthermore, with a view to lightening the work of the central administration and to encouraging local effort

192

and initiative, the Boards make considerable grants to a host of miscellaneous societies and agencies, municipal and philanthropic, engaged in the struggle against consumption and other diseases. Besides spending large sums in measures of a propagandist order, by way of instruction, advice, and warning, the Boards have also, since 1895, made loans with a free hand—at a rate of interest as low as 2 to 3½ per cent.—for the erection of hospitals and sanatoria of various kinds and the promotion of miscellaneous works having for their object the public health and welfare.

The total amount of the loans made on account of such agencies of social well-being amounted at the close of 1910 to the stately sum of £43,850,000, made up as follows :—

Building of workmen's dwellings	£15,084,050
Building of hospices, hostels, lodging-houses for single persons, &c.	£939,250
Building of hospitals, convalescent homes, sanatoria, infirmaries, &c.	£1,818,700
Provision of institutions and works in the interest of public health (baths, abattoirs, water and sewerage works, cemeteries, &c.)	£7,613,200
Popular education .. .. • ..	£4,114,500
Works in the interest of agriculture (reclamation, irrigation and drainage, afforestation, roads, light railways, cattle, breeding, &c.)	£5,479,300
Other welfare works	£5,795,350

In view of the close association of the Pension Boards with the anti-consumption crusade, and of the urgency of this crusade in all countries, it seems pertinent to refer briefly to the different orders of curative and preventive measures—all directly complementary to each other — which are adopted by the various German agencies engaged in this great work.

Social Insurance in Germany

The basis and starting-point of the movement is the large system of public dispensaries, established by municipal and other public bodies and philanthropic associations, at which persons may be examined gratuitously for signs of tuberculosis, and be advised as to the proper measures to be taken. During the year 1910 the various Pension Boards contributed towards the cost of 777 of these dispensaries in all parts of the country. The majority of the dispensaries are intended specially for men; others are for women; others, again, have departments for both sexes; and many are exclusively intended for children. The Pension Board for Berlin has, however, established its own " tuberculosis stations " for the service of consumptives living at home. Such persons, with the members of their families, are medically examined at these stations, and are advised as to the measures which they should adopt in order to ward off permanent disease. The stations also undertake the visitation and where necessary the disinfection of dwellings occupied by consumptives, and they also keep records of the cases of consumption discovered by actual investigation or notified to them by the police.

These dispensaries for consumptives proceed from the assumption that if tuberculosis is to be combated on a national scale the non-infectious cases must be prevented from becoming infectious, and the infectious cases must be prevented from becoming centres of disease; and systematic endeavours are made, wherever possible, to apply practical measures accordingly. Such measures are (1) the adoption of prophylactic methods at home or elsewhere in the case of incipient disease; (2) systematic institutional treatment where the disease has begun

The Crusade against Disease

its course, but is still in a hopeful stage; and (3) the segregation amid humane and sympathetic conditions of the incurables.

(1) If a patient can safely remain at home he is carefully advised as to the steps which he should take to protect his health—light and ventilation, food, clothing, exercise, &c. A record is kept of the character, size, and condition of his home, and by visitation by doctors or nurses, and often by the gift of money, he is helped to adapt his accommodation to the hygienic needs both of himself and his family. Thus during the first two and a half years' existence of the Berlin dispensaries not only did the doctors examine 34,800 persons, but by means of visiting nurses 18,200 homes of the working classes were put into a wholesome sanitary condition. The Leipzig Central Dispensary for consumptives is one of the most efficient institutions of this kind. It is carried on by an association, but is liberally subsidised by the Pension Board, the Municipality, and the Trade Unions. During 1910 the medical examination of 1,643 men, 1,635 women, and 835 children took place, and 460 persons were placed in institutions of various kinds, while 36 were given grants of money to enable them to live in the country for a time. In a large number of cases also articles of clothing, bedding, food, milk, wine, and medicaments were given. It may be noted that some Pension Boards make small grants of money to enable consumptives, unfit for arduous outside work, to follow light employments at home.

(2) The work of the dispensaries is supplemented by curative agencies of various kinds. Persons in the curable stages of the disease are sent to sanatoria

Social Insurance in Germany

thoroughly equipped in the best sense, and situated as a rule in rural surroundings and often in the pine forests which abound in most parts of Germany; while those who have undergone beneficial treatment or who need secondary treatment are often helped to enter equally excellent convalescent institutions.

(3) On the whole the incurable cases, in Germany as in this country, have received least attention, though there can be no doubt that their treatment is the most urgent and imperative if the crusade against consumption is to be crowned by genuine and not delusive victories. Nevertheless, a number of institutions have been established by the Pension Boards and other agencies for these cases alone, and similar provision is made in increasing amount in existing infirmaries and hospitals of various kinds.

An excellent illustration of co-ordination of effort in the combating of consumption is afforded by Charlottenburg, a town which of late years has distinguished itself in connexion not only with the anti-consumption crusade but with the crusade against infant mortality. The first agency is the municipal dispensary for consumptives, which works hand in hand with a similar and older dispensary carried on for some years by the Women's Red Cross Association. In the dispensary persons of both sexes are on request gratuitously examined and the requisite treatment is prescribed. If home treatment is sufficient, patients are required to visit the dispensary at intervals in order that the doctors may assure themselves that their advice is being faithfully followed. If admission to a sanatorium is desirable, the needful permit is given without formalities. It is a condition that no

The Crusade against Disease

insured person in Charlottenburg can obtain admission to a sanatorium without first being examined at the municipal dispensary. If a certificate is given there the Pension Board, under the Invalidity Insurance Law, at once makes itself responsible for the cost. In the case of an uninsured patient without means the Poor Law Administration bears the cost of the same treatment. Another form of treatment is that of the home for recuperation, admission to which is likewise conditional upon examination at the public dispensary. In addition, Charlottenburg maintains what is known as a " Holiday Colony " for children. Finally, the incurables are dealt with as far as possible in a special Home for Incurables and in a separate section of the Municipal Hospital.

As showing the extent of the system of agencies of all kinds which have been established in Germany for the treatment of tuberculosis, it may be stated that there existed in Germany in 1909 no fewer than 99 sanatoria for the service of the working classes. These sanatoria had 6,584 beds for men, 3,802 for women, and 680 available for both sexes as required, making a total of 11,066. There were also 36 private institutions with 2,175 beds. The total number of sanatoria for adults was therefore 135, with 13,241 beds.[1] In addition, there

[1] By way of comparison it may be stated that the List of Sanatoria published by the National Association for the Prevention of Consumption enumerates 96 sanatoria for consumptives and others, with 4,031 beds, of which 40 with 2,347 beds charge no more than 25s. per week, and may thus be regarded as more or less accessible to the working classes and persons of limited means. Yet even this reduced number includes many sanatoria which are without adequate provision for outdoor treatment.

were 18 sanatoria with 837 beds for juvenile consumptives only, and 73 institutions (with 6,843 beds) of a miscellaneous kind for scrofulous children and those threatened with consumption. The usual charges made in the people's sanatoria for adults are from 2s. 3d. to 4s. 6d. daily, and predominantly 3s. 6d. There were, further, 15 convalescent homes for consumptives exclusively, and 25 hospitals and homes for incurable cases, independently of a far larger number of similar institutions intended for the victims of other diseases.

One of the most recent agencies added to the German system of provision for the sick is the "forest resort" (*Walderholungsstätte*), to which increasing attention is being given. The impetus to the "forest resort" movement was given by the first International Tuberculosis Congress, held in Berlin in 1899. Under the leadership of Dr. Pannwitz, the German Red Cross Association took up the question and formed a special branch for the purpose of propagating and materialising the new idea. In Berlin the Invalidity Pension Board and the Sickness Insurance Funds promptly offered their support, and the first of these resorts, for men, was established in Berlin in 1900, the second, for women, in 1901; quite a number of others have since been called into existence in the neighbourhood of Berlin for adults of both sexes, for young people, and for children separately. The movement spread rapidly to other parts of the country. In order to have forest resorts forests of the right kind are first necessary, and here Germany is exceptionally fortunate; most large towns have forests in their immediate vicinity, often in municipal ownership, and it was natural, therefore, that towns like Düsseldorf,

The Crusade against Disease

Munich, Dresden, Leipzig, Cassel, Carlsruhe, Frankfort-on-Main, Hanover, and many others that might be named should follow the example of Berlin. At the present time there are in various parts of Germany over a hundred of these institutions.

These "forest resorts" are not intended primarily for sick persons who are in the doctor's hands, but rather for those persons in indifferent health who need to rest and recuperate in the open air. Their frequenters are generally suffering from weak nerves, anæmia, asthma, and light heart troubles, though many convalescents are also among the number. The organisation of a forest resort is as inexpensive as possible; the usual area allotted to the purpose varies from one to five acres, and beyond a simple building of wood or half-timber work, containing provision for attendants and for refreshment, the only necessary equipment consists of shelters, benches, chairs, hammocks, with provision for light games. In some resorts, however, opportunity is furnished for light work in gardening. These resorts are always found near towns, and in fixing the site care is taken that the means of communication are convenient. Most of the forest resorts used by the working classes of Berlin are within six or seven miles of the centre of the city, and some are much nearer. As a rule, the convalescents arrive from town between the hours of 7 and 9 o'clock a.m., and by 7 p.m. all have returned to their homes.

Any attempt at a statistical estimate of the results of the Pension Boards' energetic aggressive campaign against disease would take us into a field too technical for these pages, though statistical data on the subject abound in the reports of the Imperial Insurance Office.

Social Insurance in Germany

It is characteristic of the thoroughness of the work done by that department that it has for many years, in conjunction with the Pension Boards, kept careful records of the health of patients treated by means of an elaborate case-paper system, for this purpose enlisting the services of the Sickness Funds, medical practitioners, and local authorities, and as far as possible keeping in touch with the patients themselves. The condition of all these is, wherever possible, observed for a series of years in order to determine the degree of permanence of the success originally attained. The first results were collected in 1898, and related to cases treated during the years 1894–6; these results were published in 1899. Since then results have been collected more systematically, and published in great detail year by year, not only for the Pension Boards, but for the other executive authorities which assist in administering the Infirmity Insurance Law.

The Imperial Insurance Office, which itself claims that "the curative work of the insurance organisations, and particularly those established under the Infirmity Insurance Law, forms a glorious page in the history of the German insurance legislation," states in its report for 1909 : "It is satisfactory to record that the successes in treatment attained by the multifarious methods adopted show continuously a large increase alike in number and duration." For example, of patients treated for consumption in 1897 68 per cent. were reported to be so far cured at the end of treatment that there was no immediate fear of their becoming unable to earn their livelihood; this percentage steadily increased until in 1909 it had reached 83. In the case of other diseases the percentage of relative cures increased from 69 to 84 per cent. during the same period, the upward tendency here likewise being constant. The percentage of successes which remained after the lapse of five years increased in the case of pulmonary tuberculosis from 27 in 1897–1901 to 46 in 1905–09, and in the case of other diseases from 34 to 53 respectively. It is pointed out that both the primary and the continued successes are more numerous in the case of women than men in all kinds of diseases, and this is explained by the fact that "women keep aloof from many sources of injury to which men often expose themselves, and especially the abuse of alcohol."

As to the effect of the measures taken to combat the consumption scourge a few more general figures may be given. Briefly stated, the effect has been to reduce the national mortality from this disease in the last thirty years by nearly one-half and to justify the hope that the war against tuberculosis has now become one of virtual extermination. The rate of mortality in German towns with a population of 15,000 and upwards has been as follows during that period, the rate being for pulmonary consumption up to 1904 and for tuberculosis in general since that year :— [2]

1877–1881	..	3·58 per 1,000	1897–1901	..	2·19 per 1,000
1882–1886	..	3·46 „	1902–1906	..	2·02 „ .
1887–1891	..	3·04 „	1907 ..	..	1·98 „
1892–1896	..	2·56 „	1908 ..	..	1·93 „
			1909 ..	..	1·83 „

[2] " Statistisches Jahrbuch des deutschen Reiches," 1911.

Social Insurance in Germany

The reduced death-rate in the last-named year as compared with the average for the earliest period specified would, if applied to the entire country, imply the saving of over 100,000 lives in a single year. Further, in the whole of Prussia the mortality from all forms of tuberculosis fell from 3·25 per 1,000 in 1878 to 1·65 in 1908, the fall being in this as in the other case constant throughout the whole period.[3] Figures like these leave little room for doubt that before many years have passed this scourge of the race, after baffling scientific effort for many painful centuries, will at last be robbed of the terrors and take its place as one of the minor afflictions of mankind.

It is not without significance that from 1876 to 1885, prior to the insurance era, the rate of mortality as shown above for German towns, stood still; from 1885 forward there was a steady fall from 3·1 to 2·2 per 1,000 in 1897; from that time the normal influence of the three Insurance Laws, all now in full operation, was reinforced by the anti-consumption crusade of the Pension Boards, and there was simultaneously a further fall in the mortality rate to a figure which in 1908 was little less than that of the United Kingdom.

Professor Kayserling, of Berlin, and Professor Fränkel, who rank amongst the highest German authorities upon the subject, frankly attribute the progress which has been made in the crusade against tuberculosis more to the Industrial Insurance Laws than to any other cause,

[3] It is gratifying to note that during the same period equally satisfactory progress has been made in our own country, for while the mortality from pulmonary tuberculosis was 2·90 per 1,000 of the population of the United Kingdom in 1878, it had fallen to 1·72 in 1908.

The Crusade against Disease

owing to the fact that these laws have placed within the reach of the working classes resources of healing which were never dreamt of before. The former writes: "It must be regarded as a happy dispensation for the crusade against tuberculosis that at the very time Koch pointed the way to the prevention of this disease the German Insurance Legislation came into operation, giving to the less favoured sections of the population, which are the special victims of this disease, a legal claim to treatment in the event of sickness, for in view of the long protracted nature of tuberculosis the effective protection of the healthy cannot be secured without simultaneous care for the sick. I attach special weight to the statistics (*i.e.*, the statistics showing the progressive decline in the consumption death-rate), since they show us how we may succeed in obtaining the mastery over this disease. We shall do it (*a*) on the one hand by the recognition of the fact that we have to deal with a specific infectious disease caused by the tubercle bacillus and the subordination of all measures to the one object of combating the plague, and (*b*) on the other hand by the largest possible development of the system of treating tuberculosis by means of the machinery of Industrial Insurance."

Facts and figures like the above show clearly that, thanks to the organisations and the resources created by the Insurance Laws, a work of the utmost importance is being done for a large section of the population which had beforetimes been almost entirely deprived of the manifold healing agencies within the reach of the rich. This work, indeed, affords one of the most striking illustrations of the principle of "equality of opportunity" furnished by the history of working-class movements.

Social Insurance in Germany

So important is this work regarded by the Pension Boards in particular, that they are resolutely opposed to any attempt to restrict it. When such an attempt was made in the draft of the new Insurance Consolidation Law, in a proposal that the expenditure by Pension Boards on curative measures should not henceforth exceed 7 per cent. of the yearly income from contributions, a meeting of representatives of the Boards (February 18, 1911) formally condemned it as an unjustifiable limitation of the autonomy conferred upon the Boards by the original law and as depriving the consultative committees, composed of employers and workpeople, of the influence which they had hitherto exerted upon the administration of the law. The resolution of protest stated further: "The preventive treatment of the sick forms at present one of the most important factors in the operation of the Infirmity Insurance Law, and admits of no restriction so long as the ability of the Pension Boards to discharge their liability for pensions is not directly endangered." As a result of this and similar protests the 7 per cent. limit was not pressed.

For the objects of this crusade against disease are not yet achieved : the future holds out still greater possibilities. "In the sphere of a systematic and deliberately devised prophylaxis," writes Dr. Zacher, "the German insurance system will celebrate its greatest triumphs, since it will gradually go beyond the narrow limits of mere sickness and accident prevention, and will develop the entire wide field of national hygiene, and so achieve for the nation at large incalculable benefits by the increase of its labour, strength, efficiency, vital energy, and defensive power."[4]

[4] "Arbeiterversicherung im Ausland," vol. xvii. p. 12.

The Crusade against Disease

It is not too much to claim already, indeed, that the Insurance legislation has developed into a great system of social hygiene which has produced a marked improvement upon the entire health of the community. "Not only," writes Dr. Zahn, " have the sick, the injured, and the infirm been relieved, but disease has been cured, and the incapacitated have been restored to work. The adult workers are now in general less exposed to, and appear to be more capable of resisting, the dangers of sickness, infirmity, and accident, and the rising generation is at the outset healthier and robuster. The increase of vital force thus effected benefits not only the individual but the nation as a whole. The Insurance Laws thus relieve the Poor Law of a host of cases which otherwise would have fallen to it, while they positively prevent a large amount of pauperism." The collateral effects have in many directions been very striking. The medical profession was first disposed to view the Insurance systems with suspicion, as seeming to involve something like a semi-public control of its craft. Though the fees may not always be generous, the demand for doctors has increased enormously, and the independence of the profession has not been destroyed. According to Dr. Zahn, the number of doctors increased between the years 1883 and 1906 from 15,100 to 31,346, or from a ratio of one for every 3,047 to one for every 1,952 inhabitants.[5] During the same period the number of public hospitals

[5] According to the General Medical Council the approximate number of registered medical practitioners in the United Kingdom in 1910 was 32,154, viz., 25,472 in England and Wales (6,415 in London, 17,721 in the English provinces, and 1,336 in Wales), 3,958 in Scotland, and 2,724 in Ireland.

increased from 2,024 to 3,801, the ratio to the population increasing from one for every 22,349 to one for every 16,095 persons, and the ratio of beds to population from one for 545 to one for 275 persons; while, finally, the number of apothecaries increased from 4,483 to 6,189, or from a ratio of one for every 10,264 to one for every 9,885 inhabitants.[6]

Further, the Insurance Legislation has been the parent of a host of social measures instituted by public authorities, philanthropic organisations, industrial enterprises, and private individuals. Wherever the opportunity of useful co-operation with the Insurance organisations has offered itself, it has been seized; and where in some directions the Insurance Laws have stopped short, these public and private agencies have taken up the threads, increasing, supplementing, amplifying in a hundred ways the benefits and advantages created by statute. It is only necessary to mention the dispensaries for consumptives, the dispensaries and clinics for infants, the first-aid societies, the school doctors, the day nurseries and care-rooms for children, the holiday colonies and forest resorts, the people's kitchens, the milk depôts, and the various societies and agencies for combating alcoholism and even more insidious diseases, as examples of a new and large order of hygienic endeavours which play a part of the utmost importance in the life of the German working classes. Many of these institutions directly owe their existence to the impetus given to the Insurance Laws, and all of them are carried on, more or less consciously, as part of the national health crusade for which the

[6] The apothecary's business is a licensed and valuable vested interest in Germany.

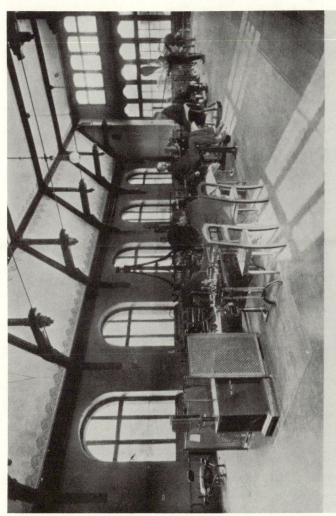

BEELITZ SANATORIUM (BELONGING TO THE BERLIN PENSION BOARD)—ZANDER HALL FOR
MEDICO-MECHANICAL APPARATUS.

The Crusade against Disease

insurance system is the rallying-ground. Without the funds created by the Insurance Institutions, also, the Co-operative and other popular Building Societies would never have been able to do their invaluable work in the better housing of working-class families. Equally important in their way are the workmen's secretariates, "People's Bureaux," and municipal information offices which were largely created for the purpose of instructing the working classes as to their duties and rights under the Insurance Laws, though their function as disseminators of knowledge and as solvents of legal and other difficulties covers the entire scope of the Civil and Industrial Codes.

I am well aware of the limitations which attach to any use of national death-rate figures, yet when every allowance has been made for other influences—as, for example, improved sanitation, a reduced birth-rate, and a higher general standard of life—it seems impossible to deny to the Insurance legislation some credit for the fact that during the past twenty-five years the rate of mortality for the whole Empire has fallen from 25·4 per 1,000 of the population (on the average of 1881–85) to 19 on the average of the years 1905–09, a decrease of 6·4 per 1,000. The rate in 1909 was 17·2, and in 1910 16·2 per 1,000.[7]

In Germany the contention is general that the effect of the Insurance legislation and of the various activities

[7] The average death-rate for England and Wales during the years 1881–90 was 19·1 per 1,000; it fell to 18·2 during the years 1890–1900, and to 15·3 during the years 1901–10, a fall in twenty years of 3·8 per 1,000. The rate in 1909 was 14·5 and in 1910 13·5 per 1,000.

Social Insurance in Germany

to which it has given rise has been a marked improvement in the physical, material, and moral condition, not
merely of the insured classes, but of the poorer sections
of the population as a whole, and that this improvement
is reflected in a higher standard of civilisation and of
economic efficiency.

CHAPTER VIII

THE COST OF INSURANCE

A QUESTION which cannot be overlooked in any estimate of the value of the Insurance Laws is the extent of the burden which these laws impose upon employers and workpeople respectively, and this will now be considered. Broadly speaking, the burden in each case is about twice that which falls upon employers and workpeople for the corresponding provision made by the National Insurance and Workmen's Compensation Acts.

(1) COST TO THE EMPLOYERS.

The general opinion prevalent in Germany is that the cost to employers of all three systems of insurance is equal to about 4 per cent. or 9½d. in the pound of the wages bill. The estimate is approximately accurate if one industry be taken with another. There is, however, considerable variation not only as between different industries but also as between undertakings in the same industry; for example, in the case of firms paying high rates of wages, as in the more skilled branches of the machinery trades, and firms engaged in trades, subject to a minimum accident risk, like the textile trades, the percentage charge is relatively low. It is understood, of course, that this estimate refers to direct charges only,

Social Insurance in Germany

and accordingly disregards the employers' share of the taxation out of which the Imperial pension subsidies, amounting now in the aggregate to about two and a half million pounds per annum,[1] are defrayed, and of the local rates in so far as the local authorities are charged with administrative functions under these laws.

The following data are based upon the operation of the Insurance Laws prior to the amendment of 1911. The radical changes which have been introduced in the organisation of the sickness insurance funds will increase rather than diminish the cost of this branch of insurance, and the same effect will naturally follow the extension of the system of invalidity insurance. Hence the figures which follow understate the cost at the present time.

Cost of Sickness Insurance.—First as to the cost of sickness insurance. There is no Government grant in aid of sickness insurance; and the cost is borne (except in the case of the Mutual Aid funds, as already explained) by the workpeople and the employers in the proportion of two-thirds and one-third respectively, though the employers usually bear a larger share in the case of the miners' funds. The contributions form a certain percentage of the average wages; this percentage may not exceed 3 in the case of parochial insurance (now abolished), to which the lower-paid workers as a rule belong, and 6 in the case of the factory, local, building workers, and Guild funds. The old law stipulated, however, that the percentage could only be levied upon a maximum wage of 4s. or 5s. a day, according to the limit which

[1] With the coming into operation of widows' and orphans' insurance in 1912 the Imperial subsidy will be increased by over a million and a quarter pounds.

The Cost of Insurance

might be adopted by the fund ; it followed that neither workman nor employer could be required to pay insuranc contributions on a higher rate than that applying to a wage of 30s. a week.[2] Subject to the foregoing limitations the amount of the levy was determined mainly by local conditions, the current level of wages, the standard of health, and the scale of benefits for which the insured were willing to pay. The principle of percentage levies is not applied separately in the case of the individual workman ; the usual practice.is to divide the insured into wages classes, graduated by 1s. to 5s. according to circumstances, and to fix for each class an "average daily wage," which serves as the basis of assessment.

The combined contributions levied on a majority of the persons insured now range from 2 to 4½ per cent. of wages. The usual rate levied by the "local" and factory funds, in which in 1910 nearly three-fourths of the workers (10,119,650 out of a total of 13,954,973) were insured, is 3½ per cent., representing a charge of 1·17 per cent. for the employer and one of 2·33 per cent. for the workman, equal to 2¾d. and 5½d. in the pound of wages respectively. In the case of the factory funds, however, the employer further bears the cost of bookkeeping. On the basis of a combined contribution of 3½ per cent. employers would pay for sickness insurance only the weekly charges shown in the first table on the following page in respect of the incomes there specified.

Cost of Invalidity Insurance.—Employers and workpeople bear the cost of invalidity and old age insurance in equal shares, the contributions being graduated, as

---

[2] Under the new law wages may be assessed up to 6s. a day.

Weekly Wages.	Weekly Contribution.	Weekly Wages.	Weekly Contribution.
s.	d.	s.	d.
30	4¼	15	2
27	3¾	12	1¾
24	3¼	9	1¼
20	2¾	6	0¾
18	2½		

has been explained, according as the workman's wages fall into one of five groups. The cost to each contributor, prior to the increase caused by the extension of insurance to survivors in 1911, was as follows in respect of the wages instanced above :—

Weekly Wages.	Weekly Contribution.	Weekly Wages.	Weekly Contribution.
s.	d.	s.	d.
30	2¼	15	1¼
27	2¼	12	1¼
24	2¼	9	1½
20	1¾	6	¾
18	1¾		

The invalidity insurance contributions hitherto payable have represented for both employers and workpeople a minimum charge of 1 per cent. upon wages in the first wages class, a minimum of 0·9 and a maximum of 1·5 per cent. in the second class, a minimum of 0·7 and a maximum of 1·1 per cent. in the third class, a minimum of 0·7 and a maximum of 0·9 per cent. in the fourth class, and a maximum of 0·8 per cent. in the fifth class.

Cost of Accident Insurance.—In the case of accident insurance the cost to the employer is assessed annually

The Cost of Insurance

on the mutual principle according to the liabilities actually incurred. This is the heaviest single charge to industry on account of insurance. The total expenditure in 1909 of Mutual Associations for industries of all kinds, with the exception of agriculture, building works and shipping, came to 16s. 4d. per person employed, equal to 1·72 per cent. of wages earned.

The cost of accident insurance in the mining industry averaged in 1909 38s. 11d. per workman insured (the total being 818,989) and 2·94 per cent. of wages.

The average cost has increased as follows during the past twenty-five years :—

Year	Per Workman.		Per cent. of Wages.
	s.	d.	
1886	7	8	0·82
1890	15	0	1·67
1895	20	5	2·28
1900	19	1	1·72
1905	33	4	2·80
1907	33	8	2·39
1908	33	5	2·39
1909	38	11	2·94

The cost of compensation only (forming 80 per cent. of the total assessment) in 1909, expressed as a percentage of wages, was 2·24 per cent. for the entire industry, and was as follows for the various branches: Coal-mining, 2·33 per cent.; lignite-mining, 1·81 per cent.; ore-mining, 2·16 per cent.; salt-mining and saline works, 1·66 per cent.; other mines, 2·23 per cent.

Combined Cost of Insurance.—Inquiries made of leading industrial firms in the principal industries in 1911 showed

213

that their insurance contributions represented the following percentages of the total wages bill :—

INSURANCE CHARGES ON EMPLOYERS—PER CENT. OF WAGES.

Industry.	Sickness.	Accident.	Invalidity.	Together.
Steel	1·04	1·76	0·60	3·4
Iron and Steel	—	—	—	3·7
Locomotives and Wagons ..	—	—	—	4·2
Locomotives..	—	—	—	3·7
Machine Tools	—	—	—	4·0
Machinery	0·9	2·2	0·6	3·7
Ditto	1·1	1·1	0·8	3·1
Ditto	—	—	—	3·5
Electrical Engineering ..	—	—	—	2·6
Ditto ..	1·1	0·7	0·6	2·4
Automobiles..	—	—	—	2·6
Shipbuilding	0·9	2·4	0·7	4·0
Coal-mining..	—	—	—	5·4
Ditto	—	2·6	—	8·2
Chemicals	—	—	—	2·9
Ditto	—	—	—	3·0
Ditto	—	—	—	4·0
Glass	1·9	2·5	0·7	5·1
Paper..	—	—	—	4·0
Cotton spinning and weaving	—	—	—	4·0
Cotton spinning	1·0	0·5	0·7	2·2
Mean of above	1·13	1·72	0·67	3·8

It is perhaps more instructive to know what these charges mean in the concrete to representative firms. Thus, in 1907, the firm of Krupp, whose enterprises include coal mines, steel works, and machine works, in addition to armament factories, paid statutory insurance contributions as follows : Sickness, £71,633 ; accident, £79,662; and infirmity, £25,545—a total of £176,840, equal to £3 2s. per head of its working staff, and to 2 per cent. of the share capital. In addition it paid £86,633 to voluntary pension and benefit funds and

The Cost of Insurance

£177,412 to works of general welfare, making a total of £440,885, or nearly 5 per cent. on the share capital paid in welfare contributions of all kinds.

The largest South German firm in the machinery trade, the Nuremberg-Augsburg Machine Works, employing over 11,000 workmen, paid in a recent year £20,276 in insurance contributions, equal to nearly £1 17s. per head, to 3·4 per cent. of the wages bill, and to 1 per cent. of the year's total turnover, and in addition paid £4,184 in voluntary subsidies to " welfare " funds for the benefit of the workpeople.

The " Vulkan " Shipbuilding Company, of Stettin, employing normally some 8,000 workpeople, paid the following amounts in insurance contributions on a wages bill of £463,000 in 1908-9 :—

	£	Per Head. £ s. d.
Sickness Insurance	4,019	0 10 6
Accident Insurance	11,332	1 9 7
Infirmity Insurance	3,097	0 8 1
Total	18,448	2 8 2

In addition the firm paid £90 on account of old claims under the Employers' Liability Act and £2,654 in free-will contributions to non-statutory provident funds for the benefit of its employees. Its insurance and other " welfare " contributions and its taxes together amounted to 7¼ per cent. of the share capital.

One of the largest mining and smelting companies of Westphalia, the " Phœnix," of Hoerde, working with an average of 33,000 workmen, paid in 1908-9 £171,700 in statutory insurance contributions and voluntary " welfare " subsidies, equal to £5 4s per head and to 7 per

215

Social Insurance in Germany

cent. of its wages bill of £2,471,000, and to nearly 3½ per cent. of its share capital of £5,000,000.

One of the smaller Westphalian colliery companies, the Kölner Bergwerksverein of Altenessen, paid in 1909 £3 12s. 1d. per head in sickness and pension contributions, £2 0s. 9d. for accident insurance, and 8s. 10d. for infirmity insurance, or a total of £6 1s. 8d. per head, the aggregate of £16,550 being equal to 5½ per cent. on the share capital.

The Arenberg Mining and Smelting Company, of Essen, paid insurance contributions as follows in the same year:—

	£	s.	d.	Per Head. £	s.	d.
Sickness, pension, and old age and infirmity ..	27,597	10	0	3	15	2¼
Accident	11,771	3	0	1	12	1
Total	39,368	13	0	5	7	3¼

These payments were equal to 4·4 per cent. on the share capital.

The Dahlbusch Colliery Company of Essen paid in 1909, on an output of 1,059,000 tons of coal, insurance contributions of £22,063, equal to 5¼d. per ton and to 3·3 per cent. on the share capital.

The Bergbaugesellschaft Neuessen of Altenessen paid in insurance charges in the same year, with an output of 665,812 tons, £13,302, or £6 3s. per head of the workpeople, equal to 6 per cent. on the share capital.

The Essener Steinkohlenbergwerke A.G., with an output of 1,814,906 tons, paid in insurance charges £81,792, equal to 4·4 per cent. on the share capital.

The Cost of Insurance

According to a return prepared in 1911 by the Association of Colliery and Smelting Works Owners of Upper Silesia, the cost of the three insurance systems to the colliery owners of that coal-field in 1909 was £7 9s. 5d. per head of all workpeople employed, 6d. per ton of the entire output, and about 12 per cent. of the wages bill. Accident insurance cost £1 15s. 4¾d. a head and 1½d. a ton, sickness insurance £4 18s. 3½d. a head and 4d. a ton, and invalidity insurance 15s. 0½d a head and ½d. a ton. In addition, these collieries paid £3 2s. 3d. a head in voluntary contributions to provident funds and other free-will benefits.

The cost to an important Saxon firm of machine builders, employing over 1,000 workmen and largely relying upon the export trade, was as follows in 1909 :—

Total Wages Bill.	EMPLOYERS' INSURANCE CHARGES.			
	Sickness.	Accident.	Infirmity.	Total.
£77,068	£ s. 868 6	£ s. 851 16	£ s. 641 3	£ s. 2,361 5
Per cent. of above	1·13	1·11	0·83 ·	3·07

It should be noted also that there is a tendency for these rates to increase slowly but automatically as wages increase and workmen become liable to higher rates of contributions, hence enjoying larger benefits. Thus the insurance contributions paid by Krupp of Essen amounted to 1·6 per cent. of wages in 1890, to 2·1 per cent. in 1895, to 1·9 per cent. in 1900, to 2·7 per cent. in 1902, and to 3·0 per cent. in 1905. The average daily wages paid in

Social Insurance in Germany

these years in the Krupp works were 3s. 10½d., 4s. 0½d., 4s. 8½d., and 5s. 0½d. The same tendency may be illustrated by the following comparative statement of the contributions paid on account of the three systems of insurance at various dates from 1885 forward by the Rheinische Stahl Industrie of Remscheid:—

	Sickness.	Accident.	Invalidity.	Together.	
				Per Head.	Per cent. of Wages.
	Marks.	Marks	Marks.	Marks.	Marks.
1885*	8·70	—	—	8·70	0·81
1886†	8·75	4·65	—	13·40	1·22
1891‡	9·23	13·11	8·59	30·93	2·55
1895	9·62	13·55	8·50	31·67	2·61
1900	10·10	13·05	8·50	31·65	2·21
1905	10·28	28·41	8·23	46·92	3·08
1906	15·40§	25·19	8·91	49·50	3·15
1907	12·87	25·28	10·02	48·17	2·91
1908	17·03§	28·69	9·77	55·49	3·39

* Introduction of Sickness Insurance.
† Introduction of Accident Insurance.
‡ Introduction of Infirmity Insurance.
§ Including special contributions.

During this period the average earnings of the work-people increased from 1,080 marks in 1885 to 1,655 marks in 1907, falling in 1908 to 1,633½ marks, but rising again in 1909 to 1,658 marks.

The cost to trades which employ for the most part unskilled labour does not increase to the same extent. The following comparative statement of the employers' insurance charges relates to a trade of this kind, the Harburg Indiarubber Company:—

The Cost of Insurance

	Sickness Insurance.	Accident Insurance.	Infirmity Insurance.	Together.	Per head of Workmen employed.
	Marks.	Marks.	Marks.	Marks.	Marks.
1890	5,025	6,432	5,205 (1901)	16,662	23·37
1895	6,262	6,725	6,017	19,004	21·90
1900	10,097	7,266	9,660	27,023·	19·22
1901	9,789	7,877	9,119	26,865	20·26
1902	10,195	10,001	9,800	29,996	21·21
1903	12,135	11,903	10,144	34,182	23·56
1904	13,245	12,723	10,510	36,478	24·53

(ii) Cost to the Workpeople.

The cost of insurance to the workmen is also considerable, for while they are relieved from liability under the
Accident Insurance Law, except to the extent that the
cost of the first thirteen weeks' care falls on the sickness
funds, they bear two-thirds of the cost of sickness insurance, the cost of infirmity insurance being divided equally.

Cost of Sickness Insurance.—The workpeople's contributions in general fall within the wide range of from
1 to 5 per cent. of their wages. For sickness insurance
they may pay from 1 to 2 per cent. if insured on the
lowest scale, which is the exception, and from 3 to 4 per
cent. if insured in the funds offering a liberal range of
benefits, which is the rule. As has been explained, the
most important groups of funds are the "local" and
factory groups. The largest "local" sickness fund in
Germany, that of Leipzig, levies on the workmen contributions equal to 2·7 per cent. of their wages, the payment
on a weekly wage of 20s. being 6¾d., on one of 25s., 7¾d.,

219

and on one of 30s., 9½d. The following are the mean rates levied on workpeople by important representative "local" and factory funds for sickness insurance only :—

	Per cent. of Wages
(*a*) *Local Funds.*	
Berlin Fund for Commercial Employees	2·8
Leipzig General Sickness Fund	2·7
Berlin Fund for Machine Builders	3·1
" " Tailoring Trade	2·0
" " Printing Trade	3·0
(*b*) *Factory Funds.*	
Berlin General Electricity Company (A.E.G.) ..	2½
Berlin Siemens Works (electrical works)	2·2
L. Loewe & Co. (machine tools, &c.), Berlin	2⅛
Royal Porcelain Manufactory	3
Hildebrand & Son (chocolate)	2
United Cement Works	2
Berlin Municipality	2⅔
Great Berlin Tramway Company	2⅝
Berlin Omnibus Company	2⅓
Düsseldorf Pipe and Iron Rolling Works ..	3
Hohenzollern Locomotive Works, Düsseldorf.. ..	2½
Heinrich Lanz, Motor Car Works, Mannheim ..	2⅔
Waldhof Paper Works, Mannheim	2⅔

An average levy for industrial workers generally will be 2⅓ per cent. (being two-thirds of a combined levy of 3½ per cent.) or 5½d. in the pound of wages, subject to the limit of assessment already explained, viz., wages 4s. or 5s. a day.

Cost of Invalidity Insurance.—To this contribution must be added the cost of infirmity insurance. Under the scale fixed by law, wage earners whose yearly earnings do not exceed £17 10s. (6s. 9d. weekly) pay about ¾d. weekly, those whose yearly earnings range from £17 11s. to £27 10s. (10s. 7d. weekly) pay 1¼d., those whose earnings range from £27 11s. to £42 10s. (16s. 4d. weekly) pay 1½d., those whose yearly earnings range from £42 11s. to £57 10s. (22s. 1d. weekly) pay 1¾d. weekly, and those

The Cost of Insurance

with higher yearly earnings pay 2¼d. The great majority
of skilled workers pay in the highest class. In general
the worker's contribution for invalidity insurance comes
to about ½ per cent. of his wages in the case of the skilled
workers, and from ¾ to 1 per cent. in the case of the
low-paid workers.

Combined Cost of Insurance.—Although, owing to the
different methods and scales of assessment, the cost to
German workpeople of sickness and disablement insurance combined, expressed as a percentage of wages, varies
greatly, it is probable that the predominant ratio is rather
over than under 3 per cent, while 4 per cent. is not
uncommon.

The following table shows the weekly contributions
payable by German workpeople for sickness and invalidity
insurance in respect of wages ranging from 30s. to 6s.
(the rates for sickness insurance being based on the assessment usual in the "local" and factory funds, say
2⅓ per cent. on wages for the workman) :—

Weekly Wages.	Sickness.	Invalidity.	Together.	Percentage of Wages.
30s.	8½d.	2¼d.	10¾d.	3·0
27s.	7¼d.	2¼d.	9½d.	3·0
24s.	6¼d.	2¼d.	9d.	3·1
20s.	5¼d.	1½d.	7¼d.	3·0
18s.	5d.	1¾d.	6¾d.	3·1
15s.	4¼d.	1¼d.	5¾d.	3·2
12s.	3¼d.	1¼d.	4¾d.	3·3
9s.	2¼d.	1¼d.	3¾d.	3·5
6s.	1¾d.	¾d.	2¼d.	3·4

The foregoing German figures are based upon the scale
rates of contribution. They may be supplemented by

Social Insurance in Germany

returns of the actual payments ascertained to have been made by workpeople in different trades and occupations. The following were the insurance contributions paid in July, 1911, by workmen engaged in a leading machine tool works in Düsseldorf as shown by the pay-sheets:—

Class of Workmen.	Weekly Wages for Full Time.	Weekly Insurance Contributions.	Per cent. of Wages.
Turners	43s. 3d.	11½d.	2·2
Planers	34s. 11d.	11½d.	2·7
Borers	40s. 8d.	11½d.	2·4
Drillers	30s. 7d.	11d.	3·1
Smiths	33s. 7d.	11d.	2·7
Fitters	25s. 11d.	10½d.	3·5
Cabinetmakers ..	34s. 8d.	11d.	2·6
Labourers.. ..	22s. 2d.	6¼d.	2·5

The following were the weekly insurance contributions paid by representative Berlin artisans at the same date, as shown by the pay-sheets:—

BUILDING TRADE.

Weekly Wages (including Overtime).	Weekly Insurance Contributions.	Per cent. of Wages.
32s. 2½d.	11½d.	2·9
26s. 5½d.	11½d.	3·6
44s. 5½d.	11½d.	2·1
37s. 3d.	11½d.	2·5
35s. 2d.	11½d.	2·7
37s. 0½d.	11½d.	2·5
30s. 2½d.	11½d.	3·1
36s. 9½d.	11½d.	2·6
37s. 7½d.	11½d.	2·5
31s. 0½d.	11½d.	3·0

In each case the charge for sickness insurance was 9d. and for invalidity insurance 2½d.

The Cost of Insurance

WOODWORKING TRADES.

Weekly Wages (including overtime).	Weekly Insurance Contributions.	Per cent. of Wages.
31s. 11½d.	11¼d.	2·7
27s. 0d.	9¾d.	2·7
33s. 5½d.	9¾d.	2·5
33s. 6d.	9¾d.	2·5
36s. 9½d.	9¾d.	2·2
18s. 6d.	9¾d.	4·4
40s. 6d.	9¾d.	2·0
39s. 6d.	9¾d.	2·1
	MACHINE WORKS.	
43s. 0d.	9¾d.	1·9
45s. 5¼d.	9¾d.	1·8
41s. 10½d.	9¾d.	2·0
43s. 8¼d.	9¾d.	1·9
42s. 2½d.	9¾d.	1·9
42s. 2¾d.	9¾d.	1·9
43s. 7d.	9¾d.	1·9
38s. 1½d.	9¼d.	2·0
40s. 2¼d.	9¼d.	1·8
	TRANSPORT WORKERS.	
30s. 3d.	11¼d.	3·1
33s. 3d.	11¼d.	2·8
33s. 1¾d.	11¾d.	3·0
28s. 2½d.	11¾d.	3·5

According to a report published by the Prussian Government the following were the average deductions for insurance charges only made from the wages of the workpeople engaged in the mines of Prussia during 1909:—

	Insurance Contributions per week (6 shifts).	Per cent. of Total Wages.	Per £ of Wages.
Coal Mining—			
Dortmund District	18½d.	5·5	13½d.
Upper Silesia ..	14¼d.	5·4	13d.
Lower Silesia ..	13½d.	5·4	13d.
Saarbrucken (State)	25½d.	8·0	19¼d.
Aix-le-Chapelle Dis.	14¾d.	4·4	11½d.
Copper Mining—			
Halle	15¾d.	6·1	14½d.
Salt Mining—			
Halle	16¾d.	5·6	13½d.
Clausthal	18½d.	6·1	14½d.

Social Insurance in Germany

The exceptionally high contributions paid by the miners are in part explained by the fact that the range of benefits is as a rule wider than that usual in other industries.

The following are the weekly insurance contributions paid by the Crefeld silk weavers, who represent a lower scale of earnings [3] :—

Weekly Wages.	Insurance Contributions.
8s.	3¼d.
8s. to 12s.	4¼d.
12s. to 16s.	5d.
16s. to 20s.	6¼d.
20s. to 24s.	8d.
24s. to 28s.	8¾d.
over 28s.	9¼d.

With the gradual advance of wages the contributions and the benefits automatically increase, so that as the workman derives all the advantages of his employer's higher payments he is getting better value for his outlay than ever before. During the years 1905–1910 the sickness contributions of workpeople alone (both sexes and all ages) increased in the case of the important "local" and factory groups of funds from 15s. 7¼d. to 19s. 2¼d. and from 19s. 2¼d. to 21s. 6¼d. respectively per head of the membership, and the increase for all statutory funds together was from 15s. 7d. to 18s. 11¼d. The contributions of the miners to their funds increased between 1905 and 1910 from 19s. 4½d. to 23s. 2d. (the employers' contributions being about equal).

[3] The employer who supplies these figures speaks of the Insurance Laws as "necessary and beneficent in their operation."

The Cost of Insurance

A concrete illustration of this steady, increase in the cost of insurance, concurrently with a rise in wages and an extension of benefits, is shown in the following table, which relates to an important firm in the Rhenish steel industry :—

INSURANCE CONTRIBUTIONS OF WORKPEOPLE.

Year.	Sickness.	Infirmity.	Per Head.	Percentage of Wages.
1904	20s. 11d.	7s. 5d.	28s. 4d.	1·96
1905	20s. 9d.	7s. 4d.	28s. 1d.	1·85
1906	22s. 3d.	7s. 9d.	30s. 0d.	1·90
1907	26s. 4d.	8s. 10d.	35s. 2d.	2·12
1908	26s. 8d.	8s. 10d.	35s. 6d.	2·17

The average annual wages of all workpeople employed by this firm were as follows in the years named : 1904, £72 8s. ; 1905, £75 19s. ; 1906, £78 13s. ; 1907, £82 15s.; 1908, £81 13s. 6d.

In support of his contention that the Insurance Laws do not impose an intolerable burden upon the workers, Dr. Zacher points to the large amounts of money which are expended on drink and sport as indicating a wide margin of income that is not entrenched upon by the absolute necessaries of life. However this may be, there is evidence that the insurance lien upon working class income established in 1885 has not arrested the upward tendency of wages which had already begun before the Insurance Laws were passed. Without citing figures for specific trades, which might be controversial, it will be sufficient to point to the fact that the workers' contributions to the cost of infirmity insurance have shown a constant tendency to pass from a lower to a higher

Social Insurance in Germany

scale. Thus, between 1891 and 1910 the proportion of the contributions in the first or lowest wages class paid to the 31 Pension Boards decreased from 253 to 91 per 1,000, the number in the second class decreased from 384 to 241, those in the third class increased from 217 to 259, those in the fourth increased from 146 to 177, and while there were none in the fifth class in 1891, there were 232 per 1,000 in 1910.

During the same period the percentage of each 100 marks of contributions paid in the lowest wages class fell from 17.1 to 4.8 per cent., the percentage in the second class fell from 36.9 to 18.5, the percentage in the third class from 25 to 24.0, and the percentage in the fourth class from 21.1 to 20.5, while that in the highest class increased from 11.6 per cent. in 1900 (when contributions are first shown as appearing in this class) to 32.2 per cent. in 1910.

To quote the words of the Imperial Insurance Office, contained in its report upon the Infirmity Insurance system for 1910: "The continuous increase of the revenue from insurance contributions is largely due to the transference of the workpeople to the higher wages classes by reason of the uninterrupted rise in wages. The revenue from contributions increases more rapidly than the number of the contributions."

(iii) Comparison of Insurance Charges, Germany and the United Kingdom.

Comparison of the cost of sickness and invalidity insurance in Germany and sickness and disablement insurance under the National Insurance Act in this country is to some extent vitiated by the fact that the benefits offered in the two cases differ very considerably. On the one hand higher maximum sickness and invalidity benefits are possible in Germany in the case of highly paid workers, but on the other hand the general average value of the corresponding benefits will at once be much higher in this country under the National Insurance Act than in Germany. Further, the maternity and sanatorium benefits offered by this Act far exceed anything achieved or even attempted in Germany or any other country. Benefits apart, however, it is possible to make a fair comparison of insurance contributions regarded as a charge upon industry, and this is done in the following table, in which the German contributions for sickness insurance have been computed, for reasons already stated, on the basis of 3¼ per cent. of wages for employers and workpeople jointly, borne in the proportion of one-third and two-thirds respectively :—

Weekly Wages.	Weekly Charge to Employers.		Weekly Charge to Workpeople.	
	Germany.	United Kingdom.	Germany.	United Kingdom.*
30s.	6½d.	3d.	10¾d.	4d. (3d.)
27s.	6d.	3d.	9¾d.	4d. (3d.)
24s.	5½d.	3d.	9d.	4d. (3d.)
20s.	4½d.	3d.	7¾d.	4d. (3d.)
18s.	4¼d.	3d.	6¾d.	4d. (3d.)
15s.	3½d.	4d. (3d.)	5¾d.	3d.
12s.	3¼d.	5d. (4d.)	4¾d.	1d.
9s.	2½d.	6d. (5d.)	3¾d.	—
6s.	1½d.	6d. (5d.)	2½d.	—

* The reduced rates shown in brackets for the United Kingdom are for women.

Social Insurance in Germany

Comparison of the cost of accident insurance is more difficult owing to the fact that in this country employers usually insure themselves with commercial companies against liability under the Workmen's Compensation Act and the Employers' Liability Act, on which account data comparable with those available for Germany do not exist. The only official published information on the subject is that contained in the "Statistics of Compensation and of Proceedings under the Workmen's Compensation Act, 1906, and the Employers' Liability Act, 1880," published by the Home Office. The report for 1909[4] contains returns relating to six and a half million workpeople coming under the provisions of the Workmen's Compensation Act, four and a half millions of these being employed in factories. Taking all the seven great groups of industries for which returns are given, viz., mines, quarries, railways, factories, harbours and docks, constructional works, and shipping, it is shown that the charge for compensation averaged in that year 6s. 10d. per person employed. It was lowest in the case of factories, viz., 3s. 5d. per head ; in the case of railways it was 7s. 1d., in that of quarries 9s. 2d., in shipping 10s. 8d., constructional works 14s. 11d., docks 16s. 8d., and miners 20s. 1d. The charge to the coal-mining industry worked out at about 0·8d. per ton of coal raised.

It must be remembered that the amount of compensation here shown does not include compensation paid

[4] The report for 1910 shows increased charges in nearly all cases, but it cannot be used for comparison owing to the fact that at the moment of writing the corresponding German data have not been published.

The Cost of Insurance

under contracting-out schemes, payments on account of outstanding claims under earlier Acts, damages recovered under the Employers' Liability Act, 1880, or at common law, employers' legal costs, &c. For purposes of comparison, however, these additional elements in the cost of accident compensation may be disregarded, inasmuch as corresponding or other charges fall upon German employers independently of the expenditure shown in the accounts of the Mutual Associations which administer the Accident Insurance Law.

The following table showing for 1909 the cost of accident compensation per person employed in important industries in the United Kingdom, and the expenditure per person insured in the same year by the German Mutual Associations for the same industries, is given subject to the foregoing reservations, and to the further fact that the figures for the United Kingdom do not include costs of administration and the profits of the Insurance Companies :—

Industry.	United Kingdom.	Germany.
Textile—	s. d.	s. d.
Cotton	1 10½ ⎫	
Wool, worsted, shoddy	1 1 ⎬	5 1¼
Other textile	0 10½ ⎭	
Metal (extraction, &c.)	7 5 ⎫	
Engine and shipbuilding	8 7 ⎬	16 1¼
Machinery, appliances, &c.	3 11½ ⎭	
Wood	7 11	16 11⅞
Paper	1 6 ⎫	17 6½
Printing	⎬	4 3½
China and earthenware	3 ·0¾	5 7¾
Mines	20 1	34 1½
Quarries	9 2	11 6⅞
Shipping	10 8	21 10⅞

229

Social Insurance in Germany

While the mean cost of compensation computed over all the industries covered by the English returns was 6s. 10d. per head of all employed, the average cost of accident compensation in the case of undertakings insured through the industrial Mutual Associations was in the same year 16s. 4d. per person.

The charge to the mining industry of 0·8d. per ton of coal raised compares more than favourably with the corresponding charge in Germany. The cost of accident insurance to the mining undertakings comprised in the German Mutual Associations for the entire mining industry (coal, lignite, ore, salt, &c.), was 1½d. per ton of output in 1909, and this was the cost of accident insurance to the colliery owners of Upper Silesia in the same year.

(iv) The Burden upon Industry.

The question whether and to what extent German industry is handicapped by the three insurance charges is one that cannot be answered by the help of abstract argument. So far as the protected home market is concerned the cost of insurance is to some extent a matter of indifference to the employers, since all alike have to pay it and take it into account in fixing prices, with the result that in the end the consumer bears his share with the producer. In this way, of course, some portion of the employers' charge comes back to the workers themselves.

The extent to which an addition to the cost of labour of 4 per cent. (counting the employer's contributions only) constitutes a handicap in foreign markets depends upon a multitude of factors, of which the most important

The Cost of Insurance

are the compensating advantages of insurance in increasing the efficiency of labour, and the extent to which the working classes of competing countries are protected by similar legislation or by special conditions of labour, whether based on statute or agreement, of counterbalancing effect. The first of these points will be dealt with later. As to the second, it would obviously be impossible to express in terms of costs of production the various measures of a positive or restrictive order by which labour is protected against excessive and premature exhaustion; but by way of illustrating a minor adjustment as between Germany and this country which such a calculation, if possible, would entail, it may be interesting to state that the number of children under 14 years employed as half-timers in textile factories in 1907 was 32,647, or 3 per cent of the total number of textile operatives in the United Kingdom, but only 3,747 or 0·4 per cent. of the total employed in Germany. It is more pertinent to observe that as the insurance charges have increased German employers have more and more studied economy in other directions, as by the modernising of plant, the increased use of labour-saving appliances, greater specialisation, &c., and in practice it might appear from Germany's increasing export trade that the burden is not now a serious handicap.

A significant passage bearing upon this subject appeared in a work published by the Imperial Insurance Office several years ago, in which the effect of the Insurance Laws is considered from all sides. The translation used is that approved by the Insurance Office:—

"That these (insurance) charges on industrial concerns have been bearable can easily be gathered from the great

231

improvement experienced by industry and commerce, the branches most burdened on account of the insurance since the 'eighties. What is more, in many instances the contributions for insurance were the very agents that produced the improvement of our national production. The employers did their best to get even with the higher working expenses by improving the working conditions, by making technical progress, and manufacturing the same quality and quantity with less workmen than before, or producing more and better work with the same number of workmen and better tools. If the employers improved at the same time the technical conditions for the benefit of the workmen, if they arranged for better safety against accidents and for suitable personal equipment of their workmen, as by providing them with eye-preservers, &c., they were in the first line guided by their own interest and wish to have a healthy body of workmen about them who like their work and are capable of doing it." [5]

It is instructive to note also what was said by the German Government when, in the *exposé des motifs* accompanying the Private Officials Insurance Bill, it discussed the ability of industry to bear the additional insurance burden imposed by that measure. It stated :—

" The question has been asked in many quarters, can German enterprise bear this new burden? This question must be answered affirmatively. German enterprise has hitherto borne all the burdens imposed upon it by social insurance without falling behind other countries. The

[5] "The German Workmen's Insurance as a Social Institution," published by the Imperial Insurance Office for the St. Louis Exhibition of 1904 (Official English version).

The Cost of Insurance

costs of social insurance have notwithstanding continuously increased owing to the mode of assessing liability under the Accident Insurance Law, the increase of population, and the advance in wages.

"The population increased from 49·2 millions in 1890 to 63·9 millions in 1909, or about 30 per cent. ; the wages returned as paid by the Mutual Associations under the Accident Insurance Law increased from an average of £32 6s. per head in 1890 to £47 14s. in 1909, showing an increase of 47·6 per cent. The costs of social insurance increased during the same period from 139 1 million marks in 1890 to 810·7 million marks in 1909, being an increase of 483 per cent. During this time German national wealth has shown a steady growth, and all the principal departments of our economic · life have expanded. In spite of the ever-increasing competition in the international markets, Germany has maintained and strengthened its position abroad. This position will not be shaken by the new burden which the proposed new insurance will impose."

The same opinion was avowed by Dr. Kaufmann, the President of the Imperial Insurance Office, in the address which he gave at the celebration of the twenty-fifth anniversary of the passing of the first Accident Insurance Law, held October 1, 1910 :—

"When the Industrial Insurance system was introduced," he said, "grave fears were entertained that the heavy burden imposed—a burden that would for a long time increase—might overwhelm our national economy. The Emperor and his Chancellor did not share these fears, and they have been justified. Germany bore the new burden, and will be able to bear it in future, so long

233

Social Insurance in Germany

as it is kept within the limits imposed by the necessity that our industry shall retain its full capacity to compete in the markets of the world. The path-makers of social reform were confident, however, that the expenditure on industrial insurance would prove fruitful in a high degree, that the new legislation would awaken new forces in the nation, and that its effects would greatly benefit its economic life and particularly its industry. They did not ignore the fact that the State which supports its weaker members benefits itself, and that to keep the masses of the people healthy and robust is to safeguard the State's most valuable asset, the national strength. They believed that as a result of the new provision there would grow up, with advantage to our economic life, a working class happier in its toil and able to produce both more and better work. They believed also that a system of industrial insurance would generate new moral influences, and prove incalculably valuable in developing to the utmost the collective economic force by which a people holds its own in the keen rivalry of nations.

"The course of events has here, too, justified the authors of the new legislation. During the last two decades German national economy has experienced an almost unexampled development, and by the raising of its physical, intellectual, and material condition the working class has participated in this development. It was no accident that the period of this great expansion synchronised with a radical improvement in the condition of the workers, for the two are intimately connected. Unquestionably a contributory cause of our growing industrial pre-eminence may be seen in the successful treatment of social questions, and particularly that of industrial insurance."

The Cost of Insurance

An indication of what far-seeing employers think upon the subject is afforded by a striking testimony borne by Herr E. Schmidt, a prominent representative of the tobacco trade and a member of the Reichstag, at the annual meeting of the German Tobacco Manufacturers' Association, held November 24, 1907. He stated :—

" I am convinced that when the social legislation was introduced, and for the first time the large contributions for sickness insurance and later for old age and infirmity insurance had to be paid, many of us groaned. To-day, however, these contributions, which occur every year, are booked either to the general expenses account or the wages account—for they are in fact a part of wages—and they are naturally calculated as part of the cost of production, and eventually appear in the price of the goods, though perhaps not to the full extent in times of bad trade. In any event, it is certain that it is hardly possible to speak of these insurance contributions as constituting any special burden on industry, for if you regard the sum so paid, not as a percentage of wages, but of the year's turnover, it does not exceed $\frac{1}{2}$ per cent., so that in calculating the cost of goods that is the extent of the expense to be allowed for. That is so small a sum that it is neither right nor just to make a noise about it, and pretend that we can no longer pay it if our workpeople are to have increased benefits by new insurance legislation. Speaking honestly, as one employer to another, I am of opinion that the investment in these insurance contributions is not a bad one."

As if the charge imposed on German industry by the insurance contributions were not already high enough to reassure those British employers who are appre-

235

Social Insurance in Germany

hensive as to the effect of the National Insurance Act, the German Government has by happy luck so timed two extensions of the insurance principle—long promised and last year carried into effect—that a new and very considerable burden will have to be met simultaneously with the coming into force of Mr. Lloyd George's measure. By reason of the further development of the existing Insurance Laws under the Consolidation Act of 1911 and the passing of a separate law insuring retirement and survivor pensions to salaried staffs (the Private *Employés'* Insurance Act), an additional charge of some twelve and a half million pounds will have to be borne by employers and employees of all classes.

Approximately the aggregate cost of social insurance, independently of State subsidies and charges upon public authorities, may now be placed at the huge figure of fifty-three and a half million pounds a year, made up as shown in the Table on the following page.

The subsidies from the Imperial Treasury in aid of pensions will also be increased by the new legislation, but to a less extent. The amount of the supplements paid by the Treasury towards the pensions granted under the Invalidity Insurance Law in 1910 (£2 10s. per pension per annum) was £2,626,900, and the extension of the law will add immediately £1,396,600 to this State subsidy. Adding the cost of the Imperial Insurance Office (over £110,000 a year), the total direct annual contribution from the public funds is now a little over four million pounds.

The expenditure of employers and workpeople here shown disregards all voluntary "shop" and other benevolent contributions made by the former, and all voluntary thrift practised by the latter by means of non-statutory

The Cost of Insurance

societies and funds of many kinds. History teaches that nations are at times capable of committing supreme acts of folly, and unless the obligatory insurance legislation of Germany, for the working of which this enormous sum of money is raised every year, and raised with evident ease, is not a gigantic benefaction, it is a gigantic imposture. If an imposture, the remarkable fact has to be explained that the German nation refuses to be persuaded of its blindness, but after thirty years of experience has so recently, through a virtually unanimous Legislature, greatly enlarged the ambit of social insurance, and voluntarily imposed upon itself additional heavy burdens.

	Cost to Employers.	Cost to Employees.	Together.
	£	£	£
I. *Sickness—*			
(a) Actual in 1910	6,491,600	13,406,600	19,898,200
(b) Extension of law (1911)	1,004,800	2,009,600	3,014,400
Totals	£7,496,400	£15,416,200	£22,912,600
II. *Invalidity and Old Age—*			
(a) Actual in 1910	4,933,800	4,933,800	9,867,600
(b) Extension of law (1911)	979,300	979,300	1,958,600
Totals	£5,913,100	£5,913,100	£11,826,200
III. *Accident—*			
Actual in 1910	£11,391,000	—	£11,391,000
IV. *Insurance of Salaried Staffs—*			
New measure (1911)	£3,750,000	£3,750,000	£7,500,000
Totals	£28,550,500	£25,079,300	£53,629,800

CHAPTER IX

ATTITUDE OF EMPLOYERS AND WORKPEOPLE

ANY consideration of the attitude of employers and work-people towards the Insurance Laws raises at once, besides the question of cost, that of results—in other words, the practical influence of these laws upon labour and the conditions of working-class life.

And first, from the standpoint of the employer, can it be said, and to what extent can it be said, that the Insurance Laws have "paid" as a "business proposition"? It would be easy to advance a multitude of emphatically favourable testimonies both from official sources and from writers whose interest in social insurance is that of the onlooker sympathetic to labour and all that is implied in social reform. Such testimonies, however, would not be convincing if they stood alone. Upon such a subject the only opinions which are of absolute value are the opinions of those directly interested—the men who bear the burden, know its weight by the feel of it, and who are able by observation and experience to estimate the actual effects of the benefits which this burden purchases for their work-people. Hence it is desirable, in considering this extremely practical aspect of the question, to give only a secondary place to the views of outside experts and theorists, and to go direct to the German employers themselves.

The statements from these sources published in a Parliamentary Paper in 1911 are most impressive, representing as they do large undertakings in the principal export industries. Their effect is to substantiate the view universally held by Poor Law workers, social investigators, and all who are in touch with the working classes, that this legislation has increased the economic efficiency, the material prosperity, and the entire standard of life of the masses of the population.

The President of a large Association of Employers in the iron and steel industry is reported as stating:—

"The Insurance Laws have influenced the condition of life of the working classes in that they are free from anxiety by reason of sickness, infirmity, and accidents. It cannot be denied that in many cases the workman's feeling of confidence increases his productive power and his efficiency."

Representative employers in the engineering and allied trades write:—

(*a*) "In my opinion there can be no doubt that the standard of life and the efficiency of German workmen have greatly improved in recent decades. Various causes have contributed to produce this result, the most important being higher wages, the better training of the worker by technical education, and the careful training of apprentices, but also, without doubt, the security for the future which is afforded by the Infirmity and Accident Insurance Laws and the better care provided by Sickness Insurance."

(*b*) "The three Insurance Laws have unquestionably

had a beneficent influence upon the conditions of life and the efficiency of the working classes. The workman and his family are no longer, as was formerly the case, exposed to philanthropy or to hunger in the eventuality of sickness or accident."

(c) " There can be no doubt that the Insurance Laws, together with the increase of wages, have exercised an enormously beneficent influence on the health, the standard of life, and the efficiency of the working classes."

(d) " The Insurance Laws have undoubtedly had a good influence on the position of the working man. His standard of life has decidedly been raised, and with it his efficiency has increased, since, in time of sickness, his fund provides free medical attendance for the man and his family, with such a payment during sickness as averts extreme want."

(e) " The operation of the German insurance legislation has, in the course of time, greatly improved the condition of the workers and also increased their efficiency, and has had, in general, a very beneficent influence."

(f) "The cost of the Insurance Laws indirectly benefits *entrepreneurs* owing to the resulting economic effects. They gain considerably and directly by the creation and maintenance of a more productive and more efficient working force."

The same testimony is borne by other industries :—

Chemical Industry.—(a) " The obligatory systems of insurance have unquestionably influenced the standard of life and the efficiency of the workers favourably, since these are protected against want in any of the even-

Attitude of Employers and Workpeople

tualities contemplated." (*b*) Thanks to the system of State insurance the standard of life of the German working classes has most markedly improved." (*c*) "The Insurance Laws have decidedly improved the conditions of life of the workers and increased their efficiency."

Glass Industry.—"The Insurance Laws have undoubtedly improved the condition of the working classes in a high degree, inasmuch as the workman and his family are protected against want in the event of protracted sickness and meantime receive expert medical treatment. It is difficult to decide whether these laws have favourably influenced the efficiency of the workers."

Paper and Wood Pulp Industry.—"The Insurance Laws have a decidedly favourable influence on the condition of life and also the efficiency of our workpeople."

Rubber Industry.—"In our opinion the Insurance Laws have advantageously influenced the standard of life and the efficiency of the German workers."

A firm in the steel goods industry points to some of the unanticipated effects of the Insurance Laws :—

"The insurance legislation has contributed to the solution of many problems which were hardly talked of before ; for example, the combating of pulmonary tuberculosis, housing reform, general dental care, and similar care for school children, the protection of mothers and infants, and more recently the insurance of private employees, of widows and orphans, the provision of free medical and midwife assistance for the uninsured wives of members of sickness funds, &c."

The following remarks on the inter-relationship which exists between the various insurance authorities—an

Social Insurance in Germany

inter-relationship which is not based on statutory provisions, but has been created by the force of circumstances—will be of interest to those employers of labour in this country who would welcome the conversion of the present system of accident compensation into a form of direct accident insurance on the mutual principle under State direction :—

" The German industrial insurance system comprises at the present time the three branches of sickness, accident, and infirmity and old age insurance. For each of these branches separate authorities have been created for the administration of insurance. These authorities are independent within their respective spheres ; nevertheless, the nature of their duties requires that they should keep in continuous contact with each other. The objects of the insurance laws are the more completely attained in proportion to the intimacy of this reciprocal relationship and to the degree in which the several insurance authorities work hand in hand."

The same authorities testify with equal agreement that the cost of insurance, heavy though it is, has hitherto been borne willingly by the employers. Thus the President of the Association of Employers in the iron and steel industry already cited states :—

" According to our observation the employers willingly bear the costs which the Insurance Laws impose on them, and it is doubtful whether a single employer would wish to be without these laws so far as the cost goes. The laws ' pay ' employers from their own standpoint, since they, too, are given a feeling of greater security ; they are freed from moral and material burdens which the individual standing alone would hardly be able to

Attitude of Employers and Workpeople

bear; and they are protected against constant disputes with exacting claimants."

The opinions obtained from representative firms in the engineering and allied trades are to the same effect. For example :—

(a) "The greater proportion of German employers have willingly borne the expense of Industrial Insurance, since there can be no question that by this insurance much good has been done, and distress and misfortune have been greatly ameliorated in the homes of the working classes. Most employers have recognised that the workman is not able alone to assure himself against the vicissitudes of life, and that, to a certain degree, a moral obligation rests on them to contribute to the costs of insurance."

(b) "German industry has from the beginning co-operated in the building up of the system of insurance. It has also never hesitated to bear the burden which has in this way been laid upon it."

(c) "It must be admitted that a healthy working class is far more useful to industry than one that is physically enfeebled. Hence the expenditure incurred by employers on account of these laws is more willingly borne than the burdens which are imposed upon industry in other directions by laws and institutions in the alleged interest of the working classes."

(d) "The best proof that the expense caused to employers by the compulsory insurance laws is borne most willingly is furnished by the fact that so many firms in addition carry on voluntary welfare institutions on behalf of their employees."

In other industries, not dependent in the same degree

Social Insurance in Germany

upon skilled labour, equal readiness to pay for the benefits of insurance is shown by the employers : —

Chemical Industry.—" In general, it may be assumed that the cost of insurance is borne willingly by the employers. The many voluntary welfare institutions (pension funds, relief funds, supplements to sickness insurance benefits, convalescent homes, &c.) maintained by the large industrial undertakings prove that a large section of the employers are even willing to go beyond the sacrifice required of them by law."

Paper and Wood Pulp Industry.—" The laws and the provision which they make for the workers are directly advantageous to employers."

Rubber Industry.—" It may be affirmed that employers are not merely satisfied with the high costs of insurance, but pay them gladly in the interest of their workpeople, knowing that the latter are as a consequence protected against need and anxiety."

The following statement from the head of a firm of locomotive builders reflects the genuine social spirit which, as I can testify from personal knowledge, inspires many of the great leaders of industry in Germany at the present time :—

" In considering these laws one should not ask whether they are advantageous to employers, nor was that the standpoint from which the laws proceeded. The ruling idea was, by means of these laws, to do a great social work and to banish much of the prevailing want. The progress of the nation in civilisation is closely bound up with protective legislation of this kind, and, even from the standpoint of the employer, these laws can only be regarded as beneficial."

244

Attitude of Employers and Workpeople

To one aspect of the employers' attitude towards the Insurance Laws it is impossible for the employers themselves to do justice : it is the great amount of self-sacrificing voluntary service which even the busiest of their number have for a quarter of a century been ever ready to render in the several branches of administrative work in which their active co-operation, with that of the workpeople, is sought. Upon this subject Dr. Kaufmann, President of the Imperial Insurance Department, referring especially to the Accident and Infirmity Insurance Laws, said a short time ago :—

" If we review the participation of the employers in the carrying out of these two systems of insurance, it must be acknowledged that the high expectations of the legislator have not been disappointed. The cost of insurance has been willingly borne by the employers—even those for whom it was not easy; while those who have given personal service in the work of administering the accident and infirmity insurance schemes have readily and gladly discharged their often laborious honorary duties. But the sacrifice of the employers has gone much farther. In a spirit of magnanimity many of them have voluntarily extended the provision for their workpeople far beyond the requirements of the law. This has been one of the happy incidents of the new legislation to be ranked along with the social activity of our State and communal authorities and the large development of philanthropic activity peculiar to our time for the welfare of the poorer classes of society. Thus Industrial Insurance, which opened up so many new ways, has proved in truth a socio-political school for the nation."

Social Insurance in Germany

It is a fair assumption that if the Insurance Laws were found to be unremunerative and excessively burdensome, German employers would not be so ready as they are to supplement the benefits conferred by these laws by voluntary benevolence on the same and allied lines. The "welfare" work done by many of the best known firms in the iron and steel, coal-mining, engineering, chemical, textile, and other trades forms one of the most honourable chapters in the history of German industry. Much of this work was being done long before the Insurance Laws were passed, and it is highly creditable to those concerned that the introduction of new obligatory duties towards their workers was made in comparatively few cases a pretext for abandoning provident and other benevolent schemes which had hitherto been maintained voluntarily. On the contrary, these have since been developed on still more generous lines, even where the only reward has been an uncharitable suspicion of motive or outspoken ingratitude. Some of the larger industrial companies assign truly princely benefactions to work of this kind, but its general character can perhaps be exemplified better by reference to a firm of medium size than to one with unlimited resources at command, and such a firm is the Bergische Stahl-Industrie of Remscheid, employing some 2,000 workpeople. This firm maintains a special "welfare" department under the management of a skilled and sympathetic official, and the yearly report upon the various activities of this department makes a volume of over 100 pages. In addition to its obligatory contributions to the statutory insurance systems, the firm subsidises separate supplementary pension funds for officials and workpeople, with their

widows and orphans. Every year an amount equal to
1½ per cent. of the total amount of the wages paid is
allotted out of profits to the workpeople's voluntary
pension fund alone, and the firm's contributions to both
funds actually exceed its contributions under the Insurance
Laws. The special sickness benefits given embrace free
medical assistance to all members of families, including
assistance to women in child-birth. Further, the firm
maintains canteens, provides pure tested milk for its workpeople and their families at cost price, and subsidises a
savings bank to which all juveniles and all unmarried
men under twenty-five years are required to belong; the
other institutions include a fund out of which help in
money or kind is given to workpeople in times of special
need, a loan fund to meet similar emergencies, a special
office at which mothers are advised as to the nursing of
infants, and a general advice office at which information
is given on all questions affecting the working classes.
Further, the firm helps the workmen to buy their own
houses; the arrangements provided at the works for
washing and bathing are exceptional—there are 194 wash-
basins and 19 baths; and finally, the firm subscribes to
the workpeople's musical societies. The entire voluntary
" welfare " service of this firm costs £4,000 a year.

None of these benefits need be given. That they are
given, at yearly increasing cost, demonstrates not only
the existence of a high conception of responsibility, but
the ability of industry, when well organised and directed,
to bear very considerable burdens beyond those created
by statutory authority, and unquestionably also a conviction that care for the welfare of the working classes is
from the employer's standpoint a good investment.

Social Insurance in Germany

Nevertheless, a certain amount of dissatisfaction is felt by employers on the ground that the Insurance Laws are believed to be to some extent abused, as the best laws often are. This feeling is expressed in the following extracts from the statements already alluded to, though it is fair to say that in conversation with employers the same views are often avowed with far more emphasis :—

"The laws have been accompanied by one petty drawback—an increase of querulousness and of simulation on the part of the injured and sick ; but these abuses are negligible when compared with the great advantages of the laws."

Again : "It is inevitable that these great agencies of social welfare and the conspicuous services which they render should be accompanied by less desirable effects. Among these one need not count the fact that in times of reduced employment the claims upon the sickness funds at once multiply, since workpeople who have either lost their situations, or fear the loss of them, regard any kind of sickness, which otherwise would be disregarded, as a pretext for falling on the funds with a view to obtaining sick money while out of work. For such people the sickness funds might, indeed, serve as a sort of unemployment insurance.

"More serious is the fact that the facility with which sickness benefits are obtained, and still more the chances of obtaining a permanent pension by reason of accident (a pension the amount of which, even in the case of partial incapacity, means a valuable addition to the earnings that still may be obtained), encourage in certain persons a tendency to be treated as invalids and to magnify slight ailments and injuries, while they create in

248

those who are not fond of work a diseased craving for pensions—wherever possible for life—on account of trivial disablement. This disposition has been called 'pension hysteria,' and it is a characteristic of the accident insurance system to which medical men have emphatically drawn attention.

" Phenomena of this kind naturally reduce somewhat the value of the insurance systems for the improvement of the national health and strength; yet, in spite of all, the advantages of these systems are, in my opinion, so great that the disadvantages alluded to, while it is necessary to combat them, cannot be mentioned in comparison."

It would be idle to pretend that attempts are not made, and often made successfully, to obtain benefits improperly. For example, the sickness insurance organisations connected with the building trades experience an unusually heavy drain upon their funds during the winter months, and in spite of every effort to discourage illegitimate claims it is admitted that many men engaged in these trades deliberately endeavour to obtain sickness benefits in time of seasonal employment on the pretext of ailments which, when real, are of so trivial a nature that in times of good trade they would be passed over without a moment's thought. Under the Accident Insurance Laws, too, many claims for compensation of a trivial and even of a fictitious nature are unquestionably made, and there is the greater inducement to malinger in this case since the benefits paid for accidents are in general very liberal.

Similarly the pensions granted under the Infirmity Insurance Act are a source of great temptation to misrepresentation; yet where this takes place the best that can be hoped is one of those doles for partial-incapacity which are indeed small yet mean much when added to meagre earnings. Thus in its report for 1910 the Berlin Infirmity Insurance Board explains a largely increased number of applications for pensions in 1908 and 1909 as compared with previous years by " the general depression in trade which caused many insured persons of reduced working capacity to seek infirmity pensions in the absence of employment."

Admitting that the insurance funds are thus abused, however, it would be unfair to generalise on the subject. After all, the records of the English friendly societies contain evidence to the same effect, and these societies deal in the main with selected cases and with the *élite* of the working classes, while the German insurance organisations embrace all the bad as well as all the good in the entire labouring population. Moreover, attempts to assert exaggerated claims, made with the knowledge that the facts will be carefully sifted, do not necessarily imply dishonesty. It may be presumed that the ordinary insurance claims for fire compensation, personal injury, and the like made in a different rank of life seldom err on the side of leniency to the companies liable.

When a man knows that his claim will be probed to the bottom, with a view to restricting it to his irreducible legal right, he is justified in making out the best case for himself. In asking for insurance benefits workpeople do not forget that they are getting back what they have paid for, and there is probably at the back of every claimant's mind the conviction that he has an honest right to the benefit of any doubt that may arise.

Granting, however, that the insured are, as a rule, both

Attitude of Employers and Workpeople

willing and desirous to obtain from the insurance funds all the returns possible, the exaggeration of rightful claims is in the main a sin of intent more than of deed, for it rests with the controlling authorities to grant benefits or not according to the facts of the case, and serious abuse of the funds would argue gross collusion, to which it would be necessary to suppose that the medical staff themselves would be a party. Widespread abuse does not, in fact, occur, and the working-man's frailty in this matter of malingering has unquestionably been painted in too dark colours.

No less an authority than Dr. Zacher, who was for some years engaged in the administration of the Insurance Laws as an official of the Imperial Insurance Office, states :—.

" The writer feels it his duty to assert emphatically, as the result of his twelve years' experience as President of Senate of the Imperial Insurance Office, that to the honour of the German working classes the cases in which claims to compensation are fictitious and pensions are obtained fraudulently, against better knowledge and without justification, are rare exceptions, and, as compared with the millions of claims which are settled yearly under the Insurance Legislation, prove no more than that there are bad characters among the working classes just as amongst other classes of society."

Further, Dr. Kaufmann, President of the Imperial Insurance Office, recently pointed out how small, after all, is the possibility of effective fraud when he called attention to the conscious work of the senates of arbitration connected with his Department in the following complimentary words :—

Social Insurance in Germany

" The members of the senates have always to keep in view the fact that it is not a question of granting to a destitute person relief which he may greatly need, but of determining whether a definite legal claim against a definite Insurance authority is justified by legal conditions. If on the whole it has been possible to take the right course in all these relationships, the reason lies in the high conception of their duties entertained by all the members of the arbitration bodies, and in particular the lay members."

A further objection sometimes advanced by employers against the Insurance Laws is that they have weakened in the working classes the spirit of self-help and self-reliance. This view likewise finds expression in several of the statements cited above. Thus :—

" That the standard of life of the workers has been raised by the Insurance Laws admits of no doubt whatever. On the other hand, the sense of responsibility has been weakened owing to the fact that these laws have relieved the workers of anxiety, and will do so in a still greater degree when the projected insurance of widows and orphans is introduced."

Again : " The sense of responsibility has been weakened owing to the fact that the Insurance legislation relieves them of all care."

Another employer says :—

" Personally I cannot resist the feeling that the excessive provision made for the worker by legislation tends to weaken in him the consciousness of his personal obligation . to provide independently for himself and his family. Many men who under other circumstances (*i.e.*, in the absence of the Insurance and similar protective laws) would so act, from their own sense of responsibility, unquestionably rely on the assurance that the law provides for all the vicissitudes which may befall them, and will intervene on their behalf under all circumstances in case of need. In this way the feeling of responsibility is weakened in many workers, and this I regard as the most serious defect of these laws."

It would be unwise to underrate the importance of objections of this kind—though in my opinion they are by no means generally or even very widely entertained—but even if the Insurance Laws did to some extent discourage voluntary providence, it would neither be surprising nor altogether undesirable. The thrift within the power of the working classes is at best limited, and when a working man has the assurance that the more serious risks and vicissitudes of life to which he and his family are exposed are met with tolerable completeness by public institutions provided largely at his own expense, he is fairly justified in bidding dull care begone and in spending more than he would otherwise do upon present satisfactions. One may fairly ask, if the Insurance Laws have not this effect, what is their purpose and value? After all, thrift, laudable and valuable though it is, should not be regarded as an end but as a means. A thrift which is allowed to degenerate into an unintelligent and short-sighted parsimony may well do more harm than good to those who practise it. If the urgent purposes of working-class providence are met by compulsory measures, it can only be a gain to the workers as a class—and most assuredly and more directly to the employers whom they serve—if they are able and disposed to spend more freely in the maintenance and improvement of their standard of life and

Social Insurance in Germany

comfort. The fundamental question whether it is possible to say with any certainty what working people or any others would do or not do under a different set of conditions must be left undiscussed. It is at least conceivable that in the absence of the helpful influence of the Insurance Laws there might be to-day far less voluntary providence than actually exists. It is certainly significant that many German authorities on the Insurance Laws, after long study and observation of their operation and influence, have come to the conclusion that these laws have encouraged and not discouraged voluntary thrift, have strengthened and not weakened the sense of self-respect, self-reliance, and responsibility, and in general have proved educative and morally stimulative to a marked degree.

"As is the case with insurance in general," writes Dr. Zahn, "the German social insurance legislation educates the working classes in providence, self-control, and prudence, and it is well known that the social causes of poverty are specially operative where these qualities are lacking, for wholesale poverty is due not merely to a faulty organisation of production, but to the absence of education and foresight on the part of the workman. . . . The moral influence of industrial insurance must not be overlooked. To a large extent the self-help of the workers is promoted by the insurance institutions; the sense of frugality, prudence, and self-control is extended, and voluntary benevolence is vitalised and stimulated to a degree which would have been inconceivable without the Insurance Laws."

By way of complement the following testimony may be quoted from a recent article in a Labour newspaper, the

254

Attitude of Employers and Workpeople

Deutscher Holzarbeiter (November 6, 1908). Replying to the direct charge that under the influence of the Insurance Laws the working classes had become both less provident and less strenuous, the editor of this journal says :—

" The serious objection is made against the Insurance Legislation that it has destroyed the workman's consciousness of responsibility. It is contended that the workman is so well provided for by insurance that he no longer feels under any necessity to care for the future. This complaint is unfounded. In the first place, it must be pointed out that the insurance benefits supply but a fraction of what a working-class family needs in time of sickness. To the extent that this is the case, providence is actually impossible except in isolated cases. In many reactionary circles, however, spectres are seen everywhere, though none exist. Here and there the idea seems to prevail that the workman's strength should be strained to the utmost by exposing him and those dependent upon him to abject want directly his health gives way. But a contented and efficient working class will never be created by any such means. Experience teaches every day that the workman is happiest in his work and brings the greatest interest to the welfare of the community when he has the tranquillising thought that he has a certain security even in bad times. The contention that his feeling of responsibility is disappearing is absolutely unfounded. Rather the contrary is true."

It is unfortunately impossible to put to any conclusive test of figures the thrift spirit of the German working classes either now or at any earlier date. The common test of the public savings bank deposits if applicable would altogether support the case for increasing providence; it is a test, however, which no one with respect for accuracy would knowingly apply if once aware of the fallacy inherent in it. For these banks are very largely used by the middle and lower middle classes, and no data exist to show the extent to which the accumulated funds represent working-class savings. At a time when, during the last period of trade depression, the deposits in the Berlin Municipal Savings Bank were falling alarmingly and the withdrawals increasing, the official organ of the Socialist party, the *Vorwärts*, unswervingly honest according to its lights as ever, in spite of its perversity and truculence, warned its readers, for the reason above stated, against using these figures as a test of social conditions. Nevertheless, that there is much saving amongst the working classes is undeniable, and there would be far more if the large house system and the restriction of shares in public companies to the high denomination of £50 did not close to them two avenues of thrift so attractive to the working classes in this country.

A large number of German employers successfully encourage their workpeople to save by receiving money on deposit at a higher rate of interest than can be obtained from the public savings banks. The Rheinische Stahl-Industrie of Remscheid makes membership of the factory savings banks compulsory in the case of juveniles and unmarried workers under twenty-five years, while it is voluntary for others. In the year 1909–10 1,015 out of a total of 1,817 workers had accounts with the firm, and more than half of them were voluntary depositors. Most of the accounts were small, but 328 depositors had over

Attitude of Employers and Workpeople

£5 to their credit, 116 had over £15, 21 had over £50, and 5 over £100. The deposits of the year exceeded £3,300, and the firm paid, in addition to interest of 5½ and 6 per cent. (2 per cent. more than is paid by the municipal savings bank), a bonus of £136. The withdrawals were for the most part on account of marriage, military service, urgent domestic need, and house purchase. Herr Kolluk, the able director of the "welfare" department of this firm, writes to me: "That the Insurance Laws have weakened the spirit of thrift cannot be maintained; on the contrary, we are of opinion that the benefits secured to the workers by these laws have enabled the working classes to use their surplus money in contributions to other provident funds. The idea of co-operation has also made great progress in the form of stores. While formally the Social Democrats discouraged the idea of saving, inasmuch as it would have seemed to discredit their theory of the progressive impoverishment of the people, they now embrace the idea, and endeavour to persuade their colleagues not only to take up dividend-yielding shares in their co-operative societies, but to become depositors in the savings banks carried on by these societies. If workpeople were as frugal in their habits as in the days of our youth the opportunities for saving would be greatly increased."

After all, obligatory insurance, practised under State direction, is only thrift systematised and protected by ampler guarantees than can be offered by private action and commercial enterprise. The six million pounds a year now contributed by the working classes under the Invalidity Insurance Law are as truly savings as though they had been premiums paid to insurance companies on

Social Insurance in Germany

behalf of endowments or deferred annuities, and with the advantage that the credit of the State is involved in their security. If stock were to be taken of the capital of the German working classes, not the least considerable item would be the accumulated fighting fund against sickness, amounting to sixteen million pounds sterling, and the further eighty-five millions sterling lying in readiness for old age and invalidity pensions when needed.

The question may properly be asked, Do the work-people bear their part of the cost of insurance as willingly as the employers; and are they contented with the benefits secured to them? Unquestionably the working classes overwhelmingly value the Insurance Laws highly and do not grudge the payment of their contributions. At the same time there is a certain dissatisfaction with some of the benefits paid; those obtained under the Infirmity Insurance Law in particular are not regarded as adequate, though they are as large as the contributions justify.

The attitude of the German working classes towards the Insurance Laws has undergone a complete change since the earliest of these laws was passed. The original Sickness Insurance Law was strongly opposed by the Socialist-Labour Party in the Reichstag, and in the final division (May 31, 1883) the Socialists were among 99 deputies who voted against it, the votes in favour being 216. The Socialist Party also criticised severely the first Old Age and Invalidity Law which was passed with the small majority of 20 votes in 1889. When this law was amended ten years later the voting in its favour was almost unanimous; and the Socialist members then for the first time voted as a body in favour of an

258

Attitude of Employers and Workpeople

Insurance Law. Since then the Labour Party in the Reichstag has warmly supported every development of the Insurance legislation, though often disagreeing with the Government and the parties in power on matters both of principle and detail.

It is safe to say that of all the laws passed in the interest of labour since the Empire was established the Insurance Laws are most valued by the working classes, and this holds good particularly of the Sickness and Invalidity Insurance Laws. Not only so, but the German workman bears the cost of insurance, heavy though it is when compared with that which will fall upon the working classes of this country under the National Insurance Act, with marked willingness, and regards the weekly deduction of his high contributions as perfectly equitable and self-evident.

A fairly intimate knowledge of the German working classes in various parts of the country justifies the statement that these laws are regarded by them as constituting a social charter of labour. What makes the German workman specially attached to the laws is the knowledge that the benefits which they confer are, in virtue of his large contributions, a right and not a benefaction.

During the discussion of the new Insurance Consolidation Law in 1911 the Socialist deputies endeavoured to widen the scope of insurance in many directions, while insisting on behalf of the working classes that these should bear their share of the increased cost. Thus one Socialist deputy proposed that the proportion of wages which might be levied on account of sickness insurance should be increased to 7½ per cent. (two-thirds falling on the workman), and that the invalidity insurance

259

Social Insurance in Germany

contribution should be increased as much as might be necessary in order to make old age pensions claimable at the age of sixty-five instead of seventy years. Speaking on the third reading of the Bill (May 27, 1911) the Socialist Deputy Molkenbuhr said: " It has been stated that the cost of our various proposals would be £35,000,000. These millions were required for necessary objects, however—extended maternity provision, &c.—and would have necessitated higher contributions, which the workers would willingly have taken upon themselves." One of the Government's proposals was that the employers should for the future bear one-half instead of one-third of the cost of sickness insurance and in return have half representation on the administrative bodies. This alteration would have relieved the insured workers to the extent of £2,300,000 a year, equal to 3s. 6d. per head of all persons insured, but the Socialist Party refused to accept it, and it was not pressed. The extensions introduced will, nevertheless, as we have seen, cost the working classes an additional three millions a year, and the employers an additional two millions. Already the German working classes contribute over thirteen millions a year under the Sickness Insurance Law and nearly five under the Invalidity Insurance Law. When the new law comes into full operation their, yearly expenditure on statutory insurance will exceed twenty-one million pounds.

The sentiment of the working classes is fairly and accurately reflected by the following recent statements of prominent leaders of the German trade union and labour movement. Inasmuch as the authorities quoted belong to the Socialist Party, whose general attitude

Attitude of Employers and Workpeople

towards Government measures and policy cannot be described as sympathetic, it is permissible to assume that the opinions quoted below do not go beyond the requirements of a strict regard for fact and proved experience.

Speaking at the eighth annual conference of the Socialistic Trade Unions of Germany, held at Dresden in June, 1911, Herr Robert Schmidt stated :—

"The working classes have never hesitated to pay the necessary insurance contributions. We should be foolish if we did not acknowledge the value of the Insurance legislation."

Herr A. Kersten, secretary of the Berlin Trades Council, the largest in Germany, replying to my recent invitation that he would make a frank statement upon this subject, wrote : "The workmen pay their share of the insurance contributions willingly. They are, however, dissatisfied with the provisions of the Insurance Laws to the extent that infirmity is treated in a general sense, instead of on an occupational basis; for every workman continues in his trade as long as possible and there becomes incapacitated from work." In other words, the working classes would prefer that under the Infirmity as already under the Accident Insurance Laws, every trade should bear its own special burdens, so that the compensation paid to a workman on account of incapacity would be more proportionate to the occupational risk to which he is subject.

Similarly, Herr Alex. Schlicke, Secretary of the German Metal Workers' Federation (Stuttgart), writes to me :—

"The question whether the workmen in general pay

Social Insurance in Germany

their contributions willingly can be answered in the affirmative. In Germany workmen's insurance proceeded from the workers themselves, though not to the same extent as in England. First came the 'free' benefit funds, and then the disablement funds of isolated Trade Unions, like those of the printers, sculptors, hatmakers, &c., with unemployment insurance in a large proportion of the Trade Unions. The result is that the more progressive of the workers altogether recognised the necessity of insurance, and that they willingly paid their contributions even before insurance became general. That part of the working class which did not belong to the insurance institutions created by the workers themselves, and was brought into insurance by statutory measures, has become accustomed to insurance and no longer feels the deduction of the contributions, which are as a rule retained from the wages by the employer. The Sickness Insurance Law will soon be thirty years old; a new generation has sprung up, and it takes the situation for granted.

"The workers acknowledge that the Sickness Insurance Law is a beneficent institution, the value of which is not impaired by frequent acts of chicanery on the part of officers here and there. In regard to Invalidity and Old Age Insurance the workers acknowledge the value of the preventive measures, the curative treatment, the convalescent institutions, &c., provided, but they regard the pensions as too small, and warmly deplore the struggle which is often necessary before the courts of arbitration before these pensions can be obtained."

Further, Herr Pappe, Secretary of the German Wood Workers' Federation (Berlin), states :—

Attitude of Employers and Workpeople

"The workers regard the deduction of insurance contributions from their wages as self-evident, and there is no question of either willingness or unwillingness to pay. There are, of course, workmen who would like to evade the payments, the more since their claims upon the sickness and invalidity insurance funds would not be affected (inasmuch as the employer is responsible for all payments in the first instance); on the other hand, many workmen go beyond the statutory insurance limit in insuring themselves against sickness (and in this event bear the whole of the extra cost). There are many complaints as to the inadequacy of the provision made, but it may be taken as certain that the enlightened worker would be sorry to be deprived either of sickness or disablement insurance."

Disagreement upon details is evidently compatible with satisfaction with the Insurance Laws as a whole and with readiness to pay for the benefits which they provide. The insurance premiums may or not be "withheld wages," as some doctrinaire writers have contended; it is certainly the fact that the withholding of these premiums is not regarded in Germany as either an injustice or an indignity. The truth is that the workpeople pay their weekly or fortnightly insurance contributions with neither greater nor less pleasure than any normal person feels when meeting a fair liability for an object which is not one of immediate satisfaction. All willingness to fulfil a duty of this kind is relative, but that it should be fulfilled at all presumes at least a tolerable standard of personal responsibility.

When Prince Bismarck proposed these laws he said frankly that he did not expect to make the working

Social Insurance in Germany

classes contented, for on his view of human nature a perfectly contented man was a psychological impossibility. The experience of a generation of statutory insurance has borne out this sensible estimate of things. "It cannot be said," remarks one of the employers quoted above, "that the Insurance Laws have created a more contented working class," and another says: "That the workpeople themselves are contented is not maintained. Even were the benefits under the Insurance Laws greater than they are, and granted at the employers' expense, there would be no permanent satisfaction of the workpeople's wishes; but the reason for this lies in human nature and not in the laws."

And yet while it is true that the workmen's spokesmen in the Press freely criticise the laws and make the most of their grievances, real or imaginary, yet behind all their criticism is a genuine and hearty recognition of the great benefits which the insurance legislation places within the reach of the toiling millions of the population. Not long ago a leading Socialist essayist, Herr P. Kampffmeyer, wrote in the *Sozialistische Monatshefte*: "Without doubt the German workmen's insurance legislation has greatly increased the physical strength of the working classes." The workers themselves are fully sensible of this fact, and of all the laws passed for their benefit during the past forty years none are more highly valued than the Insurance Laws. When the first President of the German Imperial Insurance Office, Dr. Boediker, retired from office in 1897, the delegate who was deputed to represent the working classes at a valedictory function stated:—

"The workers were not able to offer the retiring

264

Attitude of Employers and Workpeople

President monuments of brass or brilliant addresses, but they could assure him that his name was known in every home of labour, and that he would live in the grateful hearts of the workers."

CHAPTER X

INSURANCE OF SALARIED STAFFS

FOR many years the clerical staffs and the salaried employees engaged in private undertakings—professional, industrial, and commercial—have agitated through their powerful organisations for some sort of insurance corresponding, with the modifications called for by the different conditions of employment, education, and social status, to the provision afforded to the wage-earning classes by the Invalidity Insurance Law. This law applies, indeed, to salaried employees of certain grades—works officials, foremen, and other persons in a similar superior position—in so far as their yearly earnings do not exceed £100. The provision afforded in the event of invalidity is for the present small, however, and under that law will never be proportionate to the reasonable needs of persons accustomed and compelled to maintain a relatively high standard of life on an income which is often sadly inadequate.

Hence in agreeing to legislate for this deserving section of the population, a class probably needing provision for the time of disablement at least as urgently as the wage earners, the Government had to consider whether it would legislate for salaried employees as a separate class, withdrawing from the existing invalidity insurance system those who now come within its ambit, or simply develop this system of insurance so as to bring the salaried man and the wage-earner into one organisation, or, finally, propose a scheme which should supplement the provision already made by the Invalidity Insurance Law for salaried employees of the lower grades, and at the same time make liberal provision for those excluded by the income limit. The clerical claimants warmly pressed for independent insurance under a new law. The spokesmen of the wage-earners in the Imperial Diet as energetically objected to the institution of a new system of insurance, and refused to admit that a law which was good enough for the man who received wages was insufficient for the man who received a salary.

The Government, in a position of some difficulty, chose the middle way of compromise, and the third of the methods of procedure named above is that adopted in the " Insurance Law for Employés " (*Versicherungsgesetz für Angestellte*), bearing date December 20, 1911. So cordial was the reception of the Government's proposals when duly framed, that a Bill of 399 clauses was passed within six weeks of its first reading, thanks to the good fortune which secured its reference to the same Committee which had just completed the revision of the Consolidation Bill. Comparatively little amendment was made either by Committee or the full House, and the third reading was passed by a unanimous vote. Those portions of the law which relate to executive machinery came into operation at once, but the Federal Council was empowered to fix the date for the application of the insurance clauses.

Social Insurance in Germany

The law has many provisions in common with the Austrian law of 1906 (in operation only since the beginning of 1909), providing retirement allowances to clerks, office employees, and other salaried persons, and pensions, to their survivors; and to the earlier law the German draughtsmen were probably under important obligations. The Austrian law, however, fixes narrower limits of obligatory insurance, viz., the receipt of salaries of from £25 to £125 a year, though persons receiving a larger salary than £125 are insured in respect of this sum.

It is estimated that about two million employees of both sexes will come under the German law, of which number three-quarters already enjoy the modest provision made by the Workmen's Invalidity Insurance Act.

Scope of the Law.—The law makes insurance compulsory from the age of 16 years for the classes of persons included, conditionally upon their not being already incapable of following their callings, upon their yearly earnings from all sources not exceeding 5,000 marks (£250), and upon their age not exceeding 60 years. The benefits provided are retirement allowances to insured persons, claimable in old age or time of invalidity, and pensions to their survivors. Instead of endeavouring to define what is meant precisely by the term "private employee" or "private official" —the usually accepted synonyms for "Angestellter"— the Government has specifically applied the law to the following classes of persons, subject to the foregoing salary conditions:—

(*a*) Employees in a leading position, when this employment forms their principal calling;

(*b*) Works officials, foremen, and other employees in

268

a similar higher position without regard to training, office employees, in so far as they are not employed in meaner or wholly mechanical services, in all cases when their employment as such forms their principal calling;

(c) Assistants in shops and pharmacies;

(d) Members of theatrical and orchestral companies, whatever the artistic value of their performances;

(e) Teachers and tutors, and

(f) Captains, officers, and others employed on German sea-going ships and on vessels engaged in inland navigation.

Persons in the service of the State or public authorities (including statutory insurance authorities of all kinds), with clergymen, teachers in public schools, and certain other classes of people, are exempted from liability to insurance if otherwise guaranteed under the terms of their employment a provision equivalent to the minimum provision made by this law.

On the other hand, the Federal Council is empowered to extend liability to insurance to persons corresponding to those above specified, working on their own account, so long as they do not themselves employ persons liable to insurance.

Voluntary insurance is allowed during the first year after the coming into force of the law to persons with earnings exceeding £250, but below £500, subject to certain conditions. Further, a person withdrawing from an employment entailing liability to insure may continue his insurance voluntarily provided he has paid at least six monthly contributions. If he has paid 120 monthly contributions he may preserve the contingent claim standing to his credit up to date by the pay-

Social Insurance in Germany

ment of an acknowledgment or registration fee of
3s. a year. Subject to these conditions, insurance
may also be continued and a contingent claim be
maintained during residence abroad.

Retirement allowances are payable to those insured
persons who, having qualified for claim to benefit by
payment of the prescribed contributions, have reached
the age of 65 years or are permanently incapacitated
by physical infirmity or enfeebled physical or mental
powers from following their calling.

Inability to follow a calling is assumed "when the
working capacity of the insured person has fallen to less
than one half of that of an insured person sound in body
and mind of similar training and equal knowledge and
ability." Here the law is more liberal than the Invalidity
Insurance Law, which makes invalidity entitling to a
pension dependent upon inability to earn in any given
occupation at least one-third of the usual earnings of
normal workers of the same grade.

As in the case of the Invalidity Insurance Law, retirement allowances are also paid to insured persons not
permanently incapable of work, but incapacitated for at
least 26 weeks uninterruptedly, for the further period
of such incapacity.

Pensions are payable to survivors provided the deceased
at the time of his death had observed the waiting time
qualifying for retirement allowance and had not allowed his
contingent claim to lapse. These pensions go to widows;
on the death of a father, having been insured, to
legitimate children under 18 years ; and on the death
of an insured mother to children whether legitimate or
not. On the death of an insured wife who has been the

Insurance of Salaried Staffs

whole or main support of the family, owing to the husband's infirmity, pensions are granted to the husband and the legitimate children under 18 years so long as they are in need. It will be remembered that under the Workmen's Invalidity Insurance Law pensions to orphans cease at the age of 15 years.

Contributions.—For the purpose of contributions the insured are grouped in nine classes according to the salaries received, and the contributions for each group are uniform. The payments are made monthly; the employer pays the whole in the first instance, but deducts one-half from the salary of his employee as the monthly instalments become due. There is no assistance from the Imperial Treasury, as in the case of Invalidity Insurance for workpeople. The salary classes and the joint monthly contributions are as follows :—

	Yearly Salary.		Joint Monthly Contribution.
		Marks.	Marks.
I.		550 or under	1·60 (1s. 7½d.)
II.	Over	550 to 850	3·20 (3s. 2½d.)
III.	„	850 to 1,150	4·80 (4s. 9½d.)
IV.	„	1,150 to 1,500	6·80 (6s. 9½d.)
V.	„	1,500 to 2,000	9·60 (9s. 7½d.)
VI.	„	2,000 to 2,500	13·20 (13s. 2½d.)
VII.	„	2,500 to 3,000	16·60 (16s. 7½d.)
VIII.	„	3,000 to 4,000	20·00 (20s. 0d.)
IX.	„	4,000 to 5,000	26·60 (26s. 7½d.)

Insured persons under the age of 25 years may insure themselves in a higher salary class than that corresponding to their present earnings, and where a salary is reduced since entrance into insurance the insured person may at any time elect to contribute and receive benefits on the old basis ; but in both such cases the

Social Insurance in Germany

employer is only liable to pay on the scale prescribed by law.

The joint contributions are in general equal to about 8 per cent. of the insured income, and 7 per cent. of the average income of the persons insured.

Contributions are payable for every calendar month in which a person liable to insurance is employed. Periods of sickness for which salary is paid count for contributions. It is intended that payment shall, as a rule, be made at special pay-offices or the Post Offices, and receipts will be given in the form of stamps of different denomination which the employer must at once affix to the insurer's receipt card and deface. In the event of the voluntary continuance of insurance, or the maintenance of a contingent claim by payment of a fee, the contribution or fee respectively must be sent in by the end of the calendar year to the central authority.

Waiting Time and Lapses.—Waiting times have to be observed as follows before benefits can be claimed : For retirement allowances, 120 months, with 120 monthly contributions, in the case of male insured persons, and 60 months, with 60 monthly contributions, in the case of females; for survivor pensions 120 months and monthly contributions. Where fewer than 60 months with obligatory contributions have elapsed the waiting time qualifying for retirement allowance is extended in the case of women to 90 months, and in other cases the waiting time is 150 months.

During the first three years after the coming into force of the law the Insurance Board may allow insured persons in special cases, after undergoing medical examination, to curtail the prescribed waiting time by the

Insurance of Salaried Staffs

payment of a corresponding premium-reserve. During the first ten years also the waiting time in respect of survivor pensions is reduced to 60 contributory months, while widows' and widowers' pensions will be calculated on the basis of a retirement allowance equivalent to one-fourth of the value of the first 60 months' contributions paid. If during the first fifteen years an insured person should die without establishing any claim to benefits under the law, the amount of his own contributions will be paid to his survivors. Further, employees who have completed their 55th year when the law comes into force, and who are not allowed, or for any reason find it impossible, to curtail the waiting time, may be exempted from insurance at their request.

A contingent claim to benefits lapses if within each of the ten calendar years following the calendar year in which the first monthly contribution was paid fewer than eight such contributions are paid, and in later years four in each year, or if the registration fee is not regularly paid. But the claim is revived if the insured person pays up the contributions in arrear during the calendar year following that in which they became due. Should a contingent claim lapse during the waiting period (of 120 or 60 weeks) the contributions may be refunded. Periods of military service, of temporary disablement caused by sickness, and of attendance at a technical school count as contributory periods; and convalescence and disablement not exceeding two months due to confinement are treated as sickness.

The Benefits Provided.—The following are the benefits provided by the law :—

(a) A retirement allowance, which may be claimed in

Social Insurance in Germany

the two eventualities stated. After the payment of 120 monthly contributions within a waiting time of 120 months, this allowance amounts to one-quarter of the contributions paid in this period, plus one-eighth of all additional contributions.

In the case of females, should disablement or the age qualifying for a retirement allowance occur after the expiration of 60 and before the completion of 120 contributory weeks, the retirement allowance is one-fourth of the contributions paid during the first 60 contributory months.

Periods during which retirement allowances are received by persons insured under the Workmen's Invalidity Insurance Law count as "weeks of contribution" in preserving contingent claims under that law.

(b) Survivor pensions for widows or widowers amount to two-fifths of the retirement allowance received by the breadwinner at the time of his death or claimable by him in the event of disablement. Orphans who have lost one parent each receive one-fifth, and orphans who have lost both parents one-third, of the amount of a widow's or widower's pension. All pensions together may not exceed the amount of the breadwinner's retirement allowance, and any necessary reduction will fall proportionately to the several pensions granted. On the death of an annuitant the pension freed goes to the survivors. All payments will be made monthly through the Post Office.

Should a female insured person die after the expiration of the waiting time of 60 months with contributions and before receiving a retirement allowance or annuity, and should there be no claimants to survivor pensions in

Insurance of Salaried Staffs

respect of her insurance, the amount of her own contributions is payable to her relatives, or the Insurance Board may at discretion pay them a life annuity instead. A woman who ceases to follow an insurable employment because of marriage, and has observed the same waiting time, receives back half the contributions paid in respect of her by way of surrender value.

In general, female insured persons who have ceased to follow an insurable employment may, instead of continuing their insurance or preserving their acquired claims, or receiving back their contributions (as in case of marriage) be given an annuity proportionate to the value of their claim, with due regard to their age at the time, but at their request this annuity may be deferred and the amount be adjusted accordingly.

Persons in receipt of retirement allowances or pensions who cease to reside in Germany may be paid a surrender value equal to half the capital value of the benefits to which they are entitled.

The surrender value given to widows or widowers on remarriage is three times the amount of the yearly pension they had been receiving.

Under certain circumstances the benefits provided by the law are curtailed or suspended. Where a retirement allowance is claimable by a person in receipt of a pension under the Workmen's Insurance Laws and also of other earnings from employment, it is reduced to the extent that the total income from these combined sources would exceed the yearly earnings corresponding to the average of the 60 highest monthly contributions paid in respect of him, and pensions to survivors are not payable simultaneously with pensions under the Workmen's Insur-

Social Insurance in Germany

ance Laws in so far as they would exceed three-tenths of such yearly earnings.

Both retirement allowance and pension are suspended while a person entitled to the same is in prison or a house of correction, but if he has dependants resident in Germany the retirement allowance is payable to them under such circumstances.

These benefits are also suspended so long as the person entitled resides abroad without the consent of the Pension Committee, and before payment can be resumed a medical certificate of continued inability to work must be produced. This provision may be annulled, however, in the case of countries whose legislation affords to Germans and their survivors a provision corresponding to that made by this law.

The following table shows the retirement allowances and the survivors' pensions which will be claimable after insurance, with full contributions, for 10, 25, and 50 years in the various salary classes :—

YEARLY AMOUNT IN MARKS.

Salary Class.	Retirement Allowances.			Widows' Pensions.			Orphans' Pensions.		
	10	25 Years.	50	10	25 Years.	50	10	25 Years.	50
I.	48	84	144	19·20	33·60	57·60	3·84	6·72	11·52
II.	96	168	288	38·40	67·20	115·20	7·68	13·44	23·04
III.	144	252	432	57·60	100·80	172·80	11·52	20·16	34·56
IV.	204	357	612	81·60	142·80	244·80	16·32	28·56	48·96
V.	288	504	864	115·20	201·60	345·60	23·04	40·32	69·13
VI.	396	693	1188	158·40	277·20	475·20	31·68	55·44	95·04
VII.	498	871½	1494	199·20	348·60	597·60	39·84	69·72	119·52
VIII.	600	1050	1800	240	420	720	48	84	144
IX.	798	1396½	2394	319·20	558·60	957·60	63·84	111·72	191·52

Insurance of Salaried Staffs

(c) The Insurance Board can require a sick person to undergo curative treatment in a hospital or otherwise, with a view to preventing disablement or to restoring him to a condition of capacity if he receives a retirement pension. Provision is also made for treating sick persons in special hospitals and convalescent homes. In both these cases household money is payable to the dependants to the daily amount of 3/20ths of the monthly contribution last paid.

Existing Superannuation Funds, &c.—The law contains special provisions intended to meet the case of salaried employees entitled to benefits from superannuation funds, or insured in other ways. Existing factory, works, seamen's and similar funds established for one or several undertakings may treat their present old age, invalidity, and survivor benefits as benefits under the law and so contract out, provided these funds exist only for persons liable to insurance under the law or a separate section is formed for such persons, and that the employer makes contributions equal to at least one-half those payable under the law. Funds of this kind will be regarded or either " supplementary " or " substitutionary " funds. The same provisions apply to the statutory miners' funds and to other statutory pension funds, also funds for invalidity, old age, and survivor benefits entrance to which is compulsory in virtue of local bye-laws. Further, with certain exceptions, employees who before December 5, 1911, were insured with public or private insurance companies and societies may be similarly exempted if the insurance premiums they are already paying are equal to those which they would pay under the law in respect of the same salaries. In such a case

Social Insurance in Germany

the employer is required to pay to the Central Insurance Authority the contribution for which he is liable under the law, and in return for it half the benefits provided by the law will be given to the insured person, but if the employer contributes towards the cost of his employees' private insurance his contribution under the law will be proportionately reduced.

Administration.—The insurance will be carried out by a new public authority to be established in Berlin with the title Imperial Insurance Board (*Reichsversicherungsanstalt*), for Employees, consisting of a directorate (*Direktorium*), an administrative council, Pension Committees, and confidential delegates; courts of arbitration, upon which employers and insured persons have equal representation, are also provided. The directorate consists of the president and other permanent members, being public officials, and two representatives each of the employers and employees. The president and the official members and other higher officials are appointed for life by the Emperor on the nomination of the Federal Council. The administrative council will consist of the president of the directorate and at least 12 representatives of the employers and the same number of insured persons.

The Pension Committees will be formed according to need in such number and for such areas as the central body, with the approval of the Federal Council, may determine; a Committee will consist of a permanent chairman and representatives (assessors) of the employers and the insured persons in equal numbers to a minimum of 20 altogether. The confidential delegates will also be chosen equally by the two parties for the district of

Insurance of Salaried Staffs

each lower administrative authority, in numbers varying with the population. They will elect the representative members of the Pension Committees, the courts of arbitration, and the administrative council, and discharge such other functions as may be entrusted to them.

It has been estimated that the full operation of this system of insurance would cost ten and a quarter million pounds a year. As, however, a large number of salaried employees are already insured or otherwise provided for by superannuation and similar funds, a considerable deduction must be made from this sum in order to ascertain the extent of the new burden which will be placed upon employers and employees, and the Government actuaries conclude: "One will not perhaps be far wrong in estimating the total new burden at about 150 million marks." This would represent a yearly levy of three and three-quarter million pounds each for employers and employed.

INDEX

ACCIDENT Insurance Legislation, 8, 9, 13, 15-18, 102-127; scope, 102-106; administration, 106-109; compensation, 111-122, 126; cost, 122, 213-219, 228-230; prevention of accidents, 122-125; operations (statistics of), 125-127.

Administration of the Insurance Systems: sickness, 72-74; accident, 106-109; invalidity, 130-132; central, 173-181; salaried staffs, 278.

Aliens, treatment of, 172, 173; under sickness insurance, 72; under accident insurance, 119, 121; under invalidity insurance, 153.

Attitude of employers and workpeople towards insurance, 238-265.

BENEFITS, insurance — See under Sickness, Accident, and Invalidity Insurance respectively.

Bismarck, Prince, and Insurance Legislation, 11, 14.

CONSUMPTION, crusade against, 182-208.

Consumptives, dispensaries for, 194-196.

Contributions, insurance — See under Sickness, Accident, and Invalidity Insurance respectively.

Cost of insurance to employers, 214-219, 226-237; to workpeople, 221-226, 237.

Crusade against disease (sanatorium treatment for consumptives, &c.), 182-208.

DISEASE, crusade against, 182-208.

Dispensaries for consumptives, 194-196.

EARLY German Insurance Legislation, 6-10.

Employers, attitude toward insurance legislation, 238-247.

Employers, insurance contributions of, sickness, 43-48, 77, 99, 210, 211; accident, 122, 212, 213, 229; invalidity, 133-138, 211, 212; aggregate, 214-219, 226-237.

Employers' Liability Legislation, 8, 9.

FACTORY provident funds, 10.

Factory regulation in Germany, early, 8.

Family benefits, 62.

Forest resorts, 198, 199.

281

Index

Index